OLIVER CROMWELL was born on 25 April 1599. An East Anglian country gentleman of deep religious convictions, he was brought to prominence by his military skills and enthusiasm in the First Civil War. He coupled these qualities with political acumen and charisma to become by the end of the 1640s an indispensable force, Marvell's 'the war's and fortune's son'. In April 1653 Cromwell threw out the Rump of the Long Parliament and, after a brief experiment in government by a nominated assembly (The Barebone's Parliament, July – December 1653), he was inaugurated as Lord Protector of a united British Isles under a written constitution, the Instrument of Government. In 1657 he was offered the crown by Parliament but refused it, preferring to carry on under a revised constitution, the Humble Petition and Advice, enabling him to nominate his own successor. Cromwell was as much a speaker as a doer. His speeches and conversations, revealing his attitudes and reactions to events and developments, help to explain how it was that he made himself, and was made, in Milton's memorable phrase, 'our chief of men'. He died on 3 September 1658.

IVAN ROOTS, former President of the Cromwell Association, read history at Balliol College, Oxford. After lecturing at University College, Cardiff and Lafayette College, Easton, Pennsylvania, he was Professor of History at the University of Exeter from 1967 to 1986. He is author of, *inter alia, The Great Rebellion 1642–1660* (5th edition, 1995). On his retirement he was presented with a *festschrift* on 'People and Politics in Pre-Revolutionary England'.

SPEECHES OF
OLIVER CROMWELL

Edited and introduced by
IVAN ROOTS
Professor Emeritus of History
University of Exeter

EVERYMAN
J. M. DENT · LONDON
CHARLES E. TUTTLE
VERMONT

Introduction, selection and editorial material
© J. M. Dent & Sons Ltd, 1989

This edition first published by
Everyman Paperbacks in 1989
Reissued 2002

J. M. Dent
Orion Publishing Group
Orion House, 5 Upper St Martin's Lane,
London WC2H 9EA
and
Tuttle Publishing
Airport Industrial Park
364 Innovation Drive
North Clarendon
VT 05759-9436
USA

Typeset by Deltatype Ltd, Merseyside
Printed in Great Britain by
Clays Ltd, St Ives plc

British Library Cataloguing-in-Publication Data
is available upon request

ISBN 0 460 01254 1

Contents

Conversations

Preface

Many years of working on Oliver Cromwell have convinced me
that the Protector's own words offer the most penetrating insights
into his character, attitudes, values and intentions, and therefore
into the times in which he flourished. There are numerous letters,
formal and informal, throughout the two decades from about
1640, when he ceased to be Carlyle's mere 'private man' and Lord
Dacre's 'natural back-bencher' (if he ever was), and became
Marvell's 'the war's and fortune's son', confirming Dryden's view
that he was 'great ere fortune made him so', and Milton's 'our
chief of men'. The authenticity of most of the writings ascribed to
him – though not of his doings – has been fairly firmly established
since Thomas Carlyle first collected them (1845). Carlyle's over-
exuberant scholarship has been stabilized and much additional
material supplied by Mrs C. S. Lomas (1904) and W. C. Abbott
(1937–47). Additional pieces (and mummified heads) occasionally turn up.

The speeches, conversations and oral utterances generally
present more difficulty. We have to rely upon reporters of varying
degrees of competence. But on the major items collected in this
volume there is a large measure of agreement among the sources,
and they can be presented with reasonable confidence as a basis
for an assessment of Oliver as an orator, his style, and the thrust
and content of his attempts to persuade and dissuade groups,
notably parliaments, and individuals. They deserve to be in print
again.

There are many obligations to acknowledge. First to Peter
Shellard for letting himself be convinced that the speeches would
make an appealing Everyman History volume, and to Jocelyn
Burton and Judy Tagg, my editors, for their patience during the
more than elephantine gestation period following the conception.
My edition is largely based on C. L. Stainer's almost forgotten
compilation of 1901 and I am deeply grateful to the Oxford
University Press, who hold the copyright, for letting me use it so
freely. A succession of secretaries – Mesdames Linda Thomas,
Shelagh Banner, Janet Mills, Heather Chester, Hilary Tolley and

Margaret Gray – have coped with Cromwell and me and helped me well beyond the call of any duty. I owe an enormous debt to the students in my special subject classes on aspects of the Interregnum who have responded with unfailing courtesy to having the speeches and their virtues churned out to them year after year. Their reactions – positive and negative – in class and in examinations have enhanced my own understanding and appreciation. My wife and family, too, have lived among a litter of Cromwellian bits and pieces, ready to accept that I may have been doing something useful.

Above all I feel indebted to Oliver Cromwell himself for being what he was – a complex, many-layered human being, an individual not a type, who has sustained my interest over so many decades and is still revealing himself.

August 1988   Ivan Roots

Introduction

Though Oliver Cromwell seems essentially a man of action, even one dedicated to the sword, he was also very much a man of the word, whether written or spoken, informal or ceremonial. We are fortunate that so many of his utterances and communications, certainly since he began to assume some prominence during the Civil War, have survived in some form or other and have been reasonably accessible, especially since 1845 when Thomas Carlyle, after half-a-dozen frustrated attempts at a life-and-times, published his idiosyncratic but influential edition of *The Letters and Speeches* – 'a really pious labour' for which he thanked the gods for allowing him to get 'out of it alive'. Since then some more material has come to light, incorporated into W. C. Abbott's magisterial four-decker *The Writings and Speeches* (Cambridge, Mass., 1937–47), set out in relentless chronological order, with a vast commentary, more judicious than Carlyle's but, it must be admitted, twice as tedious. Odd fragments of Cromwelliana still turn up, though not of late anything of major significance likely to affect estimates of Oliver's outlook and character.

There are several hundred of Cromwell's splendid letters, some long, some short, every one – even those tiredly dictated at the end of a hard day's fighting or riding – full of good things, a vivid phrase, a characteristic exhortation to the recipient, as it might be the Speaker of the Commons, a friend, or a county committee. He seems like the well-organized archaeologist who never lets the sun go down without writing up the record of work done each day. There are some particularly telling flashes of the heart and mind of the man. Think, for instance, on the consolatory note he sent on 5 July 1644 to Col. Valentine Walton reporting on his son's death at Marston Moor: 'There is your precious child full of glory, never to know sin or sorrow any more. He was a gallant young man, exceeding gracious. God give you his comfort.'

Carlyle claimed – and who of the readers since of his pioneer edition would deny it? – that Cromwell's letters will convince anyone that the past really did exist and can come alive in the present through the exercise of historical imagination set going by words which, though not directed at posterity, still speak with a plangent voice. Cromwell's letters re-create particularly the man of the 1640s, the dynamic junior officer growing into the Lord General. His oral words, though overlapping the letters, bring out particularly the later Cromwell of the 1650s, 'our chief of men', 'the war's and fortune's son' facing up to the fact that if 'peace hath its victories not less renowned than war's', they are just as hard – harder perhaps – to win.

We have records, some very detailed and circumstantial, of numerous interviews and conversations. Oliver seems at all stages in his career to have been ready to speak with and to all manner of folk and to have enjoyed discussions which would sometimes go on for hours on end. There were chance meetings in St James's Park, when he would stop for a while for a friendly chat. He was a good listener as well as a talker, and the reports of even those who opposed him, not liking his views or suspicious of his personality, clinch that. Admittedly, he always gave as good as he got and occasionally the arguments would grow hectic, not always his fault. His chaplain, John Maidston, was not the only one to note that his temper could be fiery, though in the main it was kept under control, both in private and in public. John Lilburne, a former friend turned inveterate enemy, gave in 1649 a vivid account of him banging the Council table as he inveighed against the Levellers:

> I tell you, sir, you have no other way to deal with these men but to break them or they will break you and bring all the guilt of the blood and treasure spent in this kingdom upon your heads and shoulders . . . and so render you to all rational men in the world as the most contemptibilest generation of silly, low-spirited men in the earth to be broken and routed by such a despicable, contempt-ible generation of men as they are . . . You are necessitated to break them . . .

It rings true.

The Fifth Monarchist John Rogers recounts what started off as an interview but which finished up as a debate (February 1655/6). It is the longest report we have of a single episode of this nature. Rogers, writing it up, clearly wanted to portray the Lord

Protector in a distinctly unfavourable light, but in spite of himself brings out evidence of the great man's natural courtesy and capacity to command respect, both qualities sorely tried in dealing with a character who has been described as – and who, indeed, in his own 'faithful narrative', shows himself to be – 'voluble and inconsecutive . . . perhaps the most notorious man of his time for excessive verbiage and irresponsible utterance', though in the 1650s (it must be admitted) he had considerable competition. In the end the discussion, passing into heated argument, in which other Cromwellians and Fifth Monarchists intervened, broke down. Even so, on the whole the Lord Protector comes out of it very well (see pp. 228–31).

Edmund Ludlow certainly had no political affinity for the later Cromwell, but again and again in his *Memoirs* (*The Memoirs of Edmund Ludlow*, first edition 1698–9) his *bête noire* comes through as not without charm. Of course, the unforgiving republican impugns even that quality as a schooled device of an opportunist, a hypocrite driven by an urge to win friends for his own purposes, most notably to serve unwittingly his overweening ambition. Readers of these reports, setting them in context – the debate with Rogers, for instance, came at a critical hour on the eve of an anticipated royalist rising and after the disappointing failure of the first Protectorate Parliament to co-operate in 'healing and settling' – will make up their own minds about Cromwell's sincerity. George Fox, in an audience not long after Rogers's, found the Protector 'very loving', saying 'with tears in his eyes' that he wished the Quaker 'no more ill than he did his own soul' . . . 'If thou and I were but an hour of a day together, we should be nearer one to the other.' Too much should not be made of Cromwell's propensity to tears. That was something he shared with many of his contemporaries. For himself, Fox – left uncertain whether Oliver had duped him – refused an invitation to dine at Whitehall, but gave credence to a report that the Protector had said afterwards that 'I see a people [the Quakers] risen and come up that I cannot win either with gifts, honours, offices or places.' Was Fox more concerned, here, to praise himself than to give the credit to Oliver's generosity of spirit?

Bulstrode Whitelocke's *Memorials* (*Memorials of the English Affairs*, 1682, drawn upon *infra* for seemingly verbatim accounts

of vital conversations with the Protector) and the reports of
various ambassadors testify to Cromwell's dignity and impress-
iveness on formal occasions. The man who was offered a crown
and refused it clearly had kingly qualities, with 'a sweet and
plausible' oratorical skill which comes through even when
brought to us at third hand, uttered in English – he had no
foreign languages and, indeed, never went out of the British Isles
– but summarized by the envoys in Dutch or French or German
and retranslated into English (as in Abbott's collection). His
Highness, the Lord Protector, was also very adept with protocol
and appears to have had a complete mastery of the art of
wearing, doffing and replacing the hat, that seventeenth-century
symbol of what was proper in social and diplomatic relations.
'Great ere fortune made him so,' sang Dryden in a funeral ode
which he would soon repudiate – anxious like so many after
1660 to put his past behind him – but which throughout has
more than a hint of a genuine respect. Reading the record one
may feel that Cromwell deserved it, proving himself again and
again an actor of majesty in the same class as Elizabeth I, whom
he admired so much, mingling dignity with humanity, without
the clownishness that marred James I and the coldness that left
Charles I's closest servants, like Laud and Strafford, without
much affection for a prince who 'could neither be nor be made
great'.

   If a good deal of the essential Cromwell can be discerned in
these reports and conversations, so often fragmentary, con-
densed, paraphrased, even deliberately distorted, it is above all
through his speeches (particularly to Parliament) that we can
best evoke the true man. For many of these we have what are
surely long authentic passages, though generally with minor
variants and lacunae. We would have had more detail and
exactitude if he had bothered to have official printed versions
made and published hot from the important occasions on which
he delivered them, especially when he was Protector. The
practice was not unknown. Early in the Long Parliament MPs
like Sir Edward Dering, who in 1641 had inaugurated the Root
and Branch discussion seemingly in a fit of absent-mindedness,
had published collections of their speeches to exculpate themselves, even though in so doing they were flouting the Commons'

rule that the proceedings of the House were secret. The fact that Cromwell did not follow that course may tell us something about him.

The speech of 22 January 1654/5, abruptly dissolving the first Protectorate Parliament as soon as it had sat for five lunar months (a narrow interpretation of Clause viii of the Instrument of Government on the length of parliaments), is the only one 'printed by order of the Council of State' by the government printer, Henry Hills (5 February). (Hills would go on to become printer to Charles II, one of many telling examples of successful 'survivors' of the Interregnum.) Some speeches (e.g. those of 4 and 12 September 1654), also delivered to the first parliament, were taken down in shorthand by 'one who stood very near' while the Protector spoke in a stuffy Painted Chamber, into which many, though not all, MPs crowded to hear him. Some versions were published 'to prevent mistakes', not one hundred per cent successfully as shown by the number of variants and additions that can be picked up elsewhere. Evidently on occasion the Protector's harangues were taken down by relays of stenographers who now and then overlapped one another. There were both professionals and amateurs with this fast-developing skill during the seventeenth century, testifying to a growing demand in politics and elsewhere for fuller truer records than hitherto available of what was said and done. Without shorthand we would never have had what seems to be almost verbatim the Putney Debates of 1647, or the less full (but still flavoursome and none too discriminating) Diary of Thomas Burton MP, to which we owe so much of our knowledge of Oliver's second and of Richard Cromwell's sole parliament. In that Diary, incidentally, there are significant versions of some of Oliver's addresses.

One fact is clear: on almost every occasion, Cromwell spoke extempore. He may have had a few notes and obviously had in his head — and one may perhaps add, heart — an idea of the basic structure of his oration, of the topics upon which he intended to touch and the line to take upon them. Some of his openings and perorations, particularly terse final sentences, suggest a little prior preparation. It is likely, too, that he had discussed with his advisers and councillors, individually or collectively, the broad outlines at least of the remit he gave himself. But little of his actual phraseology can have been the result of the lucubrations of committees and speech-writers without whom some modern politicians would be at a loss. It is clear to the reader, and must have been to his listeners, that with him the wind blew where it listed. This man was thinking on his feet, groping for the words to express the ideas that flashed or drifted into his mind. The phrases were tumbling out even before they were formed. One thing led, directly or circuitously, to another, and sometimes, but not always, back again. Speaking to the first Protectorate Parliament on 12 September 1654, in trying to head them off from tearing into the Instrument of Government under which they had, after all, assembled, he divided its terms into 'fundamentals' (inalienable) and 'circumstantials' (open to discussion and, presumably, negotiation). He overlooked one fundamental – a most vital one relating to the control of the militia – and had to bring it in abruptly with the phrase: 'Another fundamental which I forgot!' Had it really gone out of his mind, or was this a way of minimizing its importance? Common sense suggests the former since, in fact, by dragging it in so ineptly he drew added attention to it.

The Commons asked, on 26 January 1657/8, for a copy of the optimistic speech he had delivered the previous day in opening the second session of a parliament that had now, under the provisions by the Humble Petition and Advice of 'the Other House', become bicameral. The Commons, pruned of some MPs who had been wafted upwards to 'the Other House' but also augmented by returning members previously excluded who had not taken part in the framing and passage of the new constitution, were in no mood to accept without consideration either an upper Chamber or the programme set out in the Protector's speech from what was almost a royal throne. Cromwell's reply was that he had no copy of it. He had spoken 'to the House those things that did come upon his own heart and that he did acquaint them honestly and plainly how things stood in matters of fact, but of the particulars he doth not remember four lines'. (The Venetian ambassador commented on the Commons' request that 'it seemed absurd to expect the Protector to agree to print what he had confided to it on the assumption that it would be kept secret for proper consideration and not exposed to the view of all the world to be criticized and commented upon in accordance with personal prejudices' – a suggestion that Cromwell the parliamentarian was regular and traditional in his view of proceedings, and that debates as matters – mysteries – of state were not for vulgar dissemination.)

The lack of official copies made by competent shorthand writers accounts for some of the difficulties in the way of study and appreciation of Cromwell's speeches as we have them – their occasional incoherence, ambiguity, obscurity, even downright opacity, some of which must surely be the effect of an inability to scribble down his winding but rapid sentences, or of the mishearing of a phrase. (Did he really say he was 'not *wedded* or glued' to forms of government? Or did he, as has been cogently suggested, use a less mixed metaphor: '*welded* or glued'?) There are no references by ambassadors, reporting with an urge to accuracy the substance of what he said to them, to a Cromwell faltering into mere mumbling, but they show, even sometimes confess, that they were not always clear on exactly what he had in mind to put to them. Perhaps their uncertainty was just what he intended. Moreover, even if we might have had an undisputed verbatim text of *what* he said, we would have to wrestle somewhat – a favourite and typically imprecise Oliverian term – with the problem of *how* he said it. Here we can call upon the help – though it could turn out to be the hindrance – of the impressions of people who heard him speak, impressions set down very often at a later date, and open to the impact of the after-comment of events or shot through with the reporters' own prejudices or failures of memory.

Carlyle was by no means modest about his editorial prowess in his 1845 collection. He claimed that before him Cromwell's letters and speeches were never read, were misprinted, mispunctuated, unelucidated, misinterpreted – were, in fact, unintelligible, 'defaced with the dark circumstances so well known of that period', the mid-seventeenth century. One hundred and fifty years closer to the Civil Wars than we are, he makes those decades seem utterly remote, a sort of latter-day Dark Ages. Of existing printed versions of the speeches specifically he wrote, 'they excel human belief'. 'Certainly no such agglomerate of opaque confusions, printed and reprinted; of darkness on the back of darkness, thick and threefold' was known to him elsewhere 'in the history of things spoken or printed by human creatures'. He boasts that he has put them right by collecting, collating, consolidating, elucidating – 'a good historical study in itself'. In fact, characteristically, Carlyle exaggerates both the shortcomings of what went before him and the extent and quality of his own achievement, though certainly the latter was not inconsiderable and he deserves the gratitude of all students of Cromwell, whether they are admiring of, inimical to, or detached from the man himself. Carlyle was enterprising and sometimes perceptive in his commentary. But he could be quite cavalier in making emendations of the texts. He inserted words and phrases which seemed to him necessary to a proper elucidation of difficult passages. Some are needed, but others are sometimes otiose, if not actually unhelpful. His interjections, meant to make everything more vivid, often come between the reader and the text, and therefore Cromwell himself. He made mistakes of fact and offered unlikely interpretations. His commentary tends to tell us less about Cromwell than about himself, highlighting his insufficient patience to overcome a deep ignorance of British history. It is hard to respect, too, the judgment of a critic who dismissed Burton's great parliamentary Diary as 'mere moaning wind' and the seven folios of Thurloe's State Papers, an essential source for the 1650s, as rubbish.

A distinguished historian of the period has lately suggested that it is mere pedantry for a student to look elsewhere than Carlyle for the letters and speeches. That is to go too far, and in any case there is currently no edition of Carlyle in print and the work which once could be picked up cheaply in any second-hand bookshop is increasingly hard to come by. What Carlyle is valuable for is both to tell us and in the texts themselves to show us that what Cromwell said (as far as we can ascertain it) is worthy of attention and respect. He enjoins us to come to the speeches as if they are intelligent and genuine, not just cant, and to try to remember that they were once uttered by a flesh-and-blood human being to other men – not many women could have heard them – whom he wanted to persuade. 'Oliver Cromwell always had a meaning and an honest manful meaning' – but the reader has, as the listener had, to be prepared to seek it out. It may be found more readily not by merely reading the speeches but by trying to hear them in your head.

In 1954 the BBC Third Programme broadcast under the title 'A Single Person and Parliament' my tercentenary feature on Cromwell's speeches to the first Protectorate Parliament, in which an actor, apprised of Cromwell's career and aware of the contrasting estimates of his character and open to the advice of an historian, delivered the speeches as if they were new-minted – happenings, which they certainly once were, rather than readings of a known text. The results were illuminating. Where Oliver breaks off in mid-sentence the mind of the hearer manages to finish it off for him, much as we find happens in our own conversations. The performance brought out acceptable nuances and emphases on particularly pregnant words or phrases that set the speaker off on a new tack or brought him back to an old. A few hesitations – the 'ums' and 'ers' we hardly notice – and pauses that even so fluent an orator must have tipped in, added a great sense of authenticity, as did a slight East Anglian accent. We may be sure that Cromwell, like most of his contemporaries, did not escape or even try to escape from his regional origins. (We know that Sir Walter Raleigh, that polished courtier and man of the world, spoke broad Devon to the end of his days.) Above all, the reconstruction encouraged the listener to remember that the speaker was aware of his audience, could see them, even hear them, as they could see him while hearkening to him with varying degrees of attention. A speech may be punctuated by gestures, moués, coughs. Carlyle tried rather irritatingly to impose his own visualizations on his readers – the republicans Heselrige and Scot, 'looking very grim'; Whitelocke 'endeavours to smile'; 'Lenthall tries to blush' – and he even presents a totally fabricated hearer, Dryasdust, who is inclined to emit 'stifled cries'. But readers of Cromwell, like readers of a poem, are best advised to make their own immediate responses, and, only then, to go on to the sort of individual study that makes for a more educated, more penetrating impact.

Difficulties remain. Dr Blair Worden has spoken scornfully of Oliver's 'habitual incoherence'. That is too sharp and dismissive but, even after making all allowances for possible corruptions of text, clarity is often elusive. For this there are several possible reasons. Television and radio interviews with politicians and other axegrinders have made us very aware of the truth of

Talleyrand's observation on the capacity of human speech not so much to convey thought as to conceal it, even without obvious verbiage or blatant fudge. There were certainly times when Cromwell was more concerned to keep things in train than to let people on the spot know just what he did have in mind. The best examples are in the series of speeches he gave in April and May 1657 to the Committee sent by the Commons to urge him to accept the Crown along with the rest of what became known as the Humble Petition and Advice. For a definitive answer he needed time: to explore his own mind, to gather the reactions of army and other groups, interests and factions and – he made no secret of that – to discern the direction in which the Finger of Providence was pointing. Hence the utterances described in newsheets and elsewhere as dense and 'promiscuous' 'some declaring it [his apparent rejection] positive, others infer room for a further address'. 'A speech so dark none knows whether he will accept it or no; but some think he will accept it.' The point was that for some weeks Oliver thought it politic, if not essential, to keep everyone guessing, even his Secretary of State, John Thurloe, who made it his business to know everthing. Carlyle's comparison of the Protector's behaviour with that of the young lady who would but could not, yet might, is very apt. But once the real decision was made he was clear enough in the phraseology of his rejection of the offer. There is a parallel here with the moods of Cromwell the man of action whose career was marked by long periods of apparent supineness or inertia followed by sudden decisive moves, as in the trial and execution of Charles I in 1649 and in the dissolution of the Rump in 1653.

Oratorical incoherence could, of course, be a consequence of inadequacies in the command of language, intensified by the circumstances in which he had to speak. Verbiage and prolixity, smothering clarity, came in sometimes because he did not always have, as Pascal put it, time to be brief. Thinking on his feet he could not always think things through. It must have been hard to have sustained sharpness of expression while standing for two or three hours in an atmosphere that might be both physically and morally unpleasant, among auditors hostile, indifferent, restless. Some speeches must have left Cromwell exhausted, drained. On the other hand some may have had a carthartic effect, ending with 'calm of mind, all passion spent'. There is no doubt that, over the years, Cromwell had not completely tamed the natural roughness that Sir Philip Warwick had noted in 1641 and which from time to time would still break through the schooling of an essentially emotional, even passionate, man whose feelings could run ahead of his power to conjure up the words to express them moderately. We hear of him beginning 'to spit fire', trembling, laying his hand upon his sword.

Limitations upon his education, however formative that single year at Sidney Sussex may have been, inhibited his vocabulary and fields of reference. The biblical language in which he was steeped was colourful enough but could not extend right across the wide spectrum of political expression. He offered little by way of classical allusion, through which a great deal of contemporary political philosophy was approached. Nor did he, in spite of a keen interest in law reform that extended to actually doing something about it, call on legal jargon. Behind it all there was the fact that, for many of the diverse matters upon which he chose or felt he had to utter, his own understanding could at best allow him only to see as through a glass darkly.

The modern student comes up against another problem in seeking the true inwardness of what Cromwell was getting at – it is that the speaker and his hearers, being men living in a different age within a different framework of reference from ours, could catch a tone here and there and give to words meanings now lost to us. That is obvious enough, but it is not always remembered that all historians, like all political and social philosophers, should be students of language. The word 'revolution' is capable of a congeries of interpretations; so, too, are words like 'reason', 'rights', 'the people'. Even so, in spite of all the difficulties, more often than not one may be confident that Cromwell's intentions and meanings – which may be many-layered – are there to be teased out, and that it is worth the effort.

Dr Christopher Hill has called him 'the most quotable of Englishmen'. There is no doubt that he relished words, sometimes coining new phrases, at others breathing new life into old. 'Queen Elizabeth of famous memory . . . we need not be ashamed to say so. That lady, that great queen . . .' Of the execution of Charles I: 'it was not done in a corner'. Of the dissolution of the Rump:

'scarce a dog barked'. Of the major-generals: 'a little, poor invention, which I hear has been much regretted . . . to have a little inspection upon the people . . .' Of danger: 'I wish it may cause no despondency as truly I think it shall not, because we are Englishmen; that is one good account.' Of God: 'I have learned too much of God, not to dally with him and to be bold with him . . . though I can be bold with men if Christ be pleased to assist . . . It is the providence of God that does lead men in darkness.' Of the army: 'A company of poor men that had thought they had ventured their lives and that had some thoughts that they had a little interest to inquire after the things, and the rather because really they were invited out upon principles of honesty, conscience, and religion, for spiritual liberties as many as would come . . .' Or again: 'a poor unpaid army, the soldiers going barefoot at this time, in this city, this weather, and yet a peaceable people, seeking to service you with their lives, judging their pains and hazards and all, well bestowed in obeying you in their offices and serving you to keep the peace in these nations. Yea, he must be a man that hath a heart as hard as the weather that has not a due sense of this.' Of the Other House: '. . . it is not titles, it is not Lordships, it is not this or that that they have but a Christian or an English interest'. Of government: 'I would rather keep sheep under a hedge than deal with the government of men.' Elsewhere: 'the mind is the man'. 'Let us be doing, but let us be united in our doing.' The litany is endless.

Someone remarked, on first hearing Cromwell speak in the Long Parliament, about the 'sharp untuneable voice' but 'eloquence full of fervour' of this still-obscure backbencher. At about the same time John Hampden, a kinsman, forecast for him a conspicuous future, for all the present want of 'ornament' in his behaviour and speech. Clarendon, in his account (admittedly second-hand, but he was not without well primed informants) of the debates on the Self-Denying Ordinance, reports Cromwell as 'not yet arrived at the faculty of speaking with decency and temper'. Evidently the process by which the orator emerged was a slow almost imperceptible one in which experience merged with the conscious acquisition of the skills of the rhetorician. Along the way he somehow came to enjoy speaking up and out, whether in committee rooms, council chambers or in debates on the floor of the Commons, appealing to or chiding assemblies of MPs in the Painted Chamber. 'A king by long succession born,' said Andrew Marvell, and part of Oliver's claim to that encomium came from his instinct always to rise to the moment, whether as chairman in Army Council discussions, at the Putney Debates, or in any of the various challenges or opportunities which came his way in the last hectic decade of his life, when he was called upon to speak, formally and informally, again and again.

Much more might be said about these speeches. They can be analysed for their structure – of which most had at any rate somewhat of a hint, though hardly in any classical sense. Their appeal to history is characteristic. Cromwell was as fond of historical reference as Heselrige was, but he was usually more directly relevant and lacked 'the great Sir Arthur's' penchant for going back to the Anglo-Saxon heptarchy. He preferred to draw upon the years when, no longer a private man out in East Anglia, he proved an increasingly conspicuous and formative actor in the extraordinary events which left him among the best known of Englishmen, with his own folklore, but also left him among the least understood. Greater understanding can come from the student's dialogue with his speeches. Mingled with his appeal to history is his consistent tendency to spiritual exhortation and the urging of moral reformation on individuals, groups and nations. His attention to individuals is an important element, too. Cromwell was always aware of the worth of the individual soul, his own and others', to its maker. We cannot escape his insistence that it was neither covert ambition nor mere chance but Providence and necessity that called him to his great place, but which also warned him not to attempt to set the seal upon it by accepting the Crown. What he has to say (and not to say) about all these things in his speeches must be taken in the diverse contexts in which he spoke. Content and circumstance illuminate each other – and the style is the man.

This volume is entitled *Speeches of Oliver Cromwell* rather than *The Speeches*. It is not intended to be comprehensive, even if that were possible. So many of the speeches Cromwell made and conversations in which he took part survive only in fragments or reports, often belated and remote. Most of these require detailed elucidation, particularly in relation to a complex foreign policy. The core of the collection here is provided by the major speeches delivered to the Nominated Assembly of 1653 and the first two Protectorate Parliaments (1654–1654/5 and 1656–1657/8). In addition there are examples of Cromwell's interventions in the important Army debates at Putney in 1647; some reports of conversations, particularly those set down by Bulstrode White-locke, which have claims to authenticity; and a few scattered items (e.g. a circumstantial abstract of a vital speech to protesting army officers in February 1657 following the presentation in the Commons of Sir Christopher Pack's 'paper' out of which emerged the Humble Petition and Advice). These smaller pieces help to fill out the portrait of Cromwell provided by the great set-pieces. In the words of Thomas Carlyle they open 'little windows into Cromwell's mind'.

The text is based largely on *Speeches of Oliver Cromwell 1644–1658* 'collected and edited by Charles L. Stainer M.A.' of Christ Church, Oxford, published in 1904 by Henry Frowde, 'publisher to the Oxford University Press'. This work attracted little attention and was never reprinted. Little is known of Stainer, but he was certainly an assiduous and careful editor, whose work deserves a wider recognition. His annotated texts, transcribed, extracted and collated from a wide range of sources, printed and manuscript, are generally superior to Carlyle's, even if we discount Carlyle's 'embellishments'. W. C. Abbott's vast *The Writings and Speeches of Oliver Cromwell* (Cambridge, Mass., 4 vols, 1937–47) draws extensively on Stainer though no reference is made to his work in the Preface, which concentrates instead on the contribution – certainly a major one – made to the Cromwell canon by Mrs C. S. Lomas in her three-volume annotated and critical edition of Carlyle's own third (1849) edition. Piously 'unwilling to alter the Carlylean system', she put a great deal of additional material into a supplement. The Lomas edition, coming out in 1904, has an introduction on Cromwell as writer and speaker by Sir Charles Firth (C. H. Firth), then the leading historian of the epoch as the successor to S. R. Gardiner. Lomas's edition is certainly the most accessible for a (more-or-less) complete Cromwell, but in the speeches does not in general advance on Stainer in spite of a great deal of independent collation of texts. She, too, makes no reference to Stainer's volume which must have come out while she was still working on her own.

This present edition makes no claim to be definitive. Addressed to Everyman and Everywoman rather than to the specialist, to the first-degree student rather than to the postgraduate, it has not pursued every variant reading down the labyrinthine ways of copies of copies, none of which can be confidently labelled 'the original', 'authentic' or 'complete', not even the ones 'published to prevent mistakes'. Given that Cromwell, whether deliberately or by mischance, could be incoherent, it is not always sensible to dismiss this or that portion of a whole text, a paragraph or even a single sentence as corrupt; it is possible that a modern editor aspiring to come up with a polished version may, in the very act of making amendments, take us further away from what Cromwell actually said or meant. This edition has looked for the minimum of modifications to what seem the better texts, from Stainer or, for extracts from the Putney Debates, from A. S. P. Woodhouse and elsewhere. Spelling and capitalization have been modernized, and punctuation occasionally amended, to help in clinching the sense. Annotations have been kept to a minimum. A chronological table indicates the context of the speeches etc.; and prime sources for each major speech are listed in an appendix, together with suggestions for further reading, which the student will need and, one hopes, will want to pursue.

Abbreviations

B.L.	British Library
Clarke Papers	*The Clarke Papers*, ed. C. H. Firth, 4 vols (Royal Historical Society: Camden Series), 1891–1901
C.J.	*The Journals of the House of Commons*
Ludlow's Memoirs	*The Memoirs of Edmund Ludlow*, ed. C. H. Firth, 2 vols, Oxford 1894
T.S.P.	*State Papers of John Thurloe*, ed. T. Birch, 7 vols, 1742
Whitelocke, *Swedish Embassy*	B. Whitelocke, *Account of his Embassy to Sweden 1653–1654*, 1714
Whitelocke, *Memorials*	B. Whitelocke, *Memorials of the English Affairs . . . from the Reign of Charles I to Charles II*, 1732
Woodhouse, *Puritanism and Liberty*	A. S. P. Woodhouse, ed., *Puritanism and Liberty . . . the Army Debates 1647–49 from the Clarke MSS*, 3rd edn, ed. I. Roots, (Everyman History), 1986

Speeches

I.

23 March 1648/9 – Speech at the General Council at Whitehall, on being asked whether or not he would go to Ireland in command of the Parliamentary Army

The execution of Charles I (30 January 1648/9), the abolition of monarchy and the inauguration of a Commonwealth raised problems of security within and between the constituent parts of the British Isles. Of immediate concern was Ireland in rebellion since 1641 and now a potential base for a royalist comeback with or without foreign support. Ireland as an English colony was considered to be an economic asset. Everything argued for a major offensive to reduce it to obedience. Cromwell, invited by the Rump's Council of State to take command, was ready to do so.

'I told them [Council of State] also my will could not but be subject to those that were over me, barely considered as matter of will; yet inasmuch as this business is of so great importance as it is, it was fit for me in the first place to consider, how God would incline my heart to it, how I might by seeking of him receive satisfaction in my own spirit as to my own particular. Not that I would put any terms upon the State in relation to myself, but that I would be glad to see a freeness and a clearness in my spirit to the work. And a second consideration was, that if their Lordships did think that the naming of a Commander-in-Chief might be some satisfaction to persons, to officers and soldiers to go, that it was very fit for me to have a little consideration to that in relation to them, that I might not be on occasion by any interest of mine to improve that interest to draw men over, and not to be well satisfied concerning a just and fitting provision for them before they went. And in the last place, the work being so weighty, I did think that it would require many things. I had had no serious thoughts of the business, and therefore held it not fitting for me to give such an answer, that they might give the Council an answer, That they had not only made their offer of "Commander-in-Chief" but that it was accepted by him. I did think fit that they should return back this reply to them, That, I having taken time till the beginning of next week, I hope no resolution will be expected from me before that time.

I do confess, my Lord, I should desire that this business of Ireland I might not go upon it out of any personal respects whatsoever, and I would have personal respects far from this Army. I do not think that God hath blessed this Army for the sake of any one man, nor has his presence been with it upon any such ground; but that presence and blessing that God hath afforded this Army, it hath been of his own good pleasure, and to serve his own turn. That presence and blessing that he hath afforded us has been for his own name's sake, because he would do amongst the sons of men what seemed good in his eyes for the bringing of his glory and purpose to pass; and upon this score has this Army undertaken all that it hath undertaken in the presence of God. It matters not who is our Commander-in-Chief, if God be so; and if God be amongst us, and his presence be with us, it matters not who is our Commander-in-Chief. Truly I do believe that God hath so principled our Army that there is none amongst us but that if God should set us out under any man, we should come to this, to submit to one another in this for the work's sake. Therefore I would that we might think of this,—What is this business of Ireland? What are our considerations in relation to England, to Scotland, to friends here or there, or enemies anywhere? And if we, taking considerations of that kind, and seeking directions from his guidance, work together and answer the best guide that he shall give us, I doubt not but he will bless us. And therefore I shall be bold to offer to you some thoughts of mine and some considerations, which perhaps will best serve to ripen your resolutions as to this undertaking, that so you may have your undertaking from the Lord.

You know how it hath pleased God to beat down all your enemies under your feet, both in this kingdom and the kingdom of Scotland; and you have with simplicity of heart made this opposition to those enemies upon those honest and religious grounds, and that it is fit for godly, and honest, and religious men to propose to themselves. And God hath brought the war to an issue here, and given you a great fruit of that war, to wit, the execution of exemplary justice upon the prime leader of all this quarrel into the three kingdoms, and upon divers persons of very great quality who did co-operate with him in the destruction of this kingdom. Truly notwithstanding you have brought this work to this issue, yet it seems your work is not at an end. You have yet another enemy to encounter with, and friends to stand by. The interest you have fought for you have yet further to make good, not only to the end you may be able to resist those that have been heretofore your enemies, and are still your enemies, and are more enraged, and are not warned by those examples and those witnesses that God hath witnessed for you. But, some will say, they are removed at a further distance! But they are joined together in strong combination to revive the work here again, that is certainly they are in the kingdom of Scotland, and in the kingdom of Ireland. In the kingdom of Scotland you cannot so well take notice of what is done, nor of this that there is a very angry, hateful spirit there against this Army, as an Army of Sectaries, which you see all their papers do declare their quarrel to be against. And although God hath used us as instruments for their good, yet hitherto they are not sensible of it, but they are angry that God brought them his mercy at such an hand; and this their anger,—though without any quarrelling of ours with them,—will return into their own bosoms, for God did do the work without us; and they that are displeased with the instruments, their anger reaches to God and not to those that serve him. And you see they have declared the Prince of Wales their King, and endeavours are both here and there with that party to do what they can to co-operate with them to cause all this work to return again, and to seek the ruin and destruction of those that God hath ordained to be instrumental for their good. And I think you are not ignorant that a great party here does co-operate in the work and their spirits are embittered against us, even though they might know, that if God had not used this poor Army instrumentally to do what they have done, they had not had a being at this time. But such is the good pleasure of God as to leave them to the blindness of their minds.

I must needs say I do more fear,—not that I do think there is a ground to fear it will be,—but as a poor man that desires to see the work of God to prosper in our hands, I think there is more cause of danger from disunion amongst ourselves than by anything from our enemies; and I do not know anything greater danger than that. And I believe, and I may speak with confidence, till we admire God and give him glory for what he has done there is such danger; for all the rest of the world, Ministers and profane persons, all rob God of all the glory and reckon it to be a thing of chance that has befallen them. Now if we do not depart from God and disunite by that departure and fall into disunion amongst ourselves, I am confident, we doing our duty and waiting upon the Lord, we shall find he will be as a wall of brass round about us till we have finished that work that he has for us to do. And yet not to be sensible that this is the rage and malice of our enemies. . . . I wish that they may see their error, those that are good amongst them, and repent, but certainly this wrath of theirs shall turn to their hurt, and God will restrain the remainder that it shall not hurt us.

In the next place we are to consider Ireland. All the Papists and the King's party, I cannot say all the Papists but the greatest party of them, are in a very strong combination against you, and they have made an union with those apostate forces that were under Inchiquin and the Confederate Catholics of Ireland; and all that party are in a very strong combination against you. The last letters that the Council of State had from thence do plainly import, that Preston has 8,000 foot and 800 horse, that Taaffe has as many, that my Lord Clanricarde has the same proportion, that my Lord Inchiquin and my Lord Ormond have a matter of 3,000 foot and 800 horse, that these are all agreed and ready in conjunction to root out the English interest in Ireland and to set up the Prince of Wales his interest there likewise, and to endeavour as soon as they can to attempt upon our interest in Leinster and Ulster and Connaught. In all which provinces we have an interest, but in Munster none at all. And though we are fortunate in that interest we have in these three provinces, it is not so considerable but if these Confederate forces shall come upon them, it is more than probable, without a miracle from heaven, that our interest will easily be eradicated out of those parts. And truly this is really believed, if we do not endeavour to make good our interest there, and that timely, we shall not only have, as I said before, our interest rooted out there, but they will in a very short time be able to land forces in England, and to put us to trouble here. And I confess I have had these thoughts with myself, that perhaps may be carnal and foolish. I had rather be over-run with a Cavalierish interest than a Scotch interest; I had rather be over-run with a Scotch interest than an Irish interest; and I think of all, this is the most dangerous, and if they shall be able to carry on this work they will make this the most miserable people in the earth. For all the world knows their barbarism,—I speak not of any one religion, almost any of them but in a manner are as bad as Papists,—and you see how considerable they are at this time. And truly it is thus far, that the quarrel is brought to this state, that we can hardly return unto that tyranny that formerly we were under the yoke of, which through the mercy of God hath been lately broken, but we must at the same time be subject to the kingdoms of Scotland, or the kingdom of Ireland for the bringing in of the King. Now it should awaken all Englishmen, who perhaps are willing enough he should have come in upon an accommodation. But now he must come from Ireland or Scotland!

This being so, I would not have this Army now so much to look at considerations that are personal, whether or no we shall go if such a Commander go or such a Commander go, and make that any part of our measure or foundation: but let us go, if God go. If that we be still in our calling, prosecuting that cause that hitherto we have been engaged in, and if the opposing those enemies be a part of that cause,—wherein we desire that there may be no personal respects in it,—and if we be satisfied in our judgments and consciences that he is in it, I would that you would let this be your motive. And I do profess it as before the Lord of Heaven, and as in his presence, I do not speak this to you that I would shift at all from the command or in any sneaking way or in any politic way lead you to an engagement, before I declare my thoughts in the thing, whether I go or stay, as God shall incline my heart to it. And if you undertake it upon these grounds, I am confident there will not be so much dispute amongst those who shall go as who shall stay. My meaning is, you will, every honest heart that sees a freedom of their ways, will rather be whetted on out of love to God and duty to God, to go where he may do him most service, rather than stay, besides I say, except it be that God cast hindrances in men's ways by necessity of relations or laying any law upon men's hearts, and besides that that may otherwise hinder them. I do not speak this as thinking but that he may be as

honest a man that does desire to go or stay. Doing service to God
and giving glory to God will be the best motive to this work, aye, it
will be much better to have considerations of this kind, than to lay
this as the foundation, who shall command in chief. For my own
part though the Council of State hath put that upon me, yet I have
desired them to give me till Tuesday to give in my answer. I desire
you therefore now to give your resolutions as to the particular
regiments that are to go in that kind, and to state what other
demands you will make for your going that will enable those to go
and to have a subsistence when they go.'

Somebody, unstated, then gave details of the proposed force as
'8,000 foot, 3,000 horse, and 1,200 dragoons'. Sir Hardress Waller
objected that he thought 'the work would not go forward till it be
known whether the Commander-in-Chief named will go or not'.

Cromwell. 'I offer this, that the Army do move for such
provisions as may be fit for honest men to ask; and if you go upon
that account I think my resolution will be known before yours,
and that will be properly in the nature of things. It will be best and
fittest for you to consider of that first, if there be a designed part of
the Army to go, as there will probably. I hope we are such a
generation of men. I am sure God so binds us about as with a
garment, therefore we are to look one upon another, all of us
being ready to do it as if it were our own case. And therefore I
think, in order to your proceedings, it will be better to consider
who shall go and what is due to him and to provide for him. And
truly this will spend as much time as Tuesday next comes to, as to
the point of arrears, and of provision what will serve for honest
men to carry on the work.'

2.

4 July 1653 – Speech in the Council Chamber to the persons then assembled and intrusted with the Supreme Authority of the Nation

After a long period of holding back, though pressed hard from the
Army, Cromwell finally forcibly dissolved the Rump Parliament as

'no parliament', following indications that it was rushing through
an unsatisfactory Bill for a new representative. Unwilling to appear
as a military dictatorship, he and his Council of Officers, after
considering various alternatives, decided to summon a Nominated
Assembly as an interim measure. This speech offers Cromwell's
justification of developments. The Assembly then declared itself a
parliament, later nicknamed Barebone's, but it proved a disappointment to many of its members and to Cromwell, and on 12
December it too resigned. The Protectorate was shortly inaugurated under a written constitution – the Instrument of Government
– devised by Major-General John Lambert.

'Gentlemen,

I suppose the Summons that hath been instrumental to bring
you hither gives you well to understand the cause of your being
here. Howbeit, having something to impart, which is an Instrument drawn up by the consent and advice of the principal Officers
of the Army,—which is a little, as we conceive, more significant
than the letter of summons,—we have that here to tender you.
And we have somewhat likewise further to say to you for our own
exoneration, and we hope it may be somewhat further to your
satisfaction; and therefore seeing you sit here somewhat uneasy
by reason of the scantiness of the room and the heat of the
weather, I shall contract myself with respect to that.

I have not thought it amiss a little to mind you of that series of
providences, wherein the Lord hitherto hath dispensed wonderful
things to these nations, from the beginning of our troubles to this
very day. If I should look much backward, we might remember
the state of affairs as they were before the Short, and that which
was the last Parliament. In what a posture the things of this nation
stood, doth so well I presume occur to all your memories and
knowledges, that I shall not need to look so far backward, nor yet
to the beginning of those hostile actions that passed between the
King that was and the then Parliament. And indeed should I begin
this labour, the things that would fall necessarily before you,
would rather be fit for a history than for a discourse at this
present.

But thus far we may look back. You very well know, after
divers turnings of affairs, it pleased God, much about the midst of

this war, to winnow, as I may so say, the forces of this nation and to put them into the hands of men of other principles than those that did engage at the first. By what strange providences that also was brought about, would ask more time than is allotted me to remember you of. Indeed there are stories that do recite those transactions and give narratives of matter of fact, but they are not particular in those things wherein the life and power of them lay, those strange windings and turnings of providence, those very great appearances of God in crossing and thwarting the designs of men, that he might raise up a poor and contemptible company of men, neither versed in military affairs nor having much natural propensity to them, even through the owning of a principle of godliness,—of Religion. Which so soon as it came to be owned and the state of affairs put upon the foot of that account, how God blessed them and all undertakings by the rising of that most improbable, despicable, contemptible means,—for that we must for ever own,— you very well know.

What the several successes have been is not fit to mention at this time neither, though I must confess I thought to have enlarged myself upon this subject, forasmuch as the considering the works of God, and the operation of his hands, is a principal part of our duty, and a great encouragement to the strengthening of our hands and of our faith for that which is behind those marvellous dispensations then having been given us. Amongst other ends that was a most principal end, and to us in this revolution of affairs and issues of those successes God was pleased to give this nation and the authority that then stood there were very great things brought about; besides those dints that were upon these nations and places where the war was carried on, even in the civil affairs, to the bringing offenders to justice even the greatest; to the bringing the state of this government to the name at least of a Commonwealth; to the searching and sifting of all places and persons; the King removed and brought to justice and many great ones with him; the House of Peers laid aside; the House of Commons, the representative of the people of England, itself winnowed, sifted and brought to a handful, as you may very well remember.

And truly God would not rest there,—for by the way, although it be fit for us to entitle our failings and miscarriages to ourselves, yet the gloriousness of our work may well be attributed to God himself, and may be called his strange work;—you may remember well that at the change of the government there was not an end of our troubles, although that year were such things transacted as indeed make it to be the most memorable year, I mean 1648, that ever this nation saw; so many insurrections, invasions, secret designs, open and public attempts, quashed in so short a time, and this by the very signal appearances of God himself, which I hope we shall never forget. You know also, as I said before, that as the effect of that memorable year, 1648, was to lay the foundation of bringing delinquents to punishment, so it was of the change of the government, although it be true, if we had time to speak, the carriages of some in trust, in most eminent trust, was such, as would have frustrated to us the hopes of all our undertakings had not God miraculously prevented,—I mean, by that closure that would have been endeavoured by the King, whereby we should have put into his hands all that cause and interest we had opposed, and had nothing to have secured us but a little piece of paper. But things going on, how it pleased the Lord to keep this nation in exercise both at sea and land, and what God wrought in Ireland and Scotland you likewise know, until the Lord had finished all that trouble upon the matter by the marvellous salvation wrought at Worcester.

I confess to you I am very much troubled in my spirit, that the necessity of affairs doth require that I should be so short in these things, because I told you before, this is the leanest part of the transaction, to wit an historical narration; there being,—in every dispensation, whether the King's going from the Parliament, the pulling down the Bishops, purging the House at that time by their going away to assist the King, change of government, whatever it was,—not any of those things but hath a remarkable point of providence set upon it, that he that runs may read. Therefore I am heartily sorry that in point of time I cannot be particular in those things which I did principally design this day, thereby to provoke and stir up your hearts and mine to gratitude and confidence.

I shall now begin a little to remember you the passages that have been transacted since Worcester fight; whence coming with my fellow officers and soldiers, we expected, and had some reasonable confidence that our expectations should not be frustrate, that the authority that then was, having such a history to look back unto, such a God that appeared for them so eminently,—so visibly that even our enemies many times confessed that god himself was engaged against them, or they should never have been brought so low, nor disappointed in every undertaking. For that may be said by the way, had we miscarried but once, where had we been?—I say, we did think, and had some reasonable confidence, that coming up then, the mercies that God had shewed, the expectations that were in the hearts of all good men, would have prompted those in authority to have done those good things, which might by honest men have been judged a return fit for such a God and worthy of such mercies, and indeed a discharge of duty to those for whom all these mercies have been shewed, that is, the interest of the three nations, the true interest of the three nations. And if I should now labour to be particular in enumerating some businesses that have been transacted from that time till the dissolution of the late Parliament, indeed I should be upon a theme which would be very troublesome to myself. For I must say for myself and fellow officers, we have rather desired and studied healing, than to rake into sores and look backward, to render things in those colours that would not be very well pleasing to any good eye to look upon. Only this we must say for our own exoneration, and as thereby laying some foundation for the making evident the necessity and duty that was incumbent upon us to make this last great change. I think it will not be amiss to offer a word or two in that, not taking pleasure to rake into the business were not there some kind of necessity so to do.

Indeed we may say, without commending ourselves,—I mean myself and those gentlemen that have been engaged in the military affairs,—that upon our return, we came fully bent in our hearts and thoughts to desire and use all fair and lawful means we could, to have had the nation to reap the fruit of all that blood and treasure that had been expended in this cause; and we have had many desires and thirstings in our spirits to find out ways and means, wherein we might anyways be instrumental to help it forward. And we were very tender for a long time so much as to petition,—till August last, or thereabouts, we never offered to petition,—but some of our then Members, and others, having good acquaintance and relation to divers Members of the

Parliament, we did from time to time solicit that which we thought, if there had been nobody to prompt them, nobody to call upon them, would have been listened to out of ingenuity and integrity in them that had opportunity to have answered our expectations. And truly when we saw nothing would be done, we did, as we thought according to our duty, remind them by a petition, which petition I suppose the most of you have seen, which we delivered either in July or August last. What effect that had, is likewise very well known. The truth is, we had no return at all that was satisfaction for us, but a few words given us. The business petitioned for, most of them, we were told, were under consideration; and those that were not, had very little or no consideration at all.

Finding the people dissatisfied in every corner of the nation, and bringing home to our doors the non-performance of those things that had been promised and were of duty to be performed, we did think ourselves concerned. We endeavoured, as became honest men, to keep up the reputation of honest men in the world, and therefore we had divers times endeavoured to obtain a meeting with divers Members of Parliament; and truly we did not begin this till October last, and in those meetings did in all faithfulness and sincerity beseech them, that they would be mindful of their duty to God and man, and of the discharge of the trust reposed in them. I believe these gentlemen, that are many of them here, can tell that we had at the least ten or twelve meetings, most humbly begging and beseeching them, that of their own accords they would do those good things that had been promised, that so it might appear they did not do them by any suggestion from the Army but of their own ingenuity: so tender were we to preserve them in the reputation and opinion of the people to the uttermost. And having had many of those meetings, and declaring plainly that the issue would be the judgment and displeasure of God against them, the dissatisfaction of the people and the putting things into a confusion, yet how little we did prevail, we well know, and we believe is not unknown to you.

At the last, when we saw indeed that things would not be laid to heart, we had a serious consideration amongst ourselves what other way to have recourse unto. And when indeed we came to those close considerations, they began to take the Act for the New

Representative to heart and seemed exceeding willing to put it on; the which, had it been done, with that integrity, with that caution, that would have saved this cause and the interest we have been so long engaged in, there could nothing have happened to our judgments more welcome than that would have been. But finding plainly that the intendment of it was not to give the people that right of choice, all thought it had been but a seeming right; the seeming to give the people that choice which was intended and designed to recruit the House the better to perpetuate themselves. And truly divers of us being spoken to, to that end that we should give way to it,—a thing to which we had a perpetual aversion, which we did abominate the thoughts of,—we always declared our judgments against it and our dissatisfaction. But yet, they that would not hear of a Representative before,—it lay three years before them without their proceeding with one line considerably in it,—they, that would not endure to hear of it, then, when we came to our close considerations, then, instead of protracting, they did make as much preposterous haste on the other hand and ran into that extremity. And finding that this spirit was not according to God, and that the whole weight of this cause, which must needs have been very dear unto us who have so often adventured our lives for it, and we believe is so to you, when we saw plainly that there was not so much as any consideration how to assert it, or to provide security for it, as indeed to cross these that they reckoned the most troublesome people they had to deal with, which was the Army, which by this time was sufficiently their displeasure; when we saw this, truly, that had power in our hands,—to let the business go to such an issue as this, was to throw back the cause into the hands of them we first fought with,—we came to this first conclusion amongst ourselves, that if we had been fought out of it, necessity would have taught us patience; but that if it were to be taken from us so unworthily, we should be rendered the worst people in the world, and we should become traitors both to God and man. And when God had laid this to our hearts, and we found that the interest of his people was grown cheap and not laid to heart, and that if we came to competition of things the cause, even among themselves, would even almost in everything go to the ground, this did add more consideration to us that there was a duty incumbent upon us. And

truly, I speak it in the presence of some that are here, that were at
the close consultations,—held I may say as before the Lord,—the
thinking of an act of violence was to us worse than any
engagement that ever we were in yet, and worse to us than the
utmost hazard of our lives that could be, so unwilling were we, so
tender were we, so desirous were we, if it were possible, that these
men might have quit their places with honour. And truly this I am
the longer upon because it hath been in our hearts and consciences, our justification, and hath never yet been imparted
thoroughly to the nation. And we had rather begin with you to do
it, than to have done it before, and do think indeed that these
transactions be more proper for a verbal communication, than to
have put it into writing. I doubt, whosoever had put it on paper
would have been tempted to have dipt his pen in vinegar and
wrath. But affairs being at this posture that we saw plainly and
evidently in some critical things, that the cause of the people of
God was a despised thing, truly then we did believe that the hands
of other men, must be the hands that must be trusted with it, and
then we thought it high time for us to look about us and to be
sensible of our duty.

If I should take up your time to tell you what instances we have
to satisfy our judgments and consciences, that these were not vain
imaginations and things that were petitioned for, but things that
fell within the compass of our certain knowledge and sense,
should I repeat these things to you, I should do that which I would
avoid, to rake into these things too much. Only this. If any body
were in competition for any place of real and signal trust, how
hard and difficult a thing it were to get anything to be carried
without making parties, without things indeed unworthy of a
Parliament! And when things must be carried so in a supreme
authority, indeed I think it is not as it ought to be. But when it
came to other trials, as in that case of Wales, which I must confess
for my own part I set myself upon, if I should inform you what
discountenance that business of the poor people of God there had,
who had watchings over them, men like so many wolves ready to
catch the lamb as soon as it was brought out into the world; if I
should inform you how signally they threw that business under
foot to the discountenancing of the honest people there, and to the
countenancing of the malignant party of this Commonwealth—I

need but say it was so. Many have felt by sad experience it was so, who will better impart that business to you. Which, for myself and fellow officers, I think it was as perfect a trial of their spirits as anything, it being known to many of us that God kindles a seed there, indeed hardly to be paralleled since the primitive times. I would this had been all the instances, but finding which way their spirits went, and finding that good was never intended to the people of God,—I mean, when I say so, that large comprehension of them under the several forms of godliness in this nation,— when I saw that tenderness was forgotten to them all, though it was very true that by their hands and means, through the blessing of God, they sat where they did, and the late affrays, not to speak it boastingly, had been instrumentally brought to that issue they were brought to by the hands of those poor creatures, we thought this an evil requital. I will not say that they were at the uttermost pitch of reformation, although I could say that in regard to one thing, the regulation of the Law, so much groaned under in that posture it now is in. There were many good words spoken for it. But we know that many months together was not time enough to pass over one word called "Incumbrances". I say, finding that this was the spirit and complexion of them, although these were faults for which no man should have dared to lift his hand simply for their faults and failings, yet when we saw their intendment was to perpetuate themselves and men of this spirit,—for some had it from their own mouths, from their own designs, who could not endure to hear of being dissolved,—we thought this was an high breach of trust. If they had been a Parliament never violated, sitting as free and as clear as ever any sat in England, yet if they would go about to perpetuate themselves, we did think this to be so high a breach of trust, as greater could not be. And we did not go by guess in this, and to be out of doubt in it we did, having had that conference among ourselves whereof we gave account, we did desire once more the night before the dissolution, and it had been in our desires some two or three days before, that we might speak with some of the principal persons of the House, that we might with ingenuity open our hearts to them, to the end that we might be either convinced of the ground of their principles and intentions to the good of the nation, or if we could not be convinced that they would hear our offer or expedient to prevent this mischief. And indeed we could not prevail for two or three days, till the night before the dissolution. There is a touch of this in that our Declaration, we had often desired it and at that time we attained it. There were above twenty of them, who were Members, not of the least consideration for interest and ability, with whom we desired to discourse those things, and had discourse with them. And it pleased the gentlemen, the Officers of the Army, to desire me to offer their sense to them, and indeed it was shortly carried thus. We told them, that the reason of our desire to wait upon them was that we might know from them, what security lay in the way of their proceeding so hastily with their Representative, wherein they had made a few qualifications, such as they were, and how the whole business should be executed we had no account of. And we desired them they would be pleased to inform us; and we thought we had an interest in our lives, estates, and families, as well as the worst people of the nation, and that we might be bold to ask satisfaction in that; and we told them if they did proceed in honest ways, as might be safe to the nation, we might acquiesce therein. When we pressed them to give satisfaction in this, the answer was made, that nothing could be good for the nation but a continuance of this Parliament. We wondered that we should have such a return, yet we said little to that, but seeing that they would not give us that which might satisfy us that their way was honest and safe, we begged they would give us leave to make our objections. We did tell them, that we thought that way they were going in would be impracticable; we could not tell them how it would be brought to pass, to send out an Act of Parliament into the country, to have such qualifications to be the rules of electors and elected, and not to know who should execute this. We desired to know whether the next Parliament were not like to consist of all Presbyterians? Whether those qualifications would hinder them or Neuters? And though it be our desire to value and esteem those of that judgment, only, they having been as we know, having deserted this cause and interest upon the King's account and upon that closure between them and the neighbour nation, we do think, we must profess we had as good as delivered up our cause into the hands of any, as into the hands of interested and biased men. For it is one thing to live friendly and brotherly, to bear with and love a person of another judgment in religion, another thing to have any so far set into the saddle upon that account, as that it should be in them to have all the rest of their brethren at mercy.

Having had this discourse, making these objections, of bringing in Neuters, or such as should impose upon their brethren, or such as had given testimony to the King's party; and objecting to the danger of it, in drawing the concourse of all people to arraign every individual person, which indeed did fall obviously in; and objecting that the issue would certainly have been the putting it into the hands of men that had little affection to this cause, the answer again was made,—and it was confessed by some that these objections did lie,—but answer was made by a very eminent person at the same time as before, that nothing would save the nation but the continuance of this Parliament. This being so,— when neither our counsels and objections to their proceedings, nor their answers to justify them, did give us satisfaction; nor did we think they ever intended to give any, as some of them have since declared,—we humbly proposed an expedient of ours, which was indeed to desire, that the government being in that condition it was, and the things being under so much ill sense abroad and so likely to come to confusion in every respect if it went on, so we desired they would devolve the trust over to persons of honour and integrity that were well known, men well affected to religion and the interest of the nation; which, we told them—and it was confessed,—had been no new thing when these nations had been under the like hurly-burly and distractions. And it was confessed by them, it had been no new thing. We had been at labour to get precedents to convince them of it, and we told them that these things we offered out of that deep sense we had of the good of the nations and the cause of Christ. And being answered to that, that nothing would save the nation but the continuance of that Parliament—although they would not say they would perpetuate it at that time least of all, but we finding their endeavours did directly tend to it,—they gave us this answer, that the things we had offered were of a tender and very weighty consideration; they did make objections how we should raise the money and some other objections. We told them, that that we offered as an expedient, because we thought it five times better than that for which no reason was, or we thought would be given. We desired them to lay the thing seriously to heart. They told us they would take consideration of these things till the morning, that they would sleep upon them, and consult some friends, though, as I said, there was about twenty there and I think that there was scarce any day that there sat above fifty or fifty-two or fifty-three. At the parting two or three of the chief ones, the very chiefest of them, did tell us that they would endeavour the suspending the proceeedings of the Representative the next day, till they had a further conference; and upon this we had great satisfaction, and we did acquiesce, and had hope, if our expedient would take up a loving debate, that the next day we should have some such issue of our debate as would have given satisfaction to all. They went away late at night, and the next morning, we considering how to order that which we had to offer to them when they were to meet in the evening, word was brought they were proceeding with a Representative with all the eagerness they could. We did not believe persons of such quality could do it. A second and a third messenger told us they had almost finished it, and had brought it to that issue with that haste that had never been before, leaving out the things that did necessarily relate to due qualifications, as we have heard since, resolved to make it a paper bill, not to engross it, that they might make the quicker dispatch of it, thus to have thrown all the liberties of the nation into the hands that never bled for it. Upon this account we thought it our duty not to suffer it, and upon this the House was dissolved even when the Speaker was going to put the question.

This we tell you that you may so know, that what hath been done in this dissolution of this Parliament, was as necessary to be done as the preservation of this cause; and that the necessity that led us to do that, hath brought us to this issue of exercising an extraordinary way and course to draw yourselves together upon this account, that you are men who know the Lord, and have made observations of his marvellous dispensations, and may be trusted as far as men may be trusted with this cause.

It remains, for me to acquaint you further with that that relates to your taking upon you this great business, that being contained in this paper in my hand, which I do offer presently to you to read. Having done that which we thought to have done upon this ground of necessity, which we know was not feigned necessity but real and true, to the end that the government might not be at a loss, to the end that we might manifest to the world the singleness of our hearts and integrity, who did those things not to grasp after the power ourselves, to keep it in a military hand, no not for a day, it remains, as far as God enables us with strength and ability, to put it into the hands that might be called from the several parts of the nation. This necessity I say, and we hope we may say for ourselves, this integrity of labouring to divest the sword of the power and authority in the civil administration of it, hath moved us to conclude of this course of bringing you hither; and having done that, we think we cannot with the discharge of our consciences but offer somewhat unto you, as I said before, for our own exoneration, it having been the practice of others, who have voluntarily and out of sense of duty divested themselves of authority and devolved the government into the hands of others, it having been the practice where such things have been done, and very consonant to reason, together with the authority to lay a charge in such a way as we hope we do, and to press to the duty: concerning which we have a word or two to offer to you.

Truly God hath called you to this work by, I think, as wonderful providences as ever passed upon the sons of men in so short a time; and truly I think, taking the argument of necessity, for the government must not fall, taking the appearances of the will of God in this thing, I am sure you would have been loth it should have been resigned into the hands of wicked men and enemies. I am sure God would not have it so. It comes therefore to you by way of necessity, it comes to you by the way of the wise providence of God, though through weak hands. And therefore I think, it coming through our hands, though such as we are, it may not be taken ill if we offer to you something as to the discharge of that trust which is incumbent upon you. And although I seem to speak that which may have the face of a charge, it is a very humble one, and he that means to be a servant to you, who are called to the exercise of the supreme authority, desires only to discharge that which he conceives is his duty in his own and his fellows' names to you, I hope who will take it in good part. And truly I shall not hold you long in that, because I hope it is written in your hearts to approve yourselves to God only.

This Scripture I shall remember to you, which hath been much upon my spirit, Hosea 11th and 12th verse, *Yet Judah ruleth with*

God, and is faithful among the Saints; it is said before, *Ephraim did compass God about with lies and Israel with deceit.* How God hath been compassed about with fastings and thanksgivings, and other exercises and transactions, I think we have all cause to lament. Why truly you are called by God to rule with him and for him, and you are called to be faithful with the Saints, who have been somewhat instrumental to your call. He that ruleth over men, the Scripture saith, he must be just, ruling in the fear of God. And truly it is better to pray for you than to counsel you in that, that you may exercise the judgment of mercy and truth. I say it is better to pray for you to do it, than to advise you; better to ask wisdom from heaven for you, which I am confident many thousands of Saints do this day, and have done and will do through the permission of God and his assistance, than to advise you. Only truly I thought of a Scripture likewise that seems to be but a Scripture of common application to every man as a Christian, wherein he is counselled to ask wisdom. And he is told what is that wisdom that is from above; it is pure, peaceable, gentle, easy to be entreated, full of good fruits, without partiality, without hypocrisy. And my thoughts ran thus upon this, that the executing of the judgment of truth,—for that is the judgment, —that you must have wisdom from above for; and that is pure. That will teach you to execute the judgment of truth; it is without partiality. And then, if God give you hearts to be easy to be entreated, to be peaceable spirits, to be full of good fruits, bearing good fruits to the nation, to men as men, to the people of God, to all in their several stations, this wisdom will teach you to execute the judgment of mercy and truth. And I have little more to say to this, I shall rather bend my prayers for you in that behalf as I said before, and I know many others do also. Truly the judgment of truth will teach you to be as just towards an unbeliever as towards a believer; and it is our duty to do so. I confess I have often said it foolishly, if I would miscarry, I would rather do it to a believer than to an unbeliever. Perhaps it is a paradox, but let us take heed of doing it to either, of exercising injustice to either. If God fill our hearts with such a spirit as Moses and Paul had, which was not only a spirit for the believers among the people of God, but for the whole people he would have died for them, and so Paul to his countrymen according to the flesh he could have died for them, truly this will help us to execute the judgment of truth and mercy also.

A second thing is, to desire you would be faithful with the Saints; to be touched with them. And I hope, whatever others may think, it ought to be to us all a matter of rejoicing, that as one person, our Saviour, was touched with our infirmities that he might be pitiful, so should we be pitiful. I do think this Assembly, thus called, is very much touched with the common infirmities of the Saints, and I hope that will teach you to pity others, that so Saints of one sort may not be our interest, but that we may have respect unto all, though of different judgments. And if I did seem to speak anything that might reflect upon those of the Presbyterian judgment, I think if you have not an interest of love for them, you will hardly answer this faithfulness to his Saints. I confess in my pilgrimage and some exercises I have had abroad, I did read that Scripture often in Isaiah 41: 19, when God gave me and some of my fellows what encouragement he would there and elsewhere, which he performed for us. And what would he do? to what end? *That he might plant in the wilderness the cedar and the shittah tree, and the myrtle and palm tree together.* To what end? *That they might know and consider, and understand together that the hand of the Lord hath done this; and that the Lord hath created it,* that he wrought all salvation and deliverance which he hath wrought, for the good of the whole flock. Therefore I beseech you,—but I think I need not,—have a care of the whole flock. Love all the sheep, love the lambs, love all, and tender all, and cherish all, and countenance all in all things that are good. And if the poorest Christian, the most mistaken Christian, should desire to live peaceably and quietly under you, soberly and humbly desire to lead a life in godliness and honesty, let him be protected.

I think I need as little advise you, much less press you, concerning the propagation of the Gospel, and encouraging such Ministers and such a Ministry as be faithful in the land, upon whom the true character is; men that have truly received the spirit for such a use, which Christians will be well able to discern, and do; men that have received gifts from him, that ascended on high and led captivity captive, for the work before mentioned. And truly the Apostle, Romans 12, when he had summed up all the mercies of God and the goodness of God, and hath discoursed of the foundations of the Gospel and of the several things that are the subject of his discourse in the first eleven chapters, after he hath besought them to offer up their souls and bodies a living sacrifice to God, he beseecheth them not to esteem more highly of themselves than they ought, but that they would be humble and sober-minded, and not stretch themselves beyond their line, but they would have a care to those that had received gifts to these uses there mentioned. I speak not, I thank God, it is far from my heart, for a Ministry deriving itself through the Papacy and pretending to that which is so much insisted upon to be succession. The true succession is through the Spirit, given in that measure that the Spirit is given, and that is a right succession. But I need not discourse of these things to you; I am persuaded you are taught of God in a greater measure than myself in these things.

Indeed I have but one word more to say, and that is, though in that perhaps I shall shew my weakness, it is by way of encouragement to you to go on in this work. And give me leave to begin thus. I confess I never looked to see such a day as this,—it may be nor you neither,—when Jesus Christ shall be owned as he is this day and in this world. Jesus Christ is owned this day by your call, and you own him by your willingness in appearing here, and you manifest this, as far as poor creatures can, to be a day of the power of Christ by your willingness. I know you remember that Scripture in Psalm 110: 3, *The people shall be willing in the day of thy power*. God doth manifest it to be a day of the power of Jesus Christ, having through so much blood and so much trials as have been upon these nations, made this to be one of the great issues thereof, to have a people called to the supreme authority upon an avowed account. God hath owned his Son by this, and you by your willingness do own Jesus Christ. And therefore for my part I confess, I did never look to see such a day. Perhaps you are not known by face one to another, indeed I am confident you are strangers, coming from all parts of the nation as you do, but we must tell you this, that indeed we have not allowed ourselves in the choice of one person, in whom we had not this good hope, that there was faith in Jesus Christ and love unto all his Saints and people.

And thus God hath owned you in the face and eyes of the world, and thus by your coming hither have you owned him, as it is in Isaiah 43: 21. It is an high expression, and look to your own hearts whether, now or hereafter, God shall apply it to you. *This people*, saith he, *I have formed for myself, that they might shew forth my praise.* It is a memorable place, and I hope not unfitly applied. God apply it to each of your hearts. I shall not descant upon the words; they are plain. You are as like the forming of God as ever people were. If any man should ask you one by one and should tender a book to you, you would dare to swear, that neither directly nor indirectly did you seek to come hither. You have been passive in coming hither, in being called hither; and that is an active word, *This people have I formed*. Consider the circumstances by which you are called together, through what difficulties, through what strivings, through what blood you are come hither. Neither you nor I, nor no man living, three months ago had a thought to have seen such a company, taking upon them, or rather being called to the supreme authority. And therefore own now your call. Indeed I think, as it may be truly said, that there never was a supreme authority, consisting of so numerous a body as you are, which I believe are above 140, were ever in the supreme authority under such a notion, in such a way of owning God and being owned by him. And therefore I say also, never a people formed for such a purpose, so called, if it were time to compare your standing with those that have been called by the suffrages of the people. Who can tell how soon God may fit the people for such a thing, and who would desire anything more in the world but that it might be so? I would all the Lord's people were prophets, I would they were fit to be called and fit to call, and it is the longing of our hearts to see them once own the interest of Jesus Christ. And give me leave to say, if I know anything in the world, what is there more like to win the people to the interest of Jesus Christ and the love of Godliness? Nay, what a duty will lie upon you to have your conversation such, as that they may love you, that they may see you lay out your time and spirits for them? Is not this the most likely way to bring them to their liberties? And do you not by this put it upon God to find the time and the season for it by pouring forth his Spirit, at least by convincing them, that as men fearing God have fought them out of their thraldom and bondage under the regal power, so men fearing God rule them in the fear of God and take care to administer good unto them? But this is some digression. I say, own your call; for indeed it is marvellous and it is of God, and it hath been unprojected, unthought of by you and us. And that hath been the way God hath dealt with us all along, to keep things from our eyes, so that in what we have acted we have seen nothing before us; which is also a witness in some measure to our integrity. I say, you are called with a high call; and why should we be afraid to say or think, that this way may be the door to usher in things that God hath promised and prophesied of, and so set the hearts of his people to wait for and expect? We know who they are that shall war with the Lamb against his enemies; they shall be a people, called, chosen, and faithful. And God hath in the military way,—we must speak it without flattery, I believe you know it,—he hath acted with them and for them; and now he will act with them in the civil power and authority. These are not ill prognostications for that good we wait for. Indeed I do think something is at the door. We are at the threshold, and therefore it becomes us to lift up our heads and to encourage ourselves in the Lord. And we have some of us thought it our duty to endeavour this way, not vainly looking on that prophecy in Daniel, *And the Kingdom shall not be delivered to another people.* Truly God hath brought it into your hands by his owning and blessing, and calling out a military power. God hath persuaded their hearts to be instrumental in calling you; and this hath been set upon our hearts and upon all the faithful in the land, it may be that it is not our duty to deliver it over to any other people, and that the Scripture may be fulfilling now to us. But I may be beyond my line, these things are dark. But I thank God I have my hopes exercised in these things, and so I am persuaded are yours.

Truly seeing that these things are so, that you are at the edge of the promises and prophecies,—at least if there were neither promise for this, nor prophecy,—you should be sensible of your duty, carrying on the best things, endeavouring after the best things. And as I have said elsewhere, if I were to choose the meanest officer in the Army or Commonwealth, I would choose a godly man that hath principles; especially where a trust is to be committed, because I know where to have a man that hath principles. I believe if any man of you should choose a servant, you would do so, and I would all our Magistrates were so chosen; that may be some effects of this meeting. It is our duty to choose men that fear the Lord, who praise the Lord, yea, such as the Lord forms for himself, and he expects not praises from others. This being so, it puts me in mind of another Scripture, Psalm 68, which indeed is a glorious prophecy, and I am persuaded of the Gospel it may be of the Jews also. There it is prophesied, *He will bring his people again out of the depths of the sea*, as once he led Israel through the Red Sea; and it may be some do think God is bringing the Jews home to their station from the *isles of the sea*, but surely when God sets up the glory of the Gospel-Church it shall be a gathering of people out of deep waters, out of the multitude of waters, of such as are his people, drawn out of the multitudes of the nations and people of the world. And that Psalm will be very glorious in many other parts of it, *When he gave the word, great was the company of them that published it. Kings of the armies did fly apace and she that tarried at home divided the spoil. And although ye have lain among the pots, yet shall ye be as the wings of a dove covered with silver and her feathers with yellow gold.* And indeed the triumph of that Psalm is exceeding high and great, and God is accomplishing it. And the close of it, that closeth with my heart and I am persuaded with yours also. That God, *shakes hills and mountains and they reel*, and God hath a hill too, *and his hill is as the hill of Bashan, and the chariots of God are twenty thousand of Angels, and God will dwell upon this hill for ever*.

Truly I am sorry that I have troubled you, in such a place of heat as this is, so long. All that I have to say in mine own name and in the names of my fellow-Officers, who have joined with me in this work, is that we shall commend you to the grace of God and to the guidance of his spirit. Having thus far served you,—or rather our Lord Jesus Christ in it,—we are as we hope, and shall be, ready in our stations according as the providence of God shall lead us to be subservient to the work of God and the authority which we reckon God hath set over us. And although we have no formal thing to present you with, to which the hands and the outward visible expressions of the hearts of the Officers of the three nations are set, yet we may say for them, and we may say also with confidence for our brethren at sea,—with whom neither in Scotland, nor Ireland, nor at sea, hath any artifice been used to persuade their approbations to this work,—yet we can say, that their consent and affections have flowed into us from all parts beyond our expectations. And we are confident, we may say with all confidence, that we have had their approbations and full consent, unsought indeed to the other work, so that you have their hearts and affections in this. And not only they, but we have very many papers from the Churches of God throughout the nation, wonderfully both approving what hath been done in removing obstacles and approving what we have done in this very thing. And having said this I shall trouble you no more, but if you will be pleased that this Instrument may be read, which I have signed by the advice of the Council of Officers, we shall then leave you to your own thoughts and to the guidance of God, to order and dispose of yourselves for further meetings as you shall see cause.

At this point the Instrument was read out.

I have only this to say further, that the affairs of this nation laying on our hands to be taken care of, and knowing that both the affairs at sea, the armies in Ireland and Scotland, and the providing of things for the preventing of inconveniences and the answering of all emergencies, did require that there should be no interruption, but that care ought to be taken for these things; and foreseeing likewise, that before you could digest yourselves into such a method as you may think best, both for place, time, and other circumstances, in the way you shall purpose to proceed in, would ask some time, which the Commonwealth would not bear in respect of the managing of things, I have within a week set up a Council of State, to whom the managing of affairs is committed, who, I may say, very voluntarily and freely, before they see how the issue of things would be, engaged themselves in this business, eight or nine of them being Members of the House that late was. I say I did exercise that power, that I thought was devolved upon me at that time, to the end affairs might not have any interval; and now when you are met, it will ask some time for the settling of your affairs and your way, and a day cannot be lost, but they must be in a continual Council till such time as you shall take further order, so that the whole matter of their considerations are also at your disposal, as you shall see cause. And therefore I thought it my

duty to acquaint you with this much, that you may not be
distracted in your way, that things have been thus ordered, that
your affairs will go on till you see cause to alter this Council, they
having no authority nor longer to sit than until you shall take
further order.'

[The powers assigned to the Council of State were then read out,
and his Excellency left the room. The new Representative
adjourned after appointing the next day to being with prayer and
then to spend the whole day amongst themselves.]

3.

4 September 1654 – Speech in the Painted Chamber to the Parliament

This single-chamber parliament was called under the Instrument
of Government which provided for triennial meetings, the first to
be in September 1654, allowing a reasonable period for the new
executive of Protector and Council to establish itself, partly by
means of ordinances to be later confirmed or denied by parliament.
Cromwell, though no dictator, put before it a personal programme
of 'healing and settling', assuming the automatic acceptance of the
Instrument ('the Government') under which MPs had been elected.

'Gentlemen,
You are met here on the greatest occasion that, I believe,
England ever saw, having upon your shoulders the interest of
three great nations, with the territories belonging to them. And
truly, I believe I may say it without an hyperbole, you have upon
your shoulders the interest of all the Christian people in the
world; and the expectation is that I should let you know, as far as I
have cognizance of it, the occasion of your assembling together at
this time. It hath been very well hinted to you this day, that you
come hither to settle the interests before mentioned; for it will be
made of so large extension in the issue and consequence of it.

In the way and manner of my speaking to you I shall study plainness, and to speak to you what is truth and what is upon my heart, and what will in some measure reach to these concernments.

After so many changes and turnings which this nation hath laboured under, to have such a day of hope as this is, and such a door of hope opened by God to us, truly I believe, some months since would have been above all our thoughts.

I confess it would have been worthy of such a meeting as this, to have remembered that which was the rise, and gave the first beginning to all those turnings and tossings that have been upon these nations; and to have given you a series of transactions,—not of men, but of the providence of God,—all along unto our late changes, as also the ground of our first undertaking to oppose that usurpation and tyranny that was upon us, both in civils and spirituals, and the several grounds particularly applicable to the several changes that have been.

But I have two or three reasons, which divert me from such a way of proceeding at this time. If I should have gone in that way, that which is upon my heart to have said,—which is written there, that if I would blot it out I could not,—would have spent this day; the providences and dispensations of God have been so stupendous. As David said in the like case, *Many, O Lord my God, are thy wonderful works which thou hast done; and thy thoughts which are to usward, they cannot be reckoned up in order unto thee; if I would declare and speak of them they are more than can be numbered.*

Truly another reason, new to me, you had today in the sermon. Much recapitulation of providence, much allusion to a State, and dispensation in respect of discipline and correction, of mercies and deliverances,—the only parallel of God's dealing with us that I know in the world, which was largely and wisely held forth to you this day,—Israel's bringing out of Egypt through a wilderness, by many signs and wonders towards a place of rest: I say, towards it. And that having been so well remonstrated to you this day, is another argument why I shall not trouble you with recapitulation of those things, though they are things that I hope will never be forgotten, because written in better books than those of paper; I am persuaded written in the heart of every good man.

The third reason was this, that which I judge to be the great end of your meeting, the great end,—which was likewise remembered to you this day,—to wit, healing and settling. And the remembering transactions too particularly, perhaps instead of healing, at least in the hearts of many of you, may set the wound fresh a bleeding. I must profess this to you, whatever thoughts pass upon me, that if this day, that is this meeting, prove not healing, what shall we do? But as I said before, seeing I trust it is in the minds of you all, and much more in the mind of God, which must cause healing,—it must be first in his mind, and he being pleased to put it into yours it will be a day indeed, and such a day as generations to come will bless you for,—I say for this and the other reasons, have I forborne to make a particular remembrance and enumeration of things, and of the manner of the Lord's bringing us through so many changes and turnings, as have passed upon us.

Howbeit, I think it will be more than necessary to let you know, at the least so well as I may, in what condition this, nay these nations were, when this government was undertaken.

For order sake, it's very natural for us to consider, what our condition was in civils, in spirituals. What was our condition? Every man's hand almost was against his brother, at least his heart, little regarding anything that should cement and might have a tendency in it to cause us to grow into one. All the dispensations of God, his terrible ones,—he having met us in the way of his judgment in a ten years' civil war, a very sharp one,—his merciful dispensations, they did not, they did not work upon us but we had our humours and interests; and indeed I fear our humours were more than our interests. And certainly as it fell out, in such cases, our passions were more than our judgments.

Was not everything almost grown arbitrary? Who knew, where or how to have a right, without some obstruction or other intervening? Indeed, we were almost grown arbitrary in everything. What was the face that was upon our affairs as to the interest of the nation? to the authority of the nation? to the magistracy? to the ranks and orders of men, whereby England had been known for hundreds of years? A nobleman, a gentleman, a yeoman? That is a good interest of the nation and a great one. The magistracy of the nation, was it not almost trampled under foot, under despite and contempt by men of Levelling principles? I beseech you, for the orders of men and ranks of men, did not that Levelling principle tend to the reducing all to an equality? Did it think to do so, or did it practise towards it for propriety and interest? What was the design, but to make the tenant as liberal a fortune as the landlord? which I think if obtained, would not have lasted long. The men of that principle, after they had served their own turns, would have cried up interest and property then fast enough. This instance is instead of many, and that it may appear that this thing did extend far, is manifest, because it was a pleasing voice to all poor men, and truly not unwelcome to all bad men. To my thinking, it is a consideration, that in your endeavours after settlement you will be so well minded of, that I might have spared this; but let that pass.

Indeed in spiritual things, the case was more sad and deplorable, and that was told to you this day eminently. The prodigious blasphemies, contempt of God and Christ, denying of him, contempt of him and his ordinances and of the Scriptures. A spirit visibly acting those things foretold by Peter and Jude; yea, those things spoken of by Paul to Timothy, who,—when he would remember some things to be worse than the Antichristian state, of which he had spoken in the first to Timothy,—tells them what should be the lot and portion of the last times, and says, *In the last days perilous times should come, for men should be lovers of their own selves, covetous, boasters, proud, blasphemers, disobedient to parents, unthankful, &c.* And when he remembers that of the Antichristian state, he tells them, That in the latter days that state shall come in, *wherein there shall be a departing from the faith, and a giving heed to seducing spirits and doctrines of devils, speaking lies in hypocrisy, &c.*; by which description he makes the state of the last times worse than under Antichrist. And surely it may well be feared these are our times. For when men forget all rules of law and nature, and break all the bonds that fallen man hath upon him, the remainder of the image of God in his nature, which he cannot blot out and yet shall endeavour to blot out, having a form of godliness without the power, these are sad tokens of the last times. And indeed the character wherewith this spirit and principle is described in that place is so legible and visible, that he that runs may read it to be amongst us: for by such the grace of God is turned into wantonness, and Christ and the

Spirit of God made the cloak of all villany and spurious apprehensions.

And although these things will not be owned publicly as to practice,—they being so abominable and odious,—yet how this principle extends itself and whence it had its rise, makes me to think of a second sort of men, who it is true, as I said, will not practise nor own these things, yet can tell the magistrate that he hath nothing to do with men thus holding, for these are matters of conscience and opinion, they are matters of religion; what hath the magistrate to do with these things? He is to look to the outward man, but not to meddle with the inward. And truly it so happens that though these things do break out visibly to all, yet the principle wherewith these things are carried on, so forbids the magistrate to meddle with them, as it hath hitherto kept the offenders from punishment. Such considerations and pretensions of liberty, liberty of conscience and liberty of subjects, two as glorious things to be contended for as any God hath given us, yet both these also abused for the patronizing of villanies, insomuch as that it hath been an ordinary thing to say and in dispute to affirm, that it was not in the magistrate's power, he had nothing to do with it, not so much as the printing a Bible to the nation for the use of the people, lest it be imposed upon the consciences of men; for they must receive the same, traditionally and implicitly from the power of the magistrate, if thus received. The aforementioned abominations did thus swell to this height amongst us. The axe was laid to the root of the Ministry, it was Antichristian, it was Babylonish. It suffered under such a judgment, that the truth of it is, as the extremity was great on that, I wish it prove not so on this hand. The extremity was, that no man having a good testimony, having received gifts from Christ, might preach if not ordained. So now, many are on the other hand, that he who is ordained, hath a nullity or Antichristianism stamped upon his calling, so that he ought not to preach or not be heard. I wish it may not too justly be said that there was severity and sharpness, yea, too much of an imposing spirit in matter of conscience, a spirit unchristian enough in any times, most unfit for these, denying liberty to those who have earned it with their blood, who have gained civil liberty, and religious also, for those who would thus impose upon them.

We may reckon among these our spiritual evils, an evil that

hath more refinedness in it, and more colour for it, and hath deceived more people of integrity than the rest have done. For few have been catched with the former mistakes, but such as have apostatized from their holy profession, such as being corrupt in their consciences, have been forsaken by God and left to such noisome opinions. But I say, there are others more refined, many honest people, whose hearts are sincere, and the evil that hath deceived them is the mistaken notion of the Fifth Monarchy. A thing pretending more spirituality than anything else. A notion I hope we all honour, wait, and hope for, that Jesus Christ will have a time to set up his reign in our hearts, by subduing those corruptions and lusts, and evils that are there, which reign now more in the world than I hope in due time they shall do. And when more fullness of the Spirit is poured forth to subdue iniquity and bring in everlasting righteousness, then will the approach of that glory be. The carnal divisions and contentions amongst Christians, so common, are not the symptoms of that kingdom. But for men to entitle themselves on this principle, that they are the only men to rule kingdoms, govern nations, and give laws to people; to determine of property and liberty, and everything else upon such a pretence as this is, truly, they had need give clear manifestations of God's presence with them, before wise men will receive or submit to their conclusions. Besides, certainly though many of these men have good meanings, as I hope in my soul they have, yet it will be the wisdom of all knowing and experienced Christians to do as Jude saith, when he had reckoned up those horrible things done upon pretences, and happily by some upon mistakes. *Of some,* says he, *have compassion, making a difference; others save with fear, pulling them out of the fire.* I fear they will give opportunity too often for this exercise, and I hope the same will be for their good.

If men do but pretend for justice and righteousness, and be of peaceable spirits and will manifest this, let them be the subjects of the magistrate's encouragement. And if the magistrate by punishing visible miscarriages save them by that discipline,—God having ordained him for that end,—I hope it will evidence love, and no hatred, to punish where there is cause. Indeed, this is that which doth most declare the danger of that spirit; for if these were but notions,—I mean the instances that I have given you both of civil considerations and spiritual,—if I say they were but notions, they were to be let alone. Notions will hurt none but them that have them. But when they come to such practices,—as to tell us, that liberty and property are not the badges of the kingdom of Christ, and tell us that instead of regulating laws, laws are to be abrogated, indeed subverted, and perhaps would bring in the Judaical law instead of our known laws settled amongst us,—this is worthy every magistrate's consideration, especially where every stone is turned to bring confusion. I think, I say, this will be worthy of the magistrate's consideration.

Whilst these things were in the midst of us, and the nation rent and torn in spirit and principle from one end to another after this sort of manner I have now told you,—family against family, husband against wife, parents against children, and nothing in the hearts of men but overturning, overturning, overturning, a Scripture very much abused and applied to justify unpeaceable practices by all men of discontented spirits,—the common adversary in the meantime he sleeps not, and our adversaries in civil and spiritual respects did take advantage at these divisions and distractions, and did practise accordingly in the three nations of England, Scotland, and Ireland.

We know very well that emissaries of the Jesuits never came in those swarms, as they have done since these things were set on foot. And I tell you that divers gentlemen here can bear witness with me how they have had a Consistory abroad, that rules all the affairs of things in England, from an archbishop with other dependants upon him. And they had fixed in England,—of which we are able to produce the particular Instruments,—in most of the limits of the cathedrals, an episcopal power, with archdeacons, &c., and had persons authorized to exercise and distribute those things, who pervert and deceive the people. And all this while we were in this sad and, as I said, deplorable condition.

In the meantime all endeavours possible were used to hinder the work in Ireland, and the progress of the work of God in Scotland, by continual intelligences and correspondences both at home and abroad. From hence into Ireland, and from hence into Scotland, persons were stirred up and encouraged by these divisions and discomposure of affairs, to do all they could to encourage and foment the war in both these places.

To add yet to our misery, whilst we were in this condition, we were in war, deeply engaged in a war with the Portugal, whereby our trade ceased; and the evil consequences by that war were manifest and very considerable.

And not only this, but we had a war with Holland, consuming our treasure, occasioning a vast burden upon the people. A war that cost this nation full as much as the taxes came unto. The navy being one hundred and sixty ships, which cost this nation above one hundred thousand pounds a month, besides the contingencies which would make it six score thousand pounds a month. That very one war did engage us to so great a charge.

At the same time also we were in a war with France. The advantages that were taken at the discontents and divisions among ourselves, did also foment that war, and at least hinder us of an honourable peace, every man being confident that we could not hold out long. And surely they did not calculate amiss, if the Lord had not been exceeding gracious to us.

I say at the same time we had a war with France. And besides the sufferings in respect of the trade of the nation, it's most evident, that the purse of the nation had not been possibly able longer to bear it, by reason of the advantages taken by other States to improve their own and spoil our manufacture of cloth and hinder the vent thereof, which is the great staple commodity of this nation. This was our condition; spoiled in our trade, and we at this vast expense, thus dissettled at home, and having these engagements abroad.

These things being thus,—as I am persuaded it is not hard to convince every person here, they were thus,—what a heap of confusions were upon these poor nations! And either things must have been left to have sunk into the miseries these premises would suppose or a remedy must be applied. A remedy hath been applied; that hath been this government; a thing I shall say very little unto. The thing is open and visible, to be seen and read by all men, and therefore let it speak for itself. Only let me say this,— because I can speak it with comfort and confidence, before a greater than you all, that is, before the Lord,—that in the intention of it, (as to the approving our hearts to God, let men judge as they please,) it is calculated for the interest of the people, for the interest of the people alone and for their good, without respect had to any other interest. And if that be not true, I shall be bold to say again, let it speak for itself.

Truly I may, I hope humbly before God and modestly before you, say somewhat on the behalf of the government. That is, not to discourse of the particular heads of it, but to acquaint you a little with the effects of it; and that not for ostentation sake, but to the end that I may deal at this time faithfully with you by acquainting you with the state of things and what proceedings have been upon this government, that so you may know the state of our affairs. This is the main end of my putting you to this trouble.

It hath had some things in desire, and it hath done some things actually. It hath desired to reform the laws, to reform them; and for that end, it hath called together persons, without reflection of as great ability and as great integrity as are in these nations, to consider how the laws might be made plain and short, and less changeable to the people, how to lessen the expense for the good of the nation. And those things are in preparation and Bills prepared, which in due time, I make no question, will be tendered to you. There hath been care taken to put the administration of the laws into the hands of just men, men of the most known integrity and ability. The Chancery hath been reformed, and I hope to the just satisfaction of all good men. And as to the things depending there, which made the burden and work of the honourable persons intrusted in those services beyond their ability, it hath referred many of them to those places where Englishmen love to have their rights tried, the Courts of Law at Westminster.

It hath endeavoured to put a stop to that heady way, touched of likewise this day, of every man making himself a minister and a preacher. It hath endeavoured to settle a way for the approbation of men of piety and ability for the discharge of that work. And I think I may say, it hath committed that work to the trust of persons, both of the Presbyterian and independent judgments, men of as known ability, piety, and integrity, as I believe any this nation hath. And I believe also that in the care they have taken, they have laboured to approve themselves to Christ, the nation, and their own consciences. And indeed I think if there be anything of a quarrel against them, it is,—though I am not here to justify the proceedings of any,—I say, it is that they go upon such a character as the Scripture warrants to put men into that great employment; and to approve men for it, who are men who have received gifts from Him that ascended up on high, and gave gifts for the work of the Ministry and for the edifying of the body of Christ. It hath taken care, we hope, for the expulsion of all those who may be judged anyway unfit for this work, who are scandalous, and who are the common scorn and contempt of that administration.

One thing more this government hath done. It hath been instrumental to call a free Parliament, which, blessed be God, we see here this day. I say a free Parliament; and that it may continue so, I hope is in the heart and spirit of every good man in England, save such discontented persons as I have formerly mentioned. It is that which, as I have desired above my life, I shall desire to keep it so above my life.

I did before mention to you the plunges we were in, in respect of foreign states, by the war with Portugal, France, with the Dutch, the Dane; and the little assurance we had from any of our neighbours round about. I perhaps forgot it, but indeed it was a caution upon my mind, and I desire that it may be so understood, that if any good hath been done, it was the Lord, not we his poor instruments. I did instance in the wars which did exhaust your treasure and put you into such a condition, that you must have sunk therein, if it had continued but a few months longer. This I dare affirm, if strong probability can give me a ground.

You have now, though it be not the first in time, peace with Sweathland [Sweden], an honourable peace, through the endeavours of an honourable person here present as the instrument. I say you have an honourable peace with a kingdom that not many years since was much a friend to France, and lately perhaps inclinable enough to the Spaniard. And I believe you expect not very much good from any of your Catholic neighbours, nor that they would be very willing you should have a good understanding with your Protestant friends. Yet thanks be to God that peace is concluded, and as I said before it is an honourable peace.

You have a peace with the Dane, a State that lay contiguous to that part of this Island which hath given us the most trouble. And certainly if your enemies abroad be able to annoy you, it is likely they will take their advantage where it best lies, to give you trouble there. But you have a peace there, and an honourable one; satisfaction for your merchant ships, not only to their content, but to their rejoicing. I believe you will easily know it is so. You have the Sound open, which used to be obstructed. That which was and is the strength of this nation, the shipping, will now be supplied thence. And whereas you were glad to have anything of that kind at the second hand, &c., you have all manner of commerce, and at as much freedom as the Dutch themselves, there, and at the same rates and toll. And I think I may say, by that peace they cannot raise the same upon you.

You have a peace with the Dutch; a peace unto which I shall say little, because so well known in the benefit and consequences of it. And I think it was as desirable and as acceptable to the spirit of this nation, as any one thing that lay before us. And as I believe nothing so much gratified our enemies as to see us at odds, so I persuade myself nothing is of more terror nor trouble to them, than to see us thus reconciled. As a peace with the Protestant States hath much security in it, so it hath as much of honour and of assurance to the Protestant interest abroad, without which no assistance can be given thereunto. I wish it may be written upon our hearts to be zealous for that interest, for if ever it were like to come under a condition of suffering, it is now. In all the Emperor's patrimonial territories, the endeavour is to drive them out as fast as they can; and they are necessitated to run to Protestant States to seek their bread. And by this conjunction of interests I hope you will be in a more fit capacity to help them. And it begets some reviving of their spirits that you will help them as opportunity shall serve.

You have a peace likewise with the Crown of Portugal, which peace though it hung long in hand, yet is lately concluded. It is a peace that your merchants make us believe is of good concernment to their trade, their assurance being greater, and so their profit in trade thither, than to other places. And this hath been obtained in that treaty, which never was since the Inquisition was set up there, that our people which trade thither have liberty of conscience. Indeed peace is, as you were well told today, desirable with all men, as far as it may be had with conscience and honour. We are upon a treaty with France. And we may say this, that if

God give us honour in the eyes of the nations about us, we have reason to bless him for it, and so to own it. And I dare say, that there is not a nation in Europe, but they are very willing to ask a good understanding with you.

I am sorry I am thus tedious, but I did judge that it was somewhat necessary to acquaint you with these things. And things being thus, I hope you will be willing to hear a little again of the sharp, as well as the sweet. And I should not be faithful to you, nor to the interest of these nations which you and I serve, if I should not let you know all. As I said before, when this government was undertaken, we were in the midst of these divisions, and animosities, and scatterings; also thus engaged with these enemies round about us, at such a vast charge, six score thousand pounds a month for the very fleet, which was the very utmost penny of your assessments. Aye, and then all your treasure was exhausted and spent, when this government was undertaken; all accidental ways of bringing in treasure, to a very inconsiderable sum consumed. That is to say, the lands are sold, the treasures spent, rents, fee-farms, king's, queen's, princes', bishops', dean and chapters', delinquents' lands sold. These were spent when this government was undertaken. I think it is my duty to let you know so much. And that's the reason why the taxes do lie so heavy upon the people, of which we have abated thirty thousand pounds a month for the next three months.

Truly, I thought it my duty to let you know, that though God hath thus dealt with you, yet these are but entrances and doors of hope, wherein through the blessing of God you may enter into rest and peace. But you are not yet entered. You were told today of a people brought out of Egypt towards the land of Canaan, but, through unbelief, murmuring, repining, and other temptations and sins, wherewith God was provoked, they were fain to come back again, and linger many years in the wilderness, before they came to the place of rest.

We are thus far through the mercy of God. We have cause to take notice of it, that we are not brought into misery; but, as I said before, a door of hope is open. And I may say this to you; if the Lord's blessing and his presence go along with the management of affairs at this meeting, you will be enabled to put the top-stone to this work, and make the nation happy. But this must be by knowing the true state of affairs, that you are not yet like the People under Circumcision, but raw; your peaces are but newly made. And it is a maxim not to be despised, though peace be made, yet it is interest that keeps peace, and I hope you will trust it no further than you see interest upon it.

And therefore I wish that you may go forward, and not backward, and that you may have the blessings of God upon your endeavours. It's one of the great ends of calling this Parliament, that this ship of the Commonwealth may be brought into a safe harbour, which I assure you it will not well be without your counsel and advice. You have great works upon your hands. Your have Ireland to look unto; there is not much done towards the planting of it; though some things leading and preparing for it are. It is a great business to settle the government of that nation upon fit terms, such as will bear that work through. You have had likewise laid before you the considerations intimating your peace with some foreign States, but yet you have not made peace with all. And if they should see we do not manage our affairs as with that wisdom which becomes us, truly we may sink under disadvantages, for all that's done. And our enemies will have their eyes open and be revived, if they see animosities amongst us; which indeed will be their great advantage.

I do therefore persuade you to a sweet, gracious, and holy understanding of one another, and of your business, concerning which you had so good counsel this day, that indeed as it rejoiced my heart to hear it, so I hope the Lord will imprint it upon your spirits; wherein you shall have my prayers.

Having said this, and perhaps omitted many other material things through the frailty of my memory, I shall exercise plainness and freeness with you, in telling you that I have not spoken these things as one that assumes to himself dominion over you, but as one that doth resolve to be a fellow servant with you, to the interest of these great affairs and of the people of these nations. I shall therefore trouble you no longer, but desire you to repair to your House, and to exercise your own liberty in the choice of a Speaker, that so you may lose no time in carrying on your work.'

4.

12 September 1654 – Speech in the Painted Chamber to the Parliament

Cromwell's optimism about the Instrument's acceptability and parliament's readiness to get on with the tasks presented to it was speedily dashed. Among the MPs were Commonwealthsmen openly inimical to a subordinate role for parliament. To head off a confrontation the Protector intervened with this admonitory speech which divided the Instrument into fundamentals (inalienable) and circumstantials (for discussion and perhaps revision). This was accompanied by a requirement to take a Recognition, which effectively purged the House, in the expectation of making a fresh start.

'Gentlemen,

It is not long since I met you in this place, upon an occasion which gave me much more content and comfort than this doth. That which I have to say to you now will need no preamble to let me into my discourse, for the occasion of this meeting is plain enough. I could have wished with all my heart there had been no cause for it.

At that meeting I did acquaint you what the first rise was of this government which hath called you hither, and in the authority of which you came hither. Among other things that I told you of them, I said you were a free Parliament. And so you are, whilst you own the government and authority that called you hither. For certainly that word implied a reciprocation, or it implied nothing at all. Indeed there was a reciprocation implied and expressed, and I think your actions and carriages ought to be suitable. But I see it will be necessary for me now a little to magnify my office, which I have not been apt to do. I have been of this mind, I have always been of this mind, since first I entered upon it, that if God will not bear it up, let it sink. But if a duty be incumbent upon me to bear my testimony unto it, which in modesty I have hitherto forborne, I am in some measure now necessitated thereunto. And therefore that will be the prologue to my discourse.

I called not myself to this place. I say again, I called not myself to this place; of that, God is witness. And I have many witnesses, who I do believe could readily lay down their lives to bear witness to the truth of that, that is to say, that I called not myself to this place. And being in it, I bear not witness to myself; but God and the people of these nations have borne testimony to it also. If my calling be from God, and my testimony from the people, God and the people shall take it from me, else I will not part with it. I should be false to the trust that God hath placed upon me, and to the interest of the people of these nations, if I should.

That I called not myself to this place, is my first assertion. That I bear not witness to myself, but have many witnesses, is my second. These are the two things I shall take the liberty to speak more fully to you of.

To make plain and clear that which I have said, I must take liberty to look back. I was by birth a gentleman, living neither in any considerable height, nor yet in obscurity. I have been called to several employments in the nation,—to serve in Parliaments ,—and (because I would not be over tedious) I did endeavour to discharge the duty of an honest man in those services, to God, and his people's interest, and of the Commonwealth; having, when time was, a competent acceptation in the hearts of men, and some evidences thereof. I resolve not to recite the times and occasions, and opportunities that have been appointed me by God to serve him in, nor the presence and blessings of God bearing then testimony to me. I, having had some occasions to see, together with my brethren and countrymen, a happy period put to our sharp wars and contests with the then common enemy, hoped, in a private capacity, to have reaped the fruit and benefit, together with my brethren, of our hard labours and hazards, to wit, the enjoyment of peace and liberty, and the privileges of a Christian and of a man, in some equality with others, according as it should please the Lord to dispense unto me. And when, I say, God had put an end to our wars, at least brought them to a very hopeful issue, very near an end, after Worcester fight I came up to London to pay my service and duty to the Parliament that then sat. And hoping that all minds would have been disposed to answer that which seemed to be the mind of God, (*viz.*) to give peace and rest to his people, and especially to those who had bled more than others in the carrying on of the military affairs, I was much disappointed of my expectation, for the issue did not prove so; whatever may be boasted or misrepresented, it was not so, nor so. I can say in the simplicity of my soul, I love not, I love not, I declined it in my former speech, I say I love not to rake into sores or to discover nakedness. That which I drive at is this; I say to you, I hoped to have had leave to have retired to a private life, I begged to be dismissed of my charge, I begged it again and again, and God be judge between me and all men if I lie in this matter. That I lie not in matter of fact is known to very many, but whether I tell a lie in my heart, as labouring to represent to you that which was not upon my heart, I say, the Lord be judge. Let uncharitable men that measure others by themselves, judge as they please; as to the matter of fact, I say it is true. As to the ingenuity and integrity of my heart in that desire, I do appeal as before upon the truth of that also. But I could not obtain what my soul longed for, and the plain truth is I did afterwards apprehend that some did think, my judgment not suiting with theirs, that it could not well be. But this, I say to you, was between God and my soul, between me and that assembly.

I confess I am in some strait to say what I could say, and what is true of what then followed. I pressed the Parliament, as a member, to period themselves, once, and again, and again, and ten and twenty times over. I told them,—for I knew it better than any one man in the Parliament could know it, because of my manner of life, which was to run up and down the nation, and so might see and know the temper and spirits of all men, the best of men,—that the nation loathed their sitting; I knew it. And, so far as I could discern, when they were dissolved, there was not so much as the barking of a dog, or any general and visible repining at it. You are not a few here present that can assert this as well as myself. And that there was high cause for their dissolving is most evident, not only in regard there was a just fear of the Parliament's perpetuating themselves, but because it was their design. And had not their heels been trod upon by importunities from abroad, even to threats, I believe there would never have been thoughts of rising or of going out of that room to the world's end. I myself was sounded, and by no mean persons tempted, and addresses were made to me to that very end, that it might have been thus perpetuated, that the vacant places might be supplied by new elections, and so continue from generation to generation.

I have declined, I have declined very much, to open these things to you; yet having proceeded thus far I must tell you, that poor men under this arbitrary power were driven like flocks of sheep by forty in a morning, to the confiscation of goods and estates, without any man being able to give a reason that two of them had deserved to forfeit a shilling. I tell you the truth, on my soul, and many persons whose faces I see in this place, were exceedingly grieved at these things, and knew not which way to help it, but by their mournings and giving their negatives when occasions served. I have given you but a taste of miscarriages; I am confident you have had opportunities to hear much more of them, for nothing is more obvious.

It's true, this will be said, that there was a remedy to put an end to this perpetual Parliament endeavoured, by having a future Representative. How it was gotten, and by what importunities that was obtained, and how unwillingly yielded unto, is well known. What was this remedy? It was a seeming willingness to have successive Parliaments. What was that succession? It was, that when one Parliament had left their seat, another was to sit down immediately in the room thereof, without any caution to avoid that which was the danger, (*viz.*) perpetuating of the same Parliaments; which is a sore now that will ever be running, so long as men are ambitious and troublesome, if a due remedy be not found. So then, what was the business? It was a conversion from a Parliament that should have been and was perpetual, to a Legislative Power always sitting; and so the liberties, and interests, and lives of people not judged by any certain known laws and power, but by an arbitrary power,— which is incident and necessary to Parliaments,— by an arbitrary power, I say, to make men's estates liable to confiscation, and their persons to imprisonments, sometimes by laws made after the fact committed, often by taking the judgment both in capital and criminal things to themselves, who in former times were not known to exercise such a judicature. This I suppose was the case, and in my opinion the remedy was fitted to the disease, especially coming in the rear of a Parliament so exercising the power and authority as this had done but immediately before.

Truly I confess upon these grounds, and with the satisfaction of

divers other persons, seeing nothing could be had otherwise, that
Parliament was dissolved. And we, desiring to see if a few might
have been called together for some short time, who might put the
nation into some way of certain settlement, did call those
gentlemen out of the several parts of the nation for that purpose.
And as I have appealed to God before you already, I know and I
hope I may say it,—though it be a tender thing to make appeals to
God, yet in such exigencies as these I trust it will not offend his
Majesty, especially to make them before persons that know God,
and know what conscience is, and what it is to lie before the
Lord,—I say, that as a principal end in calling that assembly was
the settlement of the nation, so a chief end to myself was, that I
might have opportunity to lay down the power that was in my
hands. I say to you again, in the presence of that God who hath
blessed and been with me in all my adversities and successes, that
was as to myself my greatest end. A desire perhaps, and I am
afraid sinful enough, to be quit of the power God had most
providentially put into my hand, before he called for it, and before
those honest ends of our fighting were attained and settled.

I say, the authority I had in my hand being so boundless as it
was, I being by Act of Parliament General of all the forces in the
three nations of England, Scotland, and Ireland,—in which
unlimited condition I did not desire to live a day,—did call that
meeting for the ends before expressed. What the event and issue of
that meeting was, we may sadly remember: it hath much teaching
in it, and I hope will make us all wiser for the future. But this
meeting succeeding, as I have formerly said to you, and giving
such a disappointment to our hopes, I shall not now make any
repetition thereof. Only the effect was, that they came and
brought to me a parchment, signed by very much the major part of
them, expressing their resigning and redelivery of the power and
authority that was committed to them back again into my hands.
And I can say it in the presence of divers persons here, that do
know whether I lie in that, that I did not know one tittle of that
resignation, until they all came and brought it, and delivered it
into my hands; of this there are also in this presence many
witnesses. I received this resignation, having formerly used my
endeavours and persuasions to keep them together. Observing
their differences, I thought it my duty to give advices to them, that

so I might prevail with them for union, but it had the effect that I told you, and I had my disappointment. When this was so, we were exceedingly to seek how to settle things for the future. My power again by this resignation was as boundless and unlimited as before; all things being subjected to arbitrariness, and a person having power over the three nations boundlessly and unlimited, and upon the matter, all government dissolved, all civil administrations at an end, will presently be made to appear.

The gentlemen that undertook to frame this government did consult divers days together,—they being of known integrity and ability,—how to frame somewhat that might give us settlement, and they did so; and that I was not privy to their counsels, they know it. When they had finished their model in some measure, or made a very good preparation of it, it became communicative. They told me that except I would undertake the government, they thought things would hardly come to a composure and settlement, but blood and confusion would break in upon us. I denied it again and again, as God and those persons know, not complimentingly as they also know and as God knows. I confess after many arguments, and after the letting of me know that I did not receive anything that put me into any higher capacity than I was in before, but that it limited me and bound my hands to act nothing to the prejudice of the nations without consent of a Council until the Parliament met, and then limited me by the Parliament as the Act of Government expresseth, I did accept it. I might repeat this again to you, if it were needful, but I think I need not. I was arbitrary in power, having the armies in the three nations under my command, and truly not very ill beloved by them, nor very ill beloved then by the people, by the good people. And I believe I should have been more beloved if they had known the truth, as things were before God, and in themselves, and before divers of these gentlemen whom I but now mentioned unto you. I did, at the entreaty of divers persons of honour and quality, at the entreaty of very many of the chief officers of the army then present, and at their request, I did accept of the place and title of Protector, and was in the presence of the Commissioners of the Seal, the Judges, the Lord Mayor and Aldermen of the City of London, the soldiery, divers gentlemen, citizens, and divers other people and persons of quality, &c., accompanied to Westminster Hall, where I took my oath to this government. This was not done in a corner; it was open and public. This government hath been exercised by a Council, with a desire to be faithful in all things, and amongst all other trusts to be faithful in calling this Parliament. And thus I have given you a very bare and lean discourse, which truly I have been necessitated unto, and contracted in because of the unexpectedness of the occasion, and because I would not quite weary you nor myself. But this is a narrative that discovers to you the series of providence and of transactions leading me into this condition wherein I now stand.

The next thing I promised you, wherein I hope I shall not be so long, though I am sure this occasion does require plainness and freedom, is that as I brought not myself into this condition, as in my own apprehension I did not; and that I did not, the things being true which I have told you, I submit it to your judgments and there shall I leave it, let God do what he pleaseth. The other thing, I say, that I am to speak to you of, is that I have not, nor do not bear witness to myself. I am far from alluding to Him that said so; yet truth concerning a member of his, he will own though men do not. But I think, if I mistake not, I have a cloud of witnesses. I think so, let men be as froward as they will. I have witness within, without, and above. But I shall speak of them that are without, having fully spoken before of the witness above and the witness in my own conscience upon the other account, because that subject had more obscurity in it, and I in some sort needed appeals and I trust might lawfully make them, as well as take an oath where things were not so apt to be made evident. I shall enumerate my witnesses as well as I can. When I had consented to accept of the government there was some solemnity to be performed, and that was accompanied with some persons of considerableness in all respects, who were the persons before expressed, who accompanied me, at the time of my entering upon this government, to Westminster Hall to take my oath. *There* was an explicit consent of interested persons; and an implicit consent of many, showing their good liking and approbation thereof. And, gentlemen, I do not think that you are altogether strangers to it in your country; some did not nauseate it, very many did approve it. I had the approbation of the officers of the army in the three nations of England, Scotland, and Ireland; I say, of the officers. I had that by their Remonstrances, and under signature. There went along with that explicit consent, an implicit consent of persons that had somewhat to do in the world, that had been instrumental by God to fight down the enemies of God and his people in the three nations. And truly, until my hands were bound, and I limited,—wherein I took full contentment, as many can bear me witness,—when I had in my hands so great a power and arbitrariness, the soldiery were a very considerable part of the nations, especially all government being dissolved. I say, when all government was thus dissolved, and nothing to keep things in order but the sword, and yet they,—which many histories will not parallel,—even they were desirous that things might come to a consistency, and arbitrariness might be taken away, and the government put into a person, limited and bounded as in the Act of Settlement, whom they distrusted the least, and loved not the worst. This was another evidence. I would not forget the honourable and civil entertainment, with the approbation I found in the great City of London, which the City knows whether I directly or indirectly sought. And truly I do not think it is folly to remember this, for it was very great and high, and very public, and as numerous a body of those that are known by names and titles,—the several corporations and societies of citizens in this city,—as hath been at any time seen in England, and not without some appearance of satisfaction also. I had not only this witness, but I have had from the greatest county in England, and from many cities, and boroughs, and many counties, explicit approbations; not of those gathered here and there, but from the county of York, and City of York, and other counties and places, assembled in their public and general assizes; the Grand Jury in the name of the noblemen, gentlemen, yeomen, and inhabitants of that county, giving very great thanks to me for undertaking this heavy burden at such a time, and giving very great approbation and encouragement to me to go through with it. These are plain. I have them to shew, and by these in some measure it will appear, I do not bear witness to myself. This is not all. The Judges,—and truly I had almost forgotten it,—they thinking that there was a dissolution of government, met and consulted, and did declare one to another that they could not administer justice to the satisfaction of their consciences, until they had received commissions from me; and they did receive commissions from me, and by virtue of those commissions they have acted. And all the Justices of the Peace that have acted, have acted by virtue of like commissions, which was a little more than an implicit approbation. And I believe all the justice administered in the nation hath been by this authority, which also I lay before you, desiring you to think whether all these persons before mentioned must not come before you for an Act of oblivion and general pardon, who have acted under and testified to this government, if it be disowned by you.

I have two or three witnesses more, equivalent to all these I have reckoned, if I be not mistaken, and greatly mistaken. If I should say, all you that are here are my witnesses, I should say no untruth. I know you are the same persons here that you were in the country, but I will reserve to speak to this at the last, for this will be the issue of my speech.

I say, I have two or three witnesses that are more than all I have accounted and reckoned before. All the people in England are my witnesses, and many in Ireland and Scotland. All the sheriffs in England are my witnesses; and all that came in upon the process issued out by the sheriffs are my witnesses. Yea, the returns of the elections to the Clerk of the Crown, not a thing to be blown away with a breath; the returns on the behalf of the inhabitants in the counties, cities, and boroughs, all are my witnesses, of appro-bation to the condition and place I stand in. And I shall now make you my last witnesses, and ask you whether you came not hither by my writs, directed to the several sheriffs, and so to other officers in cities and liberties? To which the people gave obedi-ence, having also had the Act of Government communicated to them, to which end great numbers of copies were sent down on purpose to be communicated to them; and the government also required to be distinctly read unto the people at the place of elections to avoid surprises, where also they signed the Indenture with proviso, that the persons so chosen shall not have power to alter the government as it is now settled in one single person and a Parliament.

And thus I have made good my second assertion, that I bear not witness to myself; but the good people of England, and you all, are my witnesses.

Yea surely, and this being so, though I told you in my last

speech that you were a free Parliament, yet I thought it was understood that I was the Protector, and the authority that called you, and that I was in possession of the government by a good right from God and men. And I believe, if the learnedest men in this nation were called to show a precedent so clear, so many ways approving of a government, they would not in all their search find it.

I did not in my other speech to you take upon me to justify the government in every particular; and I told you the reason of it, which was plain. It was public and had been long published, and it might be under the most serious inspection of all that pleased to peruse it. By what I have said, I have approved myself to God and my conscience in my actions and in this undertaking; and I have given cause of approving myself to every one of your consciences in the sight of God.

If it be so, why should we sport with it, with a business so serious? May not this character, this stamp, bear equal poise with any hereditary interest, which may have, and hath had, in the common law, matters of dispute and trial of learning? wherein many have exercised more wit, and spilt more blood, than I hope ever to live to see or hear of in this nation. I say, I do not know why I may not balance this providence,—as in the sight of God,—with any hereditary interest, as being less subject to those cracks and flaws they are commonly incident unto: which titles have cost more blood in former times in this nation, than we have leisure to speak of now.

Now if this be thus,—and I am deriving a title from God and men upon such accounts as these are,—although some men be froward, yet for you in your judgments, that are persons sent from all parts of the nation under the notion of an acceptance of the government, for you to disown or not to own it; for you, to act Parliamentary authority, especially in the disowning of it, contrary to the very fundamental things, yea, against the very root itself of this Establishment; for you to sit, and not own the authority by which you sit, it is that, that I believe astonisheth more men than myself, and doth as dangerously disappoint, and discompose the nation, as anything that could have been invented by the greatest enemy to our peace and welfare, or could well have happened.

It is true, there are some things in the Establishment that are fundamental, and some things are not so, but are circumstantial. Of such, no question but I shall easily agree to vary, or leave out, as I shall be convinced by reason. Some things are fundamentals, about which I shall deal plainly with you; they may not be parted with, but will, I trust, be delivered over to posterity, as being the fruits of our blood and travail.

The government by a single person and a Parliament is a fundamental; it is the *esse*, it is constitutive. And for the person, though I may seem to plead for myself, yet I do not, no, nor can any reasonable man say it. But if the things throughout this speech be true, I plead for this nation, and all honest men therein who have borne their testimony as aforesaid, and not for myself. And if things should do otherwise than well, which I would not fear, and the common enemy and discontented persons take advantage at these distractions, the issue will be put up before God. Let him own it or disown it, as he please. In every government there must be somewhat fundamental, somewhat like a Magna Charta, that should be standing and be unalterable. Where there is a stipulation on one part, and that fully accepted, as appears by what hath been said, surely a return ought to be: else what does that stipulation signify? If I have upon the terms aforesaid undertaken this great trust and exercised it, and by it called you, surely it ought to be owned. That Parliaments should not make themselves perpetual, is a fundamental. Of what assurance is a law to prevent so great an evil, if it lie in one or the same legislator to unlaw it again? Is this like to be lasting? It will be like a rope of sand; it will give no security, for the same men may unbuild what they have built.

Is not liberty of conscience in religion a fundamental? So long as there is liberty of conscience for the supreme magistrate, to exercise his conscience in erecting what form of church-government he is satisfied he should set up, why should he not give it to others? Liberty of conscience is a natural right; and he that would have it ought to give it, having liberty to settle what he likes for the public. Indeed, that hath been one of the vanities of our contests. Every sect saith, Oh! Give me liberty. But give him it, and to his power he will not yield it to anybody else. Where is our ingenuity? Truly, that's a thing ought to be very reciprocal. The magistrate hath his supremacy, and he may settle religion according to his conscience. And I may say it to you,—I can say it,—all the money of this nation would not have tempted men to fight, upon such an account as they have engaged, if they had not had hopes of liberty, better than they had from Episcopacy, or than would have been afforded them from a Scottish Presbytery; or an English either, if it had made such steps or been as sharp and rigid as it threatened when it was first set up. This I say is a fundamental. It ought to be so: it is for us, and the generations to come. And if there be an absoluteness in the imposer, without fitting allowances and exceptions from the rule, we shall have our people driven into wildernesses, as they were when those poor and afflicted people, that forsook their estates and inheritances here, where they lived plentifully and comfortably, for the enjoyment of their liberty, and were necessitated to go into a vast howling wilderness in New England, where they have for liberty sake stript themselves of all their comfort and the full enjoyment they had, embracing rather loss of friends and want, than to be ensnared and in bondage.

Another, which I had forgotten, is the Militia; that's judged a fundamental, if anything be so. That it should be well and equally placed, is very necessary. For put the absolute power of the Militia into one without a check, what doth it? I pray you, what doth your check put upon your perpetual Parliaments, if it be wholly stript of this?

It is equally placed; and desires were to have it so, (*viz.*) in one Person, and the Parliament,—sitting, the Parliament. What signifies a provision against perpetuating of Parliaments, if this be solely in them? Whether, without a check, the Parliament have not liberty to altar the frame of government to Aristocracy, to Democracy, to Anarchy, to anything, if this be fully in them, yea, into all confusion, and that without remedy? And if this one thing be placed in one; that one, be it Parliament, be it supreme governor, they or he hath power to make what they please of all the rest.

Therefore, if you would have a balance at all, and that some fundamentals must stand which may be worthy to be delivered over to posterity, truly I think it is not unreasonably urged, that the Militia should be disposed, as it is laid down in the Act of

Government, and that it should be so equally placed, that one person, neither in Parliament, nor out of Parliament, should have the power of ordering it. The council are the trustees of the Commonwealth, in all intervals of Parliaments; who have as absolute a negative upon the supreme officer in the said intervals, as the Parliament hath whilst it is sitting. It cannot be made use of, a man cannot be raised nor a penny charged upon the people, nothing can be done without consent of Parliament; and in the intervals of Parliament, without consent of the Council it is not to be exercised.

Give me leave to say, that there is very little power, none but what is co-ordinate, in the supreme officer, and yet enough in him that hath the chief government. In that particular he is bound in strictness by the Parliament, out of Parliament by the Council, that do as absolutely bind him, as the Parliament, when Parliament is sitting.

For that of money, I told you some things are circumstantials. To have two hundred thousand pounds, to defray civil officers, to pay the Judges, and other officers, defraying the charges of the Council, in sending their embassies, in keeping intelligence, and doing that that's necessary, and for supporting the Governor-in-Chief,—all this, is by the Instrument supposed and intended, but it is not of the *esse* so much, and so limited. As to so many soldiers, thirty thousand,—twenty thousand foot, and ten thousand horse,—if the spirits of men be composed, five thousand horse and ten thousand foot may serve. These things are between the Chief Officer and the Parliament, to be moderated as occasion shall offer.

So there are many other circumstantial things, which are not like the laws of the Medes and Persians. But the things which shall be necessary to hand over to posterity, these should be unalterable, else every succeeding Parliament will be disputing to change and alter the government, and we shall be as often brought into confusion as we have Parliaments, and so make our remedy our disease. The Lord's providence, (appearing evil, appearing good,) and better judgment, will give occasion for the ordering of things for the best interest of the people; and those things are the matter of consideration between you and me.

I have indeed almost tired myself. That, that I have further to say is this, I would it had not been needful for me to have called you hither to have expostulated these things with you, and in such a manner as this is. But necessity hath no law. Feigned necessities, imaginary necessities, are the greatest cozenage that men can put upon the providence of God, and make-pretences to break known rules by. But it is deceitful and as carnal and as stupid, to think that they are no necessities, that are manifest necessities, because necessities may be abused or feigned. And truly I should be so, if I should think so; and I hope none of you think so.

I say, that the wilful throwings away of this government, (such as it is, so owned by God, so approved by men, so testified to in the fundamentals of it, as is before mentioned), and that in relation to the good of these nations and posterity;—I can sooner be willing to be rolled into my grave, and buried with infamy, than I can give my consent unto.

You have been called hither together to save a nation;— nations. You had the best people indeed in the Christian world in your trust, when you came hither. You had affairs and these nations delivered over to you in peace and quietness. You were, and we all were, put into an uninterrupted possession, nobody making title to us. Through the blessing of God our enemies were hopeless and scattered. We had peace at home, peace almost with all neighbours round about: we were fit to take advantages where God did administer them.

To have our peace and interest, that had those hopes the other day, thus shaken and under such a confusion, and we rendered hereby almost the scorn and contempt of those strangers, that are amongst us to negotiate their masters' affairs; to give them opportunity to see our nakedness, as they do, a people that have been unhinged this twelve years' day, and unhinged still;—as if scattering, division, and confusion should come upon us, as if it were desired, which are the greatest plagues God ordinarily lays upon nations for sin,—I would be loth to say they are matters of our delight, but if not, why not the matter of our care, so wisely as we ought by uttermost endeavours to avoid? Nay, when by such actions as these are, these poor nations shall be thrown into heaps of confusion, through blood, and ruin, and trouble,—upon the saddest account that ever was, if breaking should come upon us,—and all because we would not settle when we might, when God put it into our hands! Your affairs now almost settled everywhere, and to have all recoil upon us, and we ourselves shaken in our affections, loosened from all known and public interests, as I have mentioned to you! Who shall answer for these things to God? Who can answer for these things to God, or to men; to the people who sent you hither, who looked for refreshment from you, who looked for nothing but peace, and quietness, and rest and settlement?

And when we shall come to give an account to them, we shall be able to say, Oh! we have quarrelled for, and we contested for the liberty of England. Wherein, forsooth? For the liberty of the people? I appeal to the Lord, that the desires and endeavours,—and the things themselves will speak for themselves,—that the liberty of England, the liberty of the people, the avoiding of tyrannous impositions, either upon men as men, or Christians as Christians, is made so safe by this Act of Settlement, that it will speak sufficiently for itself.

And when it shall appear what hath been said and done, and what our transactions have been—for God can discover, and no Privilege will hinder the Lord from discovering, no Privilege or condition of men can hide from the Lord: he can and will make all manifest, if he see it for his glory,—and when these shall by the providence of God be manifested, and the people shall come and say, "Gentlemen, what condition are we in? We hoped for light, and behold darkness, obscure darkness! We hoped for rest after ten years' Civil Wars, we are plunged into deep confusion again. Aye! we know these consequences will come upon us, if God Almighty shall not find out some way to prevent them."

I had this thought within myself, that it had not been dishonest, nor dishonourable, nor against true liberty, no not of Parliaments,—when a Parliament was so chosen in pursuance of, in conformity to, and with such an approbation and consent to the government, so that he that runs might read by what authority you came hither,—that an owning of your call, and of the authority bringing you hither, might have been required before your entrance into the House.

But this was declined, and hath not been done, because I am persuaded scarce any man could reasonably doubt you came with contrary minds. And I have reason to believe, the people that sent you least doubted thereof at all. And therefore I must deal plainly with you. What I forbare upon a just confidence at first, you necessitate me unto now, that, seeing the authority calling you is so little valued and so much slighted,—till some assurance be given and made known, that the fundamental interest of the government be settled and approved, according to the proviso contained in the Return, and such a consent testified, as will make it appear that the same is accepted,—I have caused a stop to be put to your entrance into the Parliament House.

I am sorry, I am sorry, and I could be sorry to the death, that there is cause for this. But there is cause. And if things be not satisfied, that are reasonably demanded, I for my part shall do that that becomes me, seeking my counsel from God.

There is therefore somewhat to be offered to you, that I hope will, (being understood with the qualifications that I have told you of, reforming circumstantials and agreeing in the substance and fundamentals, which is the government settled as it is expressed in the Indenture, not to be altered), by the making of your minds known in that, by giving your assent and subscription to it, be that, that will let you in to act those things as a Parliament which are for the good of the people. And this thing showed to you, and signed as aforesaid, doth determine the controversy and may give a happy progress and issue to this Parliament. The place where you may come thus and sign, as many as God shall make free thereunto, is in this lobby without the Parliament door.

The Act of Government doth declare, that you have a legislative power without a negative from me. As the government doth express, you may make any laws, and if I give not my consent within twenty days to the passing of your laws, they are *ipso facto* laws, whether I consent or no, if not contrary to the government. You have an absolute legislative power in all things that can possibly concern the good and interest of the public. And I think you may make these nations happy by this settlement. And I for my part shall be willing to be bound more than I am, in anything that I may be convinced of may be for the good of the people, in preservation of the cause and interest so long contended for.'

5.

22 January 1654/5 – Speech in the Painted Chamber to the Parliament, at their dissolution

The purge of 12 September did not end the onslaught on the Instrument. Clause by clause a revised constitution was built up, redressing the balance in favour of parliament and away from the Council of State. Moreover, outside parliament the régime faced adverse developments, notably growing evidence of a plot for a nationwide royalist rising. Parliament was therefore dissolved at the earliest date allowed under the Instrument, five months taken as lunar (28 days) rather than calendar months. This was an 'addled' parliament, i.e. it passed no legislation, though bills had been brought in. The royalist rising failed to come off, except forlornly in the south-west. But the threat combined with other issues to justify the introduction of the system of the Major-Generals.

'Gentlemen,

I perceive you are here as the House of Parliament, by your Speaker whom I see here, and by your faces, which are, in a great measure, known to me.

When I first met you in this room, it was, to my apprehension, the hopefullest day that ever mine eyes saw, as to considerations of this world: for I did look at—as wrapt up in you, together with myself—the hopes and the happiness of though not of the greatest, yet a very great and the best people in the world. And truly and unfeignedly I thought so; as a people that have the highest and clearest profession among them of the greatest glory, to wit religion; as a people that have been, like other nations, sometimes up and sometimes down, in our honour in the world, but yet never so low, but we might measure with other nations; and as a people that have had a stamp upon them from God; God having, as it were, summed all our former glory and honour, in the things that are of glory to nations, in an *epitome*, within these ten or twelve years past, so that we know one another at home, and are well known abroad. And, if I be not very much mistaken, we were arrived,—as I, and truly as I believe many others did think,—at a very safe port, where we might sit down and contemplate the dispensations of God, and our mercies, and might know our mercies not to have been like to those of the ancients, who did make out their peace and prosperity, as they thought by their own endeavours, who could not say, as we, that all ours were let down to us from God himself, whose appearances and providences amongst us are not to be outmatched by any story.

Truly this was our condition, and I know nothing else we had to do, save as Israel was commanded in that most excellent Psalm of David, Psalm 78: 4, 5, 6, 7. *The things which we have heard and known, and our fathers have told us, we will not hide them from their children, shewing to the generation to come the praise of the Lord, and his strength, and his wonderful works which he hath done; for he established a testimony in Jacob, and appointed a law in Israel, which he commanded our fathers that they should make them known to their children, that the generation to come might know them, even the children which should be born, who should arise and declare them to their children, that they might set their hope in God, and not forget the works of God but keep his commandments.* This, I thought, had been a song and a work worthy of England, whereunto you might have happily invited them, had you had hearts unto it. You had this opportunity fairly delivered unto you; and if a history shall be written of these times and of transactions, it will be said, it will not be denied, but that these things that I have spoken are true. This *talent* was put into your hands: and I recur to that which I said at the first, I came with very great joy and contentment, and comfort, the first time I met you in this place. But we and these nations are, for the present, under some disappointment. If I had purposed to have played the orator, which I never did affect, nor do, nor I hope shall, I doubt not but upon easy suppositions, which I am persuaded every one among you will grant, I could shew we did meet upon such hopes as these.

I met you a second time here, and I confess at that meeting I had much abatement of my hopes, though not a total frustration. I confess that that which damped my hopes so soon was somewhat that did look like a parricide. It is obvious enough unto you, that the management of affairs did savour of a not-owning, too too much savour, I say, of a not-owning the authority that called you hither. But God left us not without an expedient that gave a second possibility—shall I say a possibility?—it seemed to me a probability, of recovering out of that dissatisfied condition we were all then in, towards some mutuality of satisfaction, and therefore by that Recognition, suiting with the Indenture that returned you hither. To which, afterwards, also was added your own Declaration, conformable to, and in acceptance of, that expedient, whereby you had, though with a little check, another opportunity renewed unto you to have made this nation as happy, as it could have been if everything had smoothly run on from that first hour of your meeting. And indeed,—you will give me liberty of my thoughts and hopes,—I did think, as I have formerly found in that way that I have been engaged as a soldier, that some affronts put upon us, some disasters at the first, have made way for great and happy successes. And I did not at all despond, but the stop put upon you would in like manner have made way for a blessing from God, that,—that interruption being, as I thought, necessary, to divert you from destructive and violent proceedings, to give time for better deliberations,—whereby leaving the [Instrument of] Government as you found it, you might have proceeded to have made those good and wholesome laws, which the people expected from you, and might have answered the grievances, and settled those other things proper to you as a Parliament, and for which you would have had thanks from all that entrusted you.

What hath happened since that time, I have not taken public notice of, as declining to intrench upon Parliament privileges. For sure I am, you will all bear me witness, that from your entering into the House upon the Recognition to this very day, you have had no manner of interruption or hindrance of mine in proceeding to that blessed issue which the heart of a good man could propose to himself, to this very day. You see you have me very much locked up as to what you have transacted among yourselves from that time to this, but something I shall take liberty to speak of to you. As I may not take notice what you have been doing, so I think I have a very great liberty to tell you, that I do not know what you have been doing. I do not know whether you have been alive or dead. I have not once heard from you in all this time, I have not, and that you all know; if that be a fault that I have not, surely it hath not been mine. If I have had any melancholy thoughts, and have sat down by them, why might it not have been very lawful to me, to think that I was a person judged unconcerned in all these businesses? I can assure you, I have not reckoned myself, nor did I reckon myself, unconcerned in you; and so long as any just patience could support my expectation, I would have waited to the uttermost to have received from you the issues of your consultations and resolutions. I have been careful of your safety, and the safety of those that you represented, to whom I reckon myself a servant. But what messages have I disturbed you withal? What injury or indignity hath been done or offered, either to your persons or to any privileges of Parliament, since you sat? I looked at myself, as strictly obliged by my oath, since your recognizing the government in the authority by which you were called hither and sat, to give you all possible security, and to keep you from any unparliamentary interruption. Think you I could not say more upon this subject, if I listed to expatiate thereupon? But because my actions plead for me, I shall say no more of this.

I say, I have been caring for you, your quiet sitting; caring for your privileges, as I said before, that they might not be interrupted; have been seeking of God, from the great God, a blessing upon you, and a blessing upon these nations; I have been consulting, if possibly I might in anything promote, in my place, the real good of this Parliament, of the hopefulness of which I have said so much unto you. And I did think it to be my business rather to see the utmost issue, and what God would produce by you, than unseasonably to intermeddle with you. But, as I said before, I have been caring for you, and for the peace and quiet of the nations, indeed I have, and that I shall a little presently manifest unto you.

And it leadeth me to let you know somewhat, that I fear, I fear will be through some interpretation a little too justly put upon you, whilst you have been employed as you have been, and,—in all that time expressed in the Act of Government, in that Government, I say, in that Government,—have brought forth nothing that you yourselves say can be taken notice of, without infringement of your privileges. I will tell you somewhat, that if it be not news to you, I wish you had taken very serious consideration of; if it be news, I wish I had acquainted you with it sooner.

And yet if any man will ask me why I did it not, the reason is given already, because I did make it my business to give you no interruption.

There be some trees that will not grow under the shadow of other trees. There be some that choose,—a man may say so by way of allusion,—to thrive under the shadow of other trees. I will tell you what hath thriven; I will not say what you have cherished under your shadow, that were too hard. Instead of the peace and settlement, instead of mercy and truth being brought together, righteousness and peace kissing each other, by reconciling the honest people of these nations, and settling the woful distempers that are amongst us,—which had been glorious things, and worthy of Christians to have proposed,—weeds and nettles, briers and thorns, have thriven under your shadow. Dissettlement and division, discontent and dissatisfaction, together with real dangers to the whole, has been more multiplied within these five months of your sitting, than in some years before.

Foundations have also been laid for the future renewing the troubles of these nations by all the enemies of it abroad and at home. Let not these words seem too sharp, for they are true, as any mathematical demonstrations are or can be. I say, the enemies of the peace of these nations abroad and at home, the dis-contented humours throughout these nations, which I think no man will grudge to call by that name or to make to allude to briers and thorns, they have nourished themselves under your shadow.

And that I may be clearly understood, they have taken the opportunities from your sitting, from the hopes they had, which with easy conjecture they might take up and conclude, that there would be no settlement; and therefore they have framed their designs, preparing for the execution of them accordingly. Now whether,—which appertains not to me to judge of on their behalf,—they had any occasion ministered for this, and from whence they had it, I list not to make any scrutiny or search, but I will say this, I think they had it not from me, I am sure they had not; from whence they had it is not my business now to discourse, but that they had, is obvious to every man's sense. What preparations they have made to execute their designs, in such a season as they thought fit to take their opportunity from, that I know, not as men know things by conjecture, but by certain

62

demonstrable knowledge that they have been, for some time past, furnishing themselves with arms, nothing doubting but that they should have a day for it; and verily believing, that whatsoever their former disappointments were, they should have more done for them by and from our own divisions, than they were able to do for themselves. I do not, and I desire to be understood so, that in all I have to say of this subject you will take it, that I have no reservation in my mind to mingle things of guess and suspicion with things of fact, but the things I am telling are of fact, things of evident demonstration.

These weeds, briers, and thorns, they have been preparing, and have brought their designs to some maturity by the advantages given to them, as aforesaid, from your sitting and proceedings. But by the waking eye, that watched over that cause that God will bless, they have been, and yet are disappointed. And having mentioned that cause, I say that slighted cause, let me speak a few words in behalf thereof, though it may seem too long a digression. Whosoever despiseth it, and will say it is "non causa pro causa", the all-searching eye, before mentioned, will find out that man, and will judge him as one that regardeth not the works of God, nor the operations of his hands, for which God hath threatened that he will cast men down and not build them up. That man because he can dispute and tell us, he knew not where the cause was begun nor where it is, but modelleth it according to his own intellect, and submits not to the appearances of God in the world, therefore he lifts up his heel against God, and mocketh at all his providences, laughing at the observations, made up, not without reason and the Scriptures, but by the quickening and teaching Spirit which gives life to the other, calling such observations, enthusiasms. Such men, I say, no wonder if they stumble and fall backward, and be broken and snared, and taken by the things of which they are so maliciously and wilfully ignorant. The Scriptures say, God has a voice, and he will make himself known, and he will make himself known by the judgments which he executeth. And do we not think he will, and does, by the providences of mercy and kindness which he hath for his people, and for their just liberties, whom he loves as the apple of his eye? Doth he not by them manifest himself? And is he not thereby also seen, *giving kingdoms for them, giving men for them, and people for their lives*, as it is in the forty-third of Isaiah? Is not this as fair a lecture and as clear speaking, as anything our dark reason, left to the letter of the Scriptures, can collect from them? By this voice has God spoken very loud on the behalf of his people, by judging their enemies in the late war, and restoring them a liberty to worship with the freedom of their consciences, and a freedom in their estates and persons when they do so. And thus we have found the cause of God by the works of God, which are the testimony of God, upon which rock whosoever splits shall suffer shipwreck.

But it is our glory, and it is mine, if I have any in the world, concerning the interest of those that have an interest in a better world, it is my glory that I know a cause, which yet we have not lost, but do hope we shall take a little pleasure rather to lose our lives than lose. But you will excuse this long digression.

I say unto you, whilst you have been in the midst of these transactions, that party, that Cavalier party,—I could wish some of them had thrust in here to have heard what I say,—the Cavalier party have been designing and preparing to put this nation in blood again, with a witness. But because I am confident there are none of that sort here, therefore I shall say the less to that; only, this I must tell you, they have been making great preparations of arms, and I do believe it will be made evident to you, that they have raked out many thousands of arms, even all that this city could afford for divers months last past.

But it will be said, May we not arm ourselves for the defence of our houses, will anybody find fault for that? No! For that the reason of their doing so hath been as explicit, and under as clear proof, as the fact of their doing so; for which I hope by the justice of the land, some will, in the face of the nation, answer it with their lives, and then the business will be pretty well out of doubt.

Banks of money have been framing for these and other such like uses. Letters have been issued, with Privy Seals, to as great persons as most are in the nation, for the advance of moneys, which have been discovered to us by the persons themselves. Commissions for regiments of horse and foot, and command of castles, have likewise been given from Charles Stuart since your sitting. And what the general insolences of that party have been, the honest people have been sensible of and can well testify.

It hath not been only thus. But as in a quinsy or pleurisy where the humour fixeth in one part, give it scope, it will gather to that place to the hazarding of the whole, and it is natural to do so, till it destroy nature in that person on whomsoever this befalls,—so likewise, will those diseases take accidental causes for aggravation of their distemper. And this was that which I did assert, that they have taken accidental causes for the growing and increasing of those distempers, as much as would have been in the natural body, if timely remedy were not applied. And indeed things were come to that pass, in respect of which I shall give you a particular account, that no mortal physician, if the great physician had not stepped in, could have cured the distemper. Shall I lay this upon your account or my own? I am sure I can lay it upon God's account, that if he had not stepped in, the disease had been mortal and destructive. And what is all this? Truly I must needs say, a company of men still,—like briers and thorns, and worse, if worse can be, of another sort than those before mentioned to you ,—have been, and yet are, endeavouring to put us into blood and into confusion, more desperate and dangerous confusion than England ever yet saw. And I must say, as when Gideon commanded his son to fall upon Zeba and Zalmunna and slay them, they thought it more noble to die by the hand of a man than of a stripling, which shows there is some contentment in the hand by which a man falls; so, is it some satisfaction if a Commonwealth must perish, that it perish by men, and not by the hands of persons differing little from beasts; that if it must needs suffer, it should rather suffer from rich men than from poor men, who as Solomon says, *when they oppress they leave nothing behind them, but are as a sweeping rain.*

Now, such as these also are grown up under your shadow. But it will be asked, what have they done? I hope, though they pretend Commonwealth's interest, they have had no encouragement from you, but that, as before, they have rather taken it, than that you have administered any cause unto them for so doing, from delays, from hopes that this Parliament would not settle, from pamphlets mentioning strange votes and resolves of yours, which I hope did abuse you. Thus you see, whatever the grounds were, these have been the effects. And thus I have laid these things before you, and you and others will be easily able to judge how far you are concerned.

And what have these men done? They have also laboured to pervert where they could, and as they could, the honest meaning people of the nation, they have laboured to engage some in the army; and I doubt, that not only they, but some others also very well known to you, have helped in this work of debauching and dividing the army; they have, they have. I would be loth to say, who, where, and how, much more loth to say, they were any of your own number, but I can say endeavours have been made to put the army into a distemper, and to feed that which is the worst humour in the army; which though it was not a mastering humour, yet these took their advantage from delay of the settlement, and the practices before mentioned, and stopping the pay of the army to run us into free quarter and to bring us into the inconveniences most to be feared and avoided.

What if I am able to make it appear in fact, that some amongst you have run into the City of London to persuade to petitions and addresses to you, for reversing your own votes that you have passed? Whether these practices were in favour of your liberties, or tended to beget hopes of peace and settlement from you? And whether debauching the army in England, as is before expressed, and starving it, and putting it upon free quarter, and occasioning and necessitating the greatest part thereof in Scotland to march into England, leaving the remainder thereof to have their throats cut there and kindling by the rest a fire in our own bosoms, were for the advantage of affairs here, let the world judge?

This I tell you also, that the correspondency held with the interest of the Cavaliers, was by that party of men, called Levellers, and who call themselves Commonwealthsmen. Whose declarations were framed to that purpose, and ready to be published at the time of their common rising, whereof we are possessed, and for which we have the confession of themselves now in custody; who confess also they built their hopes upon the assurance they had of the Parliament's not agreeing to a settlement.

Whether these humours have not nourished themselves under your boughs, is the subject of my present discourse, and I think I say not amiss, if I affirm it to be so. And I must say it again, that that which hath been their advantage thus to raise disturbance, hath been by the loss of those golden opportunities, that God hath put into your hands for settlement.

Judge you, whether these things were thus or no, when you first sat down. I am sure things were not thus. There was a very great peace and sedateness throughout these nations, and great expectations of a happy settlement, which I remembered to you at the beginning of my speech, and hoped that you would have entered upon your business as you found it. There was a Government in the possession of the people, I say a Government in the possession of the people, for many months,—it hath now been exercised near fifteen months,—and if it were needful that I should tell you, how it came into their possession and how willingly they received it, how all law and justice were distributed from it in every respect, as to life, liberty, and estate, how it was owned by God, as being the dispensation of his providence, after twelve years' war, and sealed and witnessed unto by the people, I should but repeat what I said in my last speech made unto you in this place, and therefore I forbear.

When you were entered upon this Government, instead of ravelling into it,—you know I took no notice what you were doing,—if you had gone upon that foot of account, to have made such good and wholesome provisions for the good of the people of these nations, for the settling of such matters in things of religion as would have upheld and given countenance to a Godly ministry, and yet would have given a just liberty to Godly men of different judgments, though men of the same faith with them that you call the orthodox ministry in England,—as it is well known the Independents are, and many under the form of baptism, who are sound in the faith, only may perhaps be different in judgment in some lesser matters, yet are true Christians, both looking at salvation only by faith in the blood of Christ, men professing that fear of God, having recourse to the name of God as to a strong tower,—I say, you might have had opportunity to have settled peace and quietness amongst all professing Godliness, and might have been instrumental, if not to have healed the breaches, yet to have kept the Godly of all judgments from running one upon another, and by keeping them from being overrun by a common enemy, to have rendered them and these nations both secure, happy, and well satisfied.

Are these things done? Or anything towards them? Is there not yet upon the spirits of men a strange itch? Nothing will satisfy them, unless they can put their finger upon their brethren's consciences, to pinch them there. To do this was no part of the contest we had with the common adversary; for religion was not the thing at the first contested for, but God brought it to that issue at last, and gave it to us by way of redundancy, and at last it proved that which was most dear to us. And wherein consisted this, more than in obtaining that liberty from the tyranny of the bishops to all species of Protestants, to worship God according to their own light and consciences? For want of which, many of our brethren forsook their native countries to seek their bread from strangers, and to live in howling wildernesses; and for which also many that remained here were imprisoned, and otherwise abused and made the scorn of the nation.

Those that were sound in the faith, how proper was it for them to labour for liberty, for a just liberty, that men should not be trampled upon for their consciences? Had not they laboured but lately under the weight of persecutions, and was it fit for them to sit heavy upon others? Is it ingenuous to ask liberty, and not to give it? What greater hypocrisy than for those who were oppressed by the bishops, to become the greatest oppressors themselves so soon as their yoke was removed? I could wish that they who call for liberty now also, had not too much of that spirit, if the power were in their hands.

As for profane persons, blasphemers, such as preach sedition, the contentious railers, evil speakers who seek by evil words to corrupt good manners, persons of loose conversations, punishment from the civil magistrate ought to meet with them. Because, if these pretend conscience, yet walking disorderly, and not according but contrary to the Gospel and even to natural light, they are judged of all, and their sins being open, makes them subjects of the magistrate's sword, who ought not to bear it in vain. The discipline of the Army was such, that a man would not be suffered to remain there, of whom we could take notice he was guilty of such practices as these. And therefore how happy would England have been, and you, and I, if the Lord had led you on to have settled upon such good accounts as these are, and to have discountenanced such practices as the other, and left men in disputable things free to their own consciences; which was well provided for by the Act of Government, and liberty left to provide against what was apparently evil.

Judge you, whether the contesting for things that were provided for by this Government hath been profitable expense of time for the good of these nations? By means whereof, you may see you have wholly elapsed your time, and done just nothing. I will say this to you in behalf of the Long Parliament, that had such an expedient as this Government been proposed to them, and that they could have seen the cause of God thus provided for, and had by debates been enlightened in the grounds by which the difficulties might have been cleared, and had the reason of the whole enforced,—the circumstances of time and persons, with the temper and disposition of the people, and affairs both abroad and at home when it was undertaken, well weighed,—as well as they were thought to love their seats, I think in my conscience that they would have proceeded in another manner than you have done, and not have exposed things to those difficulties and hazards they now are at, nor given occasion to leave the people so dissettled as now they are, who I dare say, in the soberest and most judicious part of them, did expect not a questioning, but a doing of things in pursuance of the Government. And if I be not misinformed, very many of you came up with this satisfaction, having had time enough to weigh and consider the same. And when I say, "such an expedient as this Government is",—wherein I dare assert there is a just liberty to the people of God, and the just rights of the people in these nations provided for,—I can put the issue thereof upon the clearest reason, whatsoever any go about to suggest to the contrary. But, this not being the time and place of such an averment, for satisfaction sake herein enough is said in a book, entitled, *A True State of the Case of the Commonwealth*, &c., published in January 1653. And for myself, I desire not to keep it an hour longer than I may preserve England in its just rights, and may protect the people of God in such a just liberty of their consciences, as I have already mentioned. And therefore if this Parliament have judged things to be otherwise than as I have stated them, it had been huge friendliness,—between persons that had such a reciprocation, and in so great concernments to the public,—for them to have convinced me in what particulars therein my error lay; of which I never yet had a word from you. But if, instead thereof, your time has been spent in setting up somewhat else upon another bottom than this stands, that looks as if a laying grounds of a quarrel had rather been designed, than to give the people settlement. If it be thus, it's well your labours have not arrived to any maturity at all.

The Government called you hither, the constitution whereof being so limited, a single person and a Parliament. And this was thought most agreeable to the general sense of the nation, having had experience enough by trial of other conclusions, judging this most likely to avoid the extremes of monarchy on the one hand, and democracy on the other, and yet not to found *dominium in gratia*. And if so, then certainly to make it more than a notion, it was requisite that it should be as it is in the Act of Government, which puts it upon a true and equal balance. It has been already submitted to the judicious honest people of this nation, whether the balance be not equal; and what their judgment is, is visible by submission to it, by acting upon it, by restraining their trustees from meddling with it; and it neither asks nor needs any better ratification. But when trustees in Parliament shall by experience find any evil in any parts of the government,—referred by the Act of Government itself to the consideration of the Protector and Parliament, of which time itself will be the best discoverer,—how can it be reasonably imagined that a person, or persons, coming in by election, and standing under such obligations, and so limited, and so necessitated by oath to govern for the people's good, and to make their love, under God, the best underpropping and his best interest to himself,—how can it, I say, be imagined that the present or succeeding Protectors will refuse to agree to alter any such thing in the government that may be found to be for the good of the people, or to recede from anything which he might be convinced casts the balance too much to the single person? And although for the present, the keeping up and having in his power the Militia seems the most hard, yet if it should be yielded up at such a time as this, when there is as much need to keep this cause,—which is most evident, at this time impugned by all the enemies of it,—as there was to get it, what would become of all? Or if it should not be equally placed in him and the Parliament, but yielded up at any time? It determines his power, either for doing the good he ought, or hindering Parliaments from perpetuating themselves, or from imposing what religions they please on the consciences of men, or what government they please upon the nation, thereby subjecting us to dissettlement in every Parliament, and to the desperate consequences thereof. And if the nation shall happen to fall into a blessed peace, how easily and certainly will their charge be taken off, and their forces be disbanded; and then where will the danger be to have the Militia thus instated? What if I should say, if there should be a disproportion or disequality as to the power, it is on the other hand? And if this be so, wherein have you had cause to quarrel? What demonstrations have you held forth to settle me to your opinion? Would you had made me so happy as to let me have known your grounds. I have made a free and ingenuous confession of faith to you, and I could have wished it had been in your hearts to have agreed that some friendly and cordial debates might have been towards mutual conviction. Was there none amongst you to move such a thing? No fitness to listen to it? no desire of a right understanding? If it be not folly in me to listen to town-talk, such things have been proposed, and rejected with stiffness and severity once and again. Was it not likely to have been more advantageous to the good of the nation? I will say this to you for myself,—and to that I have my conscience as a thousand witnesses, and I have my comfort and contentment in it, and I have the witness of divers here, that I think truly scorn to own me in a lie,—that I would not have been averse to any alteration, of the good of which I might have been convinced, although I could not have agreed to the taking it off the foundation on which it stands, *viz.* the acceptation and consent of the people.

I will not presage what you have been about or doing all this time, nor do I love to make conjectures, but I must tell you this, that as I undertook this Government in the simplicity of my heart, and as before God and to do the part of an honest man, and to be true to the interest, which in my conscience is dear to many of you,—though it is not always understood what God in his wisdom may hide from us as to peace and settlement,—so I can say, that no particular interest, either of myself, estate, honour, or family are or have been prevalent with me to this undertaking. For if you had upon the old government offered to me this one, this one thing,—I speak as thus advised, and before God as having been to this day of this opinion, and this hath been my constant judgment, well known to many that hear me speak,—if this one thing had been inserted, that one thing, that this Government should have been and placed in my family hereditary, I would have rejected it, and I could have done no other according to my present conscience and light. I will tell you my reason, though I cannot tell what God will do with me, nor you, nor the nation, for throwing away precious opportunities committed to us. This hath been my principle, and I liked it, when this Government came first to be proposed to me, that it put us off that hereditary way. Well looking that as God had declared what government he had delivered over to the Jews, and placed it upon such persons as had been instrumental for the conduct and deliverance of his people; and considering that promise in Isaiah, that God *would give rulers as at the first, and judges as at the beginning*, I did not know but that God might begin, and though at present with a most unworthy person, yet as to the future it might be after this manner, and I thought this might usher it in. I am speaking as to my judgment against making it hereditary, to have men chosen for their love to God, and to truth and justice, and not to have it hereditary. For as it is in Ecclesiastes, *who knoweth whether he may beget a fool or wise?* Honest or not, whatever they be, they must come in upon that account, because the government is made a patrimony. And this I do perhaps declare with too much earnestness, as being my own concernment, and know not what place it may have in your hearts and those of the good people in the nation; but however it be, I have comfort in this my truth and plainness. I have thus told you my thoughts, which truly I have declared to you in the fear of God, as knowing he will not be mocked, and in the strength of God, as knowing and rejoicing that I am kept in my speaking; especially, when I do not form or frame things without the compass of integrity and honesty, knowing that my own conscience gives me not the lie to what I say: and then, in what I say I can rejoice.

Now to speak a word or two to you of that I must profess in the name of the same Lord, and wish that there had been no cause that I should have thus spoken to you; and though I have told you that I came with joy the first time, with some regret the second, to tell you that now I speak with most regret of all. I look upon you as having among you many persons, that I could lay down my life individually for. I could, through the grace of God, desire to lay down my life for you, so far am I from having an unkind or un-Christian heart towards you in your particular capacities. I have that indeed as a work most incumbent upon me. I consulted what might be my duty in such a day as this, casting up all consider-ations. I must confess, as I told you, that I did think occasionally this nation hath suffered extremely in the respects mentioned, as also in the disappointment of their expectations of that justice that was due to them by your sitting thus long; and what have you brought forth? I did not, nor cannot apprehend what the reason of it is; I would be loth to call it a fate, that were too paganish a word, but there is something in it, that we have not our expectations. I did think also for myself, that I am like to meet with difficulties, and that this nation will not, as it is fit it should not, be deluded with pretexts of necessity in that great business of raising of money. And were it not that I can make some dilemmas upon which to resolve some things of my conscience, judgment, and actions, I should sink at the very prospect of my encounters. Some of them are general, some are more special. Supposing this cause, or this business, must be carried on, either it is of God, or of man. If it be of man, I would I had never touched it with a finger; if I had not had a hope fixed in me that this cause, and this business, is of God, I would many years ago have run from it. If it be of God, he will bear it up. If it be of man, it will tumble, as everything that hath been of man, since the world began, hath done. And what are all our histories, and other traditions of actions in former times, but God manifesting himself that he hath shaken and tumbled down, and trampled upon everything that he hath not planted? And as this is, so will the all-wise God deal with it. If this be of human structure and invention, and it be an old plotting and contrivance to bring things to this issue, and that they are not the births of providence, then they will tumble. But if the Lord take pleasure in England, and if he will do us good, he is able to bear us up; let the difficulties be whatsoever they will, we shall in his strength be able to encounter with them. And I bless God I have been inured to difficulties, and I never found God failing when I trusted in him; I can laugh and sing in my heart when I speak of these things to you, or elsewhere. And though some may think it is an hard thing without parliamentary authority to raise money upon this nation, yet I have another argument to the good people of this nation, if they would be safe, and have no better principle. Whether they prefer the having of their will, though it be their destruction, rather than comply with things of necessity? That will excuse me; but I should wrong my native country to suppose this. For I look at the people of these nations, as the blessing of the Lord; and they are a people blessed by God. They have been so, and they will be so, by reason of that immortal seed, which hath been and is among them. Those regenerated ones in the land, of several judgments, who are all the flock of Christ, and lambs of Christ, though perhaps under many unruly passions and troubles of spirit, whereby they give disquiet to themselves and others, yet they are not so to God, as to us. He is a God of other patience, and he will own the least of truth in the hearts of his people. And the people being the blessing of God they will not be so angry, but they will prefer their safety to their passions, and their real security to forms, when necessity calls for supplies. Had they not well been acquainted with this principle, they had never seen this day of gospel-liberty.

But if any man shall object, It is an easy thing to talk of necessities, when men create necessities. Would not the Lord Protector make himself great, and his family great? Doth not he make these necessities, and then he will come upon the people with this argument of necessity? This were something hard indeed; but I have not yet known what it is to make necessities, whatsoever the judgments or thoughts of men are. And I say this, not only to this assembly, but to the world, that that man liveth not, that can come to me, and charge me that I have in these great revolutions made necessities; I challenge even all that fear God. And as God hath said, *my glory I will not give unto another*, let men take heed and be twice advised, how they call his revolutions, the things of God, and his working of things from one period to another, how I say, they call them necessities of men's creation. For by so doing they do vilify and lessen the works of God, and rob him of his glory, which he hath said he will not give unto another, nor suffer to be taken from him. We know what God did to Herod, when he was applauded, and did not acknowledge God. And God knoweth what he will do with men, when they shall call his revolutions human designs,—and so detract from his glory,— when they have not been forecast, but sudden providences in

things: whereby carnal and worldly men are enraged, and under
and at which many I fear, some good, have murmured and
repined, because disappointed of their mistaken fancies. But still
they have been the wise disposings of the Almighty, though his
instruments have had their passions and frailties. And I think it is
an honour to God to acknowledge the necessities to have been of
God's imposing, when truly they have been so, as indeed they
have, when we take our sin in our actings to ourselves; and much
more safe, than to judge things so contingent, as if there were not a
God that ruled the earth. We know the Lord hath poured this
nation from vessel to vessel, till he poured it into your lap, when
you first came together. I am confident it came so into your hands,
and was not judged by you to be from counterfeited or feigned
necessity, but by divine providence and dispensation. And this I
speak with more earnestness, because I speak for God and not for
men. I would have any man to come and tell of the transactions
that have been, and of those periods of time wherein God hath
made these revolutions, and find where they can fix a feigned
necessity. I could recite particulars, if either my strength would
serve me to speak, or yours to hear. If that you would revolve the
great hand of God in his great dispensations, you would find that
there is scarce a man that fell off at any period of time, when God
had any work to do, that can give God or his work, at this day, a
good word. It was, say some, the cunning of the Lord
Protector,—I take it to myself,—it was the craft of such a man,
and his plot that brought it about. And as they say in other
countries, There are five or six cunning men in England that have
skill: they do all these things. Oh, what blasphemy is this!
Because, these are men that are without God in the world, and
walk not with him, and know not what it is to pray, or believe,
and to receive returns from God, and to be spoken unto by the
Spirit of God, who speaks without a written Word sometimes, yet
according to it: God hath spoken heretofore in divers manners, let
him speak as he pleaseth. Hath he not given us liberty? Nay, is it
not our duty to go to the Law and to the Testimonies, and there we
shall find that there have been impressions in extraordinary cases,
as well without the written Word as with it, and therefore there is
no difference in the thing thus asserted from truths generally
received, except we will exclude the Spirit, without whose

concurrence all other teachings are ineffectual. He doth speak to the hearts and consciences of men, and leadeth them to his Law and Testimonies, and there he speaks to them, and so gives them double teachings, according to that of Job, *God speaketh once, yea twice*; and that of David, *God hath spoken once, yea twice have I heard this*. Those men that live upon their *mumpsimus* and *sumpsimus*, their masses and service-books, their dead and carnal worship, no marvel if they be strangers to God, and the works of God, and to spiritual dispensations. And because they say and believe thus, must we do so too? We in this land have been otherwise instructed, even by the Word and Works, and Spirit of God. To say that men bring forth these things, when God doth them, judge you if God will bear this. I wish that every sober heart, though he hath had temptations upon him of deserting this cause of God, yet may take heed how he provokes, and falls into the hands of the living God by such blasphemies as these. According to the 10th of the Hebrews, *If we sin wilfully after that we have received the knowledge of the truth, there remains no more sacrifice for sin*,—it was spoken to the Jews, that having professed Christ apostatized from him,—what then? Nothing but *a fearful falling into the hands of the living God*. They that shall attribute to this or that person the contrivances and production of those mighty things God hath wrought in the midst of us, and say that they have not been the revolutions of Christ himself, upon whose shoulders the government is laid, they speak against God, and they fall under his hand without a mediator. That is, if we deny the spirit of Jesus Christ the glory of all his works in the world, by which he rules kingdoms and doth administer, and is the rod of his strength, we provoke the Mediator. And he may say, I will leave you to God, I will not intercede for you, let him tear you to pieces; I will leave thee to fall into God's hands; thou deniest me my sovereignty and power committed to me, I will not intercede nor mediate for thee; thou fallest into the hands of the living God. Therefore whatsoever you may judge men for, and say, this man is cunning, and politic, and subtle, take heed, again I say, how you judge of his revolutions, as the products of men's inventions. I may be thought to press too much upon this theme, but I pray God it may stick upon your hearts and mine. The worldly minded man knows nothing of this, but is a stranger to it, and because of this,

his atheism and murmurings at instruments, yea repining at God himself, and no wonder, considering the Lord hath done such things amongst us as have not been known in the world these thousand years;—and yet notwithstanding is not owned by us.

There is another necessity which you have put upon us, and we have not sought; I appeal to God, angels, and men, if I shall raise money according to the Article of the Act of Government, which had power to call you hither, and did. And instead of seasonable providing for the Army, you have laboured to overthrow the government, and the Army is now upon free quarter; and you would never so much as let me hear a tittle from you concerning it. Where is the fault? Has it not been as if you had had a purpose to put this extremity upon us and the nation? I hope this was not in your minds; I am not willing to judge so, but this is the state unto which we are reduced. By the designs of some in the Army, who are now in custody, it was designed to get as many of them as they could,——through discontent for want of money, the Army being in a barren country, near thirty weeks behind in pay, and upon other specious pretences,—to march for England out of Scotland, and in discontent to seize their general there, a faithful and honest man, that so another might head the Army. And all this opportunity taken from your delays. Whether will this be a thing of feigned necessity? What could it signify, but that the army are in discontent already, and we will make them live upon stones, and we will make them cast off their governors and discipline? What can be said to this? I list not to unsaddle myself, and put the fault upon others' backs. Whether it hath been for the good of England, whilst men have been talking of this thing or the other, and pretending liberty, and a many good words? Whether it hath been as it should have been? I am confident you cannot think it has; the nation will not think so. And if the worst should be made of things, I know not what the Cornish-men, or the Lincolnshire-men may think, or other counties, but I believe they will all think they are not safe. A temporary suspension of caring for the greatest liberties and privileges,—if it were so, which is denied,—would not have been of that damage, that the not providing against free quarter hath run the nation upon. And if it be my liberty to walk abroad in the fields, or to take a journey, yet it is not my wisdom to do so when my house is on fire.

I have troubled you with a long speech, and I believe it may not have the same resentment with all, that it hath with some. But because that is unknown to me, I shall leave it to God, and conclude with that that I think myself bound,—in my duty to God and the people of these nations, to their safety and good in every respect, I think it my duty,—to tell you, that it is not for the profit of these nations, nor fit for the common and public good, for you to continue here any longer, and therefore, I do declare unto you, That I do dissolve this Parliament.'

6.

5 March 1655/6 – Speech to the Lord Mayor, Aldermen, and Common Council of the City of London, at Whitehall

The speech took the opportunity to explain to the City authorities, with whom good relations were politically and financially essential, why the Major-Generals were established in the localities. The Major-General for London was Philip Skippon who had been closely involved with the City's military security since the outbreak of civil war. This speech survives only in a summary reported version.

His Highness on Wednesday last was near two hours in delivering a speech at Whitehall to the Lord Mayor, Court of Aldermen, and Common Council of London, wherein he told them, That since fair means would not indulge, foul should enforce the Royal party to a peaceable deportment. And seeing they were the cause, by their late endeavour, of raising the Militia troops to preserve the peace of the nation, it was thought but reasonable that their estate should be only charged therewith; that so they might be in the nature of a standing militia, and yet not go to warfare at their own charge; being at all times to be drawn forth upon occasion. That the soldiers, as well as the officers, were so many inhabitants of each Association under their respective Major-Generals, and would thereby fitly serve to be so many watchmen or spies to give notice of, or apprehend, such as were of dissolute lives and conversation, who lived like gentlemen and yet had not visible way for the same, being cheaters and the like, who were more fit to be sent beyond the seas than to remain here. That God Almighty hath given us many blessings and deliverances, and now seemingly brought us into a probability of enjoying peace, which called upon us to make some returns thereof, by endeavouring that after all our expense of blood and treasure, the same might reap some fruits thereof. And this way the Lord hath owned, by making more effectual than was expected and by receiving a good acceptation with those who of late stood at some distance with us, so that the sole end of this way of procedure was the security of the peace of the nation, the suppressing of vice and encouragement of virtue, the very end of magistracy. That there was a remissness in some of the Justices of Peace, by many of whom company keeping, etc. was countenanced; but now, that noble men, gentlemen, and all varieties and qualities, might give security for their peaceable and civil disposition, or go to prison. That we had indeed many good laws, yet that we have lived rather under the name and notion of Law, than under the thing; so that it is resolved to regulate the same, God assisting, oppose who will. That now the Major-Generals had gone through all the counties of England and Wales; and wherever the Major-Generals were present in action, these loose and vagrant persons did fly from thence to other counties, the Major-Generals' occasions not permitting them to be in action [everywhere] at one time. And for that this City was a place that gave shelter to many such idle loose persons, who had and have their recourse thereto, the same practice is intended to be set on foot in the City by their Major-General Skippon, the Lord-Lieutenant of the Tower, and others commissioned with him. And therefore his Highness thought fit to acquaint the Lord Mayor, and those gentlemen present, with the same, to the end no misunderstanding may be had thereof; for that thereby the good government of the City is intended, and not at all to supersede them or at least to diminish any of their rights, privileges or liberties. Which was all his Highness had to say to them, and so dismissed them.

7.

17 September 1656 – Speech at the opening of Parliament

The second Protectorate Parliament was called rather reluctantly to vote on supplies for the war with Spain, which Cromwell entered into in alliance with France. When parliament met, some one hundred MPs, including Commonwealthsmen believed to be hostile, were excluded. The remaining MPs, learning that some co-operation with the régime might produce positive results, were more amenable, responding well to the Protector's speech by promising aid for the war. The result was a parliament which passed a spate of legislation, public and private, secured the demise of the system of the Major-Generals and, following 'the case of James Nayler', who was tried and punished by the Commons for horrid blasphemy, went on to revise the constitution.

'Gentlemen,

When I came hither, I did think that a duty was incumbent upon me a little to pity myself, because, this being a very extraordinary occasion, I thought I had very many things to say to you; but truly now, seeing you in such a condition as you are, I think I must turn off in this, as I hope I shall in everything else, and reflect upon you as certainly not being able long to bear that condition and heat that you are in.

Rhetoricians, to whom I do not pretend, neither to them nor to the things they use to speak, speak words. Truly our business is to speak things; the dispensations of God that are upon us do require it. And that subject upon which we shall make our discourse is somewhat of very great interest and concernment both to the glory of God and with reference to his interest in the world,—I mean his peculiar, his most peculiar interest. And that will not teach any of us to exclude his general interest, which is the concernment of the living people within these three nations, with all the dependencies thereupon. I told you I should speak to things, things that concern these interests, the glory of God and his peculiar interest in the world, which is more extensive, I say, more extensive than the people of all these three nations, with the appurtenances or the countries and places belonging unto them.

The first thing therefore that I shall speak to, is that that is the first lesson of Nature, which is being and preservation,—as to that of being, I do think I do not ill style it the first consideration that Nature teacheth the sons of Adam,—and then I hope we shall enter into a field large enough when we come to consider that of well-being; and if that first be not well laid, I think the rest will hardly follow. Now in order to this, to the being and subsistence of these nations with all the dependencies, the conservation of that is either with a respect to be had to them that seek to undo it, and so make it not to be, and then with a very natural consideration to what will make it to be, will keep its being and subsistence.

Seeing that that which plainly seeks the destruction of the being of this nation, is out of doubt the endeavour and design of all the common enemies of it, I think truly it will not be hard to find out who those enemies are, nor what hath made them so. I think they are all the wicked men of the world, whether abroad or at home, that are the enemies to the very being of this nation, and that upon a common account, from that very enmity that is in them against whatsoever should serve the glory of God and the interest of his people; which they see to be more eminently, yea most eminently patronized and professed in this nation,—we will speak it not with vanity,—above all the nations in the world. This is the common ground of the common enmity had against the prosperity of these nations, against the very being of them. But we shall not I think take up much time in contemplating who these enemies are, what they are in the general notion, but to labour to specificate our enemies, to know who they be and are, that seek the very destruction and being of these nations. And truly I would not have laid this foundation but to this end, that I might very particularly communicate with you, for which end you are called hither at this time, that I might particularly communicate with you of the many dangers that this nation stands in, in respect of enemies both abroad and at home; and also to advise with you about the remedies and means to obviate these dangers, which, say I, and I shall leave it to you whether you will join with me or no, strike at the very being and interest of these nations, these nations in the general, and especially at the interest of the people of God in these nations. And therefore that I may be particular, I shall shortly represent to you the estate of your affairs in that respect; in respect of the enemies you are engaged with, and how you came to be engaged with those enemies, and how they came to be as heartily, I believe, engaged against you.

Why, truly, your great enemy is the Spaniard. He is. He is a natural enemy, he is naturally so. He is naturally so, throughout, as I said before, throughout all your enemies, through that enmity that is in him against all that is of God that is in you, or that which may be in you, contrary to that that his blindness and darkness, led on by superstition and the implicitness of his faith in submitting to the See of Rome, acts him unto. With this King and State, I say, you are at this present in hostility. We put you into this hostility. You will give us leave to tell you how, as we are ready to excuse most of our actions, aye and to justify them as well as to excuse them. Upon the grounds of necessity we put you into this hostility, the grounds of necessity being above all considerations of justification, of instituted law. And if this or any other State would go about, as I know they never will, to make laws against what may happen, against Providence, I think it is obvious to any man that they will make law against all events; events and issues of things being from God alone, to whom all issues belong.

This State is your enemy, and is your enemy, as I told you, naturally, by that antipathy that is in him providentially, and that in divers respects. You could not, you could not have an honest nor an honourable peace with him. It was sought by the Long Parliament, it was not attained; it could not be attained with honour and honesty. I say, it could not be attained with honour and honesty. And truly when I say that he is naturally throughout an enemy, an enmity is put into him by God. *I will put an enmity between thy seed and her seed*, which goes but for little among statesmen, but it is more considerable than all things. And he that considers not the providential and accidental enmity, I think he is not well acquainted with Scripture and the things of God. And he is not only so upon that account but he is providentially so, God having in his wisdom disposed it to be so when we made a breach with him, when we made attempt upon him: I shall tell you when.

No sooner did this nation reform that which is called unworthily the Reformed Religion, after the death of Queen Mary, by the Queen Elizabeth of famous memory,—we need not be ashamed to say so,—but his designs were by all unworthy unnatural means to destroy that person, and to seek the ruin and destruction of these kingdoms. And for me to instance in particular upon that account were to trouble you at a very unseasonable time. There is a Declaration extant, which very fully hath in it the original of the Spaniard's venting him upon this nation and a series of it from those very grounds to this present day. But it was so, partly upon that general account which all have agreed; the French, all the Protestants in Germany, have agreed that his design was the empire of the whole Christian world, if not more. And upon that ground he looks at this nation as his greatest obstacle. And what his attempts were to that end, I refer you to that Declaration and to the observations of men who read history. It would not be ill to remember the several assassinations designed upon that lady, that great Queen; the attempts upon Ireland, their invading it; the designs of the same nature upon this nation, public designs, private designs, all manner of designs to accomplish this great and general end. And truly, it is true King James made a peace; but whether this nation, or any interest of all the Protestant Christians, suffered not more by that peace, than ever by his hostility, I refer it to your consideration. So that a State that you can neither have peace with, nor reason from, is that State with whom you have enmity at this time and against whom you are engaged. And give me leave to say this unto you, because it is truth and most men know it, that the Long Parliament did endeavour but could not obtain satisfaction all the time they sat. For their messenger was murdered, and when they asked satisfaction for the blood of your poor people unjustly shed in the West Indies, and for the wrongs done elsewhere, when they asked liberty of conscience for your people that traded thither, satisfaction would not be given but denied. I say they denied satisfaction to be given, either for your messenger that was murdered, or the blood that was shed, or the damages that were done in the West Indies. No satisfaction at all, nor any reason given why there should not be liberty given to your people that traded thither, whose trade was very considerable there and drew many of your people thither. And this begot an apprehension in us; whether in you or no, let God judge between you and himself, I prejudge not, but all of us know that the people that went thither, to manage the trade there, were imprisoned there. We desired such a liberty as they might keep Bibles in their pockets, to exercise their liberty of religion to themselves and not to be under restraint. But there is not liberty of conscience to be had, neither satisfaction for injuries, nor for blood; but when these things were desired, the Ambassador told us it was to ask his master's two eyes. To ask both his eyes to ask these things of him!

Now if this be so, why truly then there is some little foundation laid to justify the war that was had with the Spaniard. And not only so, but the plain truth of it is, make any peace with any State that is Popish and subjected to the determination of Rome and the Pope himself, you are bound and they are loose. It is in the pleasure of the Pope at any time to tell you, that though the man may be murdered, yet he has got into the sanctuary. And it is as true, and it hath been found by common and constant experience, that peace is but to be kept so long as the Pope saith Amen to it. And truly if I should tell you that that will determine it without any further question at all, we have not to do with any Popish State except France, and in that country it is true that they do not think themselves under such a tie to the Pope, but think themselves at liberty to perform honesties with nations with whom they are agreed, and protest against the obligation of such a thing as that is. They are able to give us an explicit answer to anything reasonably demanded of them! And there is no State we can speak of save this, which is under the lash of the Pope to be determined upon anything, but will break it or keep it when they please upon these grounds. In the time when Philip the Second was married to Queen Mary, and since that time, through that power and instigation, twenty thousand Protestants were massacred in Ireland.

We thought, being denied just things, we thought it our duty to get that by the sword which we could not otherwise do. And this hath been the spirit of Englishmen; and if so, certain it is and ought to be the spirits of men that have higher spirits. With this State you are engaged, and it is a great and powerful State, though I may say that also with all other States, with all other Christian States, you are at peace. And this in spite of all those engagements that were upon you before the government were undertaken, which was war with France, Denmark, and upon the matter war with Spain. I could instance how it was said, we will have a war in the Indies, though we fight them not at home. I say we are at peace with all other nations, and have only a war with Spain. I shall say somewhat to you, that will let you see our clearness to that, by-and-by.

Having thus engaged with Spain, it is that party that brings all your enemies before you; it doth. For it is so now that Spain hath espoused that interest that you have all along hitherto been conflicting with, Charles Stuart's interest. And I would but meet that gentleman upon a fair discourse that is willing that that person should come back again, but I dare not believe any in this room is. I say it doth not detract at all from your cause, nor yet from your ability to make resistance, that God by his providence hath so disposed that the King of Spain hath espoused that person. I say no person but would be wonderfully well satisfied that it is not for the advantage of that person, and the choosing out, as was said today, of a captain to lead us back again into Egypt, if there be such a place,—I mean metaphorically and allegorically so,— that is to say, returning to all those things that we think we have been fighting against and destroying of all that good, (we have had some hints today,) we have attained unto. I am sure my speech will signify very little if such grounds go not for good. And I must say this to you, that there is not a man in England that is apt to comply with Papists and Cavaliers, but to them it is the greatest parable and absurdest discourse. And therefore we could wish they were all where Charles Stuart is, all that declare that they are of that spirit. I do with all my heart, aye, and I would help them to a boat to carry them over that are of that mind. Yea, and if you shall think it a duty to drive them over by arms, I will help in that also. You are engaged with this enemy; and this last said hath a little vehemency in it, but it is worth your consideration.

Though I seem to be all this while upon the justice of this business, yet my desire is to let you see the dangers that this nation stands in, and all the honest interest. Yea, all the interests of the Protestants in Germany, Denmark, Helvetia, the Cantons, and all the interests in Christendom are the same as yours. If you succeed well and act well, and be convinced what is God's interest and but prosecute it, you will find that you act for a very great many that are God's own. Therefore I say that as your danger is from the common enemy abroad, who is the head of the Papal interest, the head of that anti-Christian interest, that is so described in Scripture, so forespoken of,—and so fully is that charactered name given him by the Apostle in his Epistle to the Thessalonians, and also expressed throughout the Revelations, which are sure plain things, except you will deny the truth of the Scriptures, you must needs see that that State is so described in Scripture to be Papal and anti-Christian,—I say with this enemy and upon this account you have the quarrel with the Spaniard. And truly he hath an interest in your bowels, he hath so. The Papists in England they have been accounted, ever since I was born, Spaniolised. There is not a man amongst us can hold up a face against it. They never regarded France, they never regarded any other Popish State. Where any such interest was, Spain was their patron. It was so in England, Ireland, and Scotland; no man can doubt of it. Therefore I must needs say, this interest at home is a great piece of your danger. It is, and it is evidently so, and will be more so, upon that account that I told you. He hath espoused Charles Stuart, with whom he is fully at agreement; for whom he hath raised seven or eight thousand men, that are now quartered at Bruges; to whom Don John of Austria hath promised as soon as the campaign is ended, which it is conceived will be in about five or six weeks, he shall have four or five thousand; and the Duke of Neuburg, who is a Popish State, hath promised good assistance according to his power; and other Popish States the like. In this condition you are with that State, and in this condition through unavoidable necessity, because your enemy was naturally so, and is become so providentially.

This being so, that as there is a complication of these interests, so there is a complication here. Can we think that Papists and Cavaliers shake not hands in England? They will not tell you so, nor in being cozened by unworthy compliances of individuals in this nation, or any general compliance, admit it to be unworthy, un-Christian, un-English-like. Therefore I say it doth serve to let you see, and for that end I tell it you, to let you see your danger and the rise of it. It is not only thus, that we stand in this condition towards Spain, towards all that interest that would make void and frustrate all that are doing for you, it is not only in respect of the Popish interest, Papists and Cavaliers, but it is also in other respects, that is to say your danger is so great, if you be sensible of it, from persons that pretend other things; yea, who though perhaps they do not all suit in their hearts with the said interest, yet all men know, and must know, that discontented spirits end somewhere. They must expect back and support somewhere; and truly those discontentments are another piece of your danger. They must end at the interest of the Cavalier at the long run. That must be their support. I could have reckoned this upon other grounds, but I shall give you an account of things as they appear to be, for that I desire to clear them to you not discoursively but to let you see matter of fact and to let you see how the state of your affairs stands.

It is true, there was not long since an endeavour to make an insurrection in England. It was so for some time before it brake out. It was so before the last Parliament sat, the last! It was so from the time not only of the undertaking of this government, but the spirit and principle of it did work in the time of the Long Parliament. From that time till to this, hath there been nothing but enterprising and designing against you, and it is no strange nor new thing to tell you, because it is true and certain, that the Papists, the priests and Jesuits, have a great influence upon the Cavalier party. They and the Cavaliers' party have a like influence upon discontented spirits of the nation, who are not all so apt to see where dangers lie, nor to what the management of affairs tends. It is these to whom they do foment all things that tend to disservice, to propagate discontentments upon the minds of men. And if we would instance in particulars those that have manifested this, we could tell you that priests and Jesuits have insinuated themselves into the society of men, pretending the same things that they have pretended, and whose ends have been that, out of doubt, which I told you. We had that insurrection. It was intended first to the assassination of my person; which I would not remember as anything at all considerable to myself or to you, for they must cut throats beyond human consideration before they had been able to effect their design. You know that very well. It is no fable, for persons were arraigned for it before the Parliament and tried, and upon proof condemned for their designs and endeavours to cut the throat of myself and three or four more, that they singled out as being a little more than ordinary industrious to preserve the peace of the nation; and did think to make a very good issue to the accomplishment of their designs. I say this was made good upon the trial. Before the Parliament sat, all the time the Parliament sat, they were about it. We did hint these things to them by several persons, that acquainted them therewith. But what fate we lay under I know not. It was conceived, it seems, we had hinted things that rather intended to persuade agreement and consent, and monies out of the people's purses, or I know not what; but nothing was believed, though there was a series of these things distinctly and plainly communicated to many Members. The Parliament rose about the middle of January. By the twelfth of March after, they were in arms. But these were a company of mean fellows, alas, not a lord, nor a gentleman, nor a man of fortune, nor this nor that, amongst them; but it was a poor headstrong people, a company of rash fellows, that were at the undertaking of this, and this was all. And by such things have men lost their consciences and honours, by complying upon such notions as these are.

Give me leave to tell you, we know it, we are able to prove it, and I refer you to that Declaration which is for provision against Cavaliers, as I did you to the other that sets down the ground of our war with Spain, whether these things were so or no. If men will not believe, we are satisfied we do our duty. If we let you know things and the ground of them, it is satisfaction enough to us; but to see how men can reason themselves out of their honours and consciences in their compliance with those sort of people, which truly I must needs say some men had compliance with, that I thought never would for all the world, I must tell you so. These men rise in March; and that it was a general design, I think all the world must know and acknowledge. For it is as evident as the day that the King sent Sir Joseph Wagstaffe and another, the Earl of Rochester, to the North. And that it was general, we had not by suspicion and imagination, but we know individuals. We are able to make appear, that persons that carried themselves the most demurely and fairly of any men in England were engaged in this business. And he that gave our instructions lost his life for it in [another] country; I think I may now speak of it, because he is dead, but he did discover from time to time a full intelligence of these things. Therefore how men of wicked spirits may traduce us in that matter, or, notwithstanding all that hath been done, may still hold their compliances, I leave it. I think England cannot be safe, unless malignants be carried far away. We did our duty upon such an account as we are ready to give to all the world, and that done to them was truly honest, aye, to them all, and upon undeniable grounds of justice and equity, knowing that they were in the eye and judgment of all the counties of England and all honest men in separating themselves for such a work all the land over. There was never any design, but we could hear of it out of the Tower. He that watched over that, would give us an account that within a fortnight, or such a time, there would be some stirrings, for there was a great concourse of people came to them, and that they had very great elevations of spirit. It was not only there, but in all the counties of England we have had informations that they were upon designs all over, besides some particular places which came to our particular assurance and knowledge we had as from persons we had from the several counties in England. And if this be so, then as long as commotions can be held on foot, you are in danger by your war with Spain, with whom all the Papal interest is joined. This Pope [Alexander VII] is a person all the world knows to be a person of zeal for his religion, wherein perhaps he may shame us, and a man of contrivance, and wisdom, and policy, and his designs are known all over to be nothing else but endeavours to unite all the Popish interests in all the Christian world, against this nation above any, and against all the Protestant interest in the world. If this be so, and if you will take a measure of these things and we must still hold our esteem that we have had, can we be ready to shake hands with them and the Cavaliers? What doth this differ from the Archbishop of Canterbury to reconcile matters of religion, if this temper be upon us to unite with men in civil things? Give me leave to say, and I speak what I know, really I think if this nation cannot be happy upon the score of General &c., without we have this shaking of hands, if this be so I tell you plainly,—I hope I need not, I wish all the Cavaliers in England and all the Papists heard me declare it, and many here besides yourselves,—I tell you there are a company of poor men that are ready to spend their blood against such compliance; and I am persuaded the same things of you.

If this be our condition, with respect had to this, truly let us go a little further, for I would lay open the danger wherein, I think in my conscience, we stand. And if God give not your hearts to see and discern that which is obvious, we shall sink and the house will fall about our ears upon such sordid attempts as these are. Truly there are a great many people in this nation that would not reckon up every pitiful thing,—that may be like a mouse nibbling at the heel,—but of considerable dangers. I will tell you plainly, for it is not time for compliments nor rhetorical speeches; I have none truly but to tell you how we find things.

There is a generation of men in this nation that cry up nothing but righteousness, and justice, and liberty; and these are diversified in several sects and sorts of men. And though they may be contemptible, in respect they are many and so not like to make a solid vow to do you mischief, yet they are apt to agree *in aliquo tertio*; they are known, yea well enough, to shake hands together, I should be loth to say with Cavaliers, but with all the scum and dirt of this nation, to put you to trouble. And therefore when I shall come to speak to the remedies, I shall tell you what are the most apt and proper remedies in all these respects. I tell you of the very time when there was an insurrection at Salisbury,—I doubt whether it be believed whether ever there was any rising in North Wales, Shrewsbury, Rufford-Abbey, where there was about five hundred horses, Marston-Moor, Northumberland, &c. when all these insurrections were,—at that very time there was a party which was very proper and apt to come between the Papists and Cavaliers. And that Levelling party hath some access lately that goes under a finer name or notion. I think they would be called Commonwealthsmen, who perhaps have reason little enough. And it is strange that men of fortune and great estates should join with such a people, but if the fact be so, there needs no great reasons to discover it to be so, it being so by demonstration. I say, this people at that very time, they were pretty numerous and do not despise them, this people at that time the Cavaliers were risen, this very people had prepared a Declaration against all the things that had been transacted, and called them I know not by what, tyranny, oppression, things against the liberty of the subject, and cried out for justice, and righteousness, and liberty. And what was all this business for, but to join with the Cavaliers to carry on that design? And these are things, not words; that Declaration we got, and the penner of it we got, and we have got intelligence also how the business was laid and contrived, which was hatched in the time of the sitting of that Parliament. I do not accuse anybody, but I say that was the time of it, an unhappy time. And a plausible Petition was penned, that must come to me forsooth to consider of these things and to give redress and remedies: and this was so. Now indeed I must tell you plainly, we suspected a great deal of violence then, and we did hunt it out. I will not tell you these as high things, but at that time that the Cavaliers were to rise, a party was to seize upon General Monk in Scotland and to commit him to Edinburgh Castle upon this pretence of liberty. And when they had seized upon him, and clapped him by the heels and some other true and faithful officers, they were resolved upon a number at the same time to march away for London, and to leave a party behind them to have their throats cut by the Scots. Though I will not say they would have done it, yet it cannot be thought otherwise but that a considerable army would have followed them at the heels. And not only thus, but this spirit and principle designed some little fiddling things upon some of your officers to an assassination, and an officer was engaged that was upon the Guard to seize me in my bed; this was true. And other foolish designs there were, as to get in a room, to get gunpowder laid in it, and to blow up the room wherein I lay; and this, we can tell you, is truth. These are persons not worthy naming, but the things are really true, and this is the state wherein we have stood, with which we have conflicted since the last Parliament. And upon this account and in this combination that is it I say to you, that the ringleaders to all this are none but your old enemies, the Papists and Cavaliers; we have some in prison for these things.

Now we would be loth to tell you of notions more seraphical. These are poor and low conceits. We have had very seraphical notions. We have had endeavours to heal between two interests, one that was part of the Commonwealth's interest, and another that was a notion of a Fifth-Monarchy interest. Whom I do not repeat, whose condition I do not repeat, as thinking it not worth your trouble; but *de facto* it hath been so, that there hath been endeavours. As there was endeavours to make a reconciliation between Herod and Pilate that Christ might be put to death, so there hath been endeavours of reconciliation between the Fifth-Monarchy and the Commonwealthsmen, that there might be union in order to an end, no end being so bad as that of Herod's, but in order to end in blood and confusion; and that you may know. I profess, I do not believe of these two last, that of Commonwealthsmen and Fifth-Monarchy men, but that they have stood at a distance. I think they did not participate; I would be so charitable, I would be, that they did not. But this I will tell you, that for the other, they did not only set these things on work, but sent a fellow, a wretched creature, an apostate from religion and all honesty, they sent him to Madrid to advise with the King of Spain to lend forces to invade this nation; promising satisfaction, if they would comply and concur with him, to have both men and monies; undertaking both to engage the fleet to mutiny and also your Army; to raise a party, that if the Spaniard would say where he would land, they would be ready to assist him. This person was sometimes a Colonel in the Army. He went with letters to the Archduke Leopoldus and Don John. That was an Ambassador, and gave promises of much monies, and came back again and hath been soliciting and did obtain monies, that he sent thither by Bills of Exchange. And God, by his providence, we being exceeding poor, directed that we lighted on some of them and some of the monies. Now if they be payable, let them be called for. If the House shall think fit to order any, they may have an inspection into these things. We think it our duty to tell you of these things and we can make them good. Here is your danger, that is it; and here is a poor nation that hath wallowed in its blood, though thanks be to God we have had peace these four or five years. Yet here is the condition we stand in, and I think I should be false to you if I should not give you this true representation of it.

I am to tell you, by the way, a word to justify a thing that I hear is much spoken of. When we knew all these designs before mentioned, when we found that the Cavaliers would not be quiet,—no quiet there is, no peace to the wicked, saith the Scriptures, the 57th of Isaiah, they are like the troubled sea that cannot rest, whose waters cast up mire and dirt; they cannot rest, they have no peace with God and Jesus Christ in the remission of sins, they do not know what belongs to it, therefore they know not how to be at rest; therefore they can no more cease from their actions, than they can cease to be, nor so easily either,—truly when this insurrection was, and we saw it in all the roots and grounds of it, we did find out a poor little invention, which I hear has been much regretted. That was, we were resolved that those men, that put the honest and peaceable minded people that would not comply with such things as these are to such expense, should bear the charge of it. I say there was a little thing invented, which was the erecting of your Major-Generals, to have a little inspection upon the people, thus divided, thus discontented, thus dissatisfied in divers interests by the Popish party,— the Lord Taaffe and others, the most consisting of natural Irish rebels and all those men you have fought against in Ireland, and expulsed from thence as having had a hand in that bloody massacre of those that were under his power, who should have joined in this excellent business of insurrection. And to the end that this nation, upon such a rise as that was, might be settled, we invented this; so justifiable to necessity, so honest in every respect. Truly, if ever I think anything were honest, this was, as anything that ever I knew; and I could as soon venture my life with it, as anything I ever undertook. We did find out,—I mean, myself and the Council,—that it was necessary to put that people who had occasioned all this trouble, if there were need to have greater forces to carry on this work, it was a most righteous thing to put the charge upon that party which was the cause of it. And if there be any man that hath a face looking averse to this, I dare pronounce him to be a man against the interest of England. Upon this account and upon this ground of necessity, when we saw what game they were upon, and knew individual persons, and of the greatest rank not a few engaged in this business,— I knew one man that laid down his life for it,—and by letters intercepted which made it as clear as the day, we did think it our duty to make them that were in the combination of men, as evident as anything in the world, equally to bear their shares of the charge, one with another, for the raising of the forces that were so necessary to defend us against these designs. And truly if any man be angry at it, I am plain and shall use a homely expression, let him turn the buckle of his girdle behind him. If this were to be done again, I would do it! How the Major-Generals have behaved themselves in that work! I hope they are men as to their persons of known integrity and fidelity, and men that have freely adventured their blood and lives for that good cause, if it be thought so, which in my conscience is so, and it was well stated against all the humours and fancies of men. And truly England doth yet receive one day more of lengthening out its tranquillity by that occasion and action; they do say that it doth manifest a year, for it is near so much time as that they have been exercised in that service. Well, your danger is, as you have seen; and truly I am sorry it is so great. I wish it might cause no despondency, as truly I think it will not, because we are Englishmen; that is one good account. And if God give a nation propriety of valour and courage, it is honour and mercy and much more, because you all, I hope, are Christian men, Christian men that know Jesus Christ, and know that cause that hath been mentioned to you this day.

Having declared to you my sense and my knowledge, pardon me if I say so, my knowledge of the condition of these poor nations, for it hath an influence upon them all, it concerneth them all very palpably, I should be to blame if I should not a little offer to you the remedies. I would comprehend them under two considerations; they are somewhat general. The one is, considering all things that may be done and ought to be done in order to security; that is one. And truly the other is a common head. The other is, doing all things that ought to be done in order to reformation; and with that I shall close my discourse. And all that first hath been hinted at, was but to give you a sense of the danger that is most material and significant, for which you are principally called hither to advise of the remedies. I do put them into this method, not but that I think they are scarcely distinct. I do believe truly upon a serious and deliberate consideration, that a true reformation,—as it may and will, through God's acceptance and the endeavours of his poor servants, be,—that that will be pleasing in his sight, and be that, which will be not only that which shall avert the present danger, but be a worthy return for all the blessings and mercies which you have received. So in my conscience, if I were put to shew it this hour, where the security of the nations will lie, forces, arms, watchings, parts, strength, your being and freedom, be as politic and diligent and as vigilant as you can be, I would say in my very conscience, and as before Almighty God I speak it, I think your reformation, if it be honest, and thorough, and just, it will be your best security.

First, for that of security. We shall speak a little distinctly to that. You see where your war is. It is with the Spaniard. You have peace with all nations, or the most of them, Swede, Dane, Dutch. At present I say, it is well it is at present so, and so with the Portugal, France, the Mediterranean Sea, both those States both Christian and profane; the Mahometans, you have a peace with them all. Only with Spain I say you have a difference, you have a war. I pray consider it. Do I come to tell you that I would tie you to this war? No. As you shall find your spirits and reasons grounded in what hath been said, so let you and me join in the prosecution of that war, as we are satisfied, and as the cause will appear to our consciences in the sight of the Lord. But if you can come to prosecute it, prosecute it vigorously, or do not do it at all. Truly I shall speak a very great word, one may ask a very great question. *Unde*, whence shall it come? Our nation is overwhelmed in debts. But I think it my duty to deal plainly, I shall speak to that which Nature teacheth us, if we engage in a business. A recoiling man may haply recover of his enemy, but the courage of an enemy, surely, will be in the keeping of his ground. Therefore it is that which I would advise you, that we may join together to prosecute it vigorously. In the second place, I would advise you that you would deal effectually, seeing there is such a complication of interests. If you believe that there is such a complication of interests, why then, in the name of God, that excites you the more to do it! Give me leave to tell you, that I do not believe that in any war, that ever was in former times, nor any engagements that you have had with others, this nation had more obligations upon them to look to itself, to forbear expense of time, precious time. We have no time now needlessly to mind things that are not essential, to be quibbling about words and comparatively about things of no moment, and in the meantime, being in such a case as I suppose you know we are, to suffer ourselves to be wanting to a just defence against the enemies abroad, or not to be thoroughly sensible of the distempers that are at home. I know perhaps there are many considerations that may teach you, that may induce you to keep your hands tender from men of one religion and of such an interest as is so spread and rooted in the nation. Hence if they seek the eradication of the nation, if they are active as you have seen, and it hath been made manifest so as may not be denied, to the carrying on of their designs; if England must be eradicated by persons complicated with the Spaniard, if this must be brought in through distempers and falseness of men amongst themselves; then the question is no more but this, whether any consideration whatever shall lead us, for fear of eradicating of distempers, to suffer all the honest interests of this nation to be eradicated? Therefore speak but generally of any of their distempers of all sorts, and when a member cannot be cured the rule is plain, *ense rescindendum est immedicabile vulnus.* And I think it is such an advantage as that nothing could ever be more properly used, since this or any nation was.

As to those lesser distempers of people that pretend religion, though that might seem to come under my first head yet from the whole consideration of religion, which it would fall under, as one of the heads of reformation, I had rather put it under this head. And I shall the less speak to it, because you have been so well spoken to this day already. I will tell you the truth, that that which hath been our practice since the last Parliament, hath been to let all this nation see that whatever pretensions be to religion, if quiet, peaceable, they may enjoy conscience and liberty to themselves, so long as they do not make religion a pretence for arms and blood. Truly we have suffered them, and that cheerfully, so to enjoy their own liberties. Whatsoever is contrary, let the pretence be never so specious, if it tend to combinations, to interests, and factions, we shall not care, by the grace of God, whom we rue withal, though never so specious, though never so quiet. And truly I am against all liberty of conscience repugnant to this; I am. If men will profess,— be they those under Baptism, be they those of the Independent judgment simply, and of the Presbyterian judgment,—in the name of God, encourage them, countenance them, while they do plainly hold forth to be thankful to God, and to make use of the liberty given them to enjoy their own consciences. For, as it was said today, undoubtedly this is the peculiar interest all this while contended for. That men that believe in Jesus Christ,—that is the form that gives the being to true religion, faith in Christ, and walking in a profession answerable to that faith,—men that believe the remission of sins through the blood of Christ and free justification by the blood of Christ, and live upon the grace of God, that those men, that are certain they are so, are members of Jesus Christ and are to him as the apple of his eye. Whoever hath this faith, let his form be what it will, if he be walking peaceably without the prejudicing of others under another form, it is a debt due to God and Christ, and he will require it, if he may not enjoy this liberty. If a man of one form will be trampling upon the heels of another form, if an Independent, for example, will despise him under Baptism, and will revile him, and reproach, and provoke him, I will not suffer it in him. If, on the other side, those of the Anabaptists' persuasion shall be censuring the godly Ministers of the nation, that profess under that of Independency or those that profess under Presbytery, shall be reproaching or speaking evil of them, traducing and censuring of them, as I would not be willing to see the day on which England shall be in the power of the Presbytery to impose upon the consciences of others that profess faith in Christ, so I will not endure any reproach to them. But God give us hearts and spirits to keep things equal; which truly I must profess to you hath been my temper. I have had boxes and rebukes on one hand and on the other, some envying me for Presbytery, others as an in-letter to all the sects and heresies in the nation. I have borne my reproach, but I have, through God's mercy, not been unhappy in preventing any one religion to impose upon another. And truly I must needs say, I speak it experimentally, I have found it, I have, that those of the Presbyterian judgment approve of it. I speak it knowingly, as having received evidences from very many counties. I have had petitions, and acknowledgments, and professions from whole counties, as from Cornwell, Devon, Somerset, and other counties, acknowledgments that they do but desire they may have liberty and protection in the worshipping of God according to their own judgments, for the purifying of their congregations and the labouring to attain more purity of faith and repentance, that in their outward profession they will not strain themselves beyond their own line. I have had those, I have them to shew, and I confess I look at that as the blessedest thing, which hath been since the adventuring upon this government, that these times produce. And I hope I gave them fair and honest answers. And if it shall be found to be the care of the Civil Magistrate to keep thus all the professing Christians, and not to suffer all things said or done to provoke others, I think he that would have more liberty than this, is not worthy of any. This therefore I think verily, if it may be thus under consideration for reformation, if it please God to give you and me hearts to keep this even; in giving countenance to ministers, countenancing a just maintenance to them, whether by tithes or otherwise, for my part I should think I were very treacherous if I should take away tithes, till I see the Legislative power to settle maintenance to them another way. But whoever they be that shall contend to destroy them, that doth as really cut their throats, as it is a drift to take them away before a way of reparation or other maintenance be had. Truly I think all such practices and proceedings would be discountenanced. I have heard it from as gracious a minister as any is in England, I have had it professed, that it would be a far greater satisfaction to them to have it another way, if the State will provide it. Therefore I think for the keeping of the Church and people of God, and professors, in their several forms in this liberty, I think, as it hath been a thing that is the root of visible profession, the upholding this I think you will find a blessing in it, if God keep your hearts to keep things in this posture and balance, which is so honest and so necessary.

Truly there might be some other things offered to you in the point of reformation, *videlicet* a reformation of manners. But I had forgot one thing that I must remember! It is their work, you know, in some measure; yet give me leave to say, and I appeal unto your consciences, whether or no there hath not been an honest care taken for the ejecting of scandalous ministers, and for the bringing in of them that have passed an Approbation. I dare say, such an Approbation as never passed in England before. And give me leave to say it hath been with this difference, that neither Mr Doctor nor Parson in the University have satisfied those that have made their Approbations. Though, I can say so, they [the "Triers"] have a great esteem of learning and look at grace as most useful when it falls unto men with it, rather than without it, and wish with all their hearts the flourishing of all those institutions of learning as much as any, yet I must say, it hath been nothing with them that have passed the best, with them or me. I think there hath been a conscience exercised, both by myself and the ministers, towards them that have been approved; I may say, such a one, as I truly believe was never known in England. And I do verily believe, that God hath for the ministry a very great seed in the youth in the universities; and instead of studying books, they study their own hearts. I do believe, as God hath made a very great and flourishing seed to that purpose, so I believe of this ministry of England, that, I think in my very conscience, that God will bless and favour, and hath blessed it to the gaining of very many souls. It was never so upon the thriving hand since England was, as it is this day. Therefore I say in these things, that tend to the profession of the Gospel and public ministry, you will be so far from hindering, that you will further it; and I shall be willing to join with you.

I did hint to you my thoughts about the reformation of manners; and those abuses that are in this nation through disorder, is a thing that should be much in your hearts. It is that, that I am confident is a description and character of that interest you have been engaged against and pressing to, as any other, the badge and character of countenancing profaneness, disorder, and wickedness in all places. In my conscience it was a shame to be a Christian within these fifteen, sixteen, or seventeen years in this nation, either in Caesar's house or elsewhere; it was a shame, it was a reproach to a man, and the badge of Puritan was put upon it, and whatever is next of kin to that reproach, and most agrees with that which is Popery, and the profane nobility and gentry of this nation. We would keep up the nobility and gentry; and the way to keep them up is, not to suffer them to be patronizers nor countenancers of debauchery or disorders; and you will hereby be as labourers in the work. And a man may tell as plainly as can be, what becomes of us by our indifferency or lukewarmness, under I know not what weak pretensions, if it lives in us. Therefore I say, if it be in the general, it is a thing I am confident, that the liberty and profaneness of this nation depends upon reformation, to make it a shame to see men to be bold in sin and profaneness, and God will bless you. You will be a blessing to the nation, and by this be more repairers of breaches than anything in the world. Truly these things do respect the souls of men, and the spirits, which are the men. The mind is the man. If that be kept pure, a man signifies somewhat; if not, I would very fain see what difference there is betwixt him and a beast. He hath only some activity to do some more mischief.

There are some things which respect the estates of men, and

there is one general grievance in the nation. It is, the Law. Not that
the laws are grievance, but there are laws that are a grievance, and
the great grievance lies in the execution and administration. I
think I may say it, I have as eminent Judges in this land, as have
been had, or that the nation has had for these many years. Truly to
be particular I could be, as to the executive part, to administration, but that would trouble you. But the truth of it is, there are
wicked abominable laws that will be in your power to alter. To
hang a man for sixpence, thirteen pence, I know not what; to hang
for a trifle and pardon a murder, is in the ministration of the Law,
through the ill framing of it. I have known in my experience
abominable murders quitted; and to come and see men lose their
lives for petty matters! This is a thing that God will reckon for,
and I wish it may not lie upon this nation a day longer than you
have an opportunity to give a remedy; and I hope I shall cheerfully
join with you in it. This hath been a great grief to many honest
hearts and conscientious people, and I hope it is in all your hearts
to rectify it.

I have little more to say to you, being very weary, and I know
you are so. Truly I did begin with that that I thought was to carry
on this war, if you will carry it on, that we may join together in
that vigorously. And I did promise an answer to an objection. But
what will you prosecute it with? The state is hugely in debt. I
believe it comes to [————]. The treasure of the state is wasted.
We shall not be an enemy to your inspection, but desire it, that
you would inspect the Treasury, and how monies have been
expended; and we are not afraid to look the nation in the face
upon this account. And therefore we will say negatively first, no
man can say we have mis-employed the treasure of this nation and
embezzled it to particular and private uses.

It may be we have not, as the world terms it, been so fortunate
in all our successes. Truly, if we have that mind, that God may not
determine us in these things, I think we shall quarrel at that which
God will answer; and we hope we are able, it may be weakly, I do
not doubt, but to give an answer to God, and to give an answer to
every man's conscience in the sight of God of the reason of things.
But we shall tell you, that it hath been a piece of that arch-fire that
hath been in this your time, where there are flames good store, fire
enough, and it will be your wisdom and skill, and God's blessing

upon you, to quench them both here and elsewhere. I say it again, the endeavours that have been by those that have been appointed, by those that have been Major-Generals, I can repeat of them with comfort that it hath been effectual for the preservation of your peace. It hath been more effectual towards the discountenancing of vice and settling religion, than anything done these fifty years. I will abide it, notwithstanding the envy and slander of foolish men, but I say that hath been a justifiable design. I confess I speak that to you with a little vehemency, but you had not had peace two months together without it. I profess I believe it as much as ever I did anything in the world, and how instrumental they have been to your peace and for your preservation by such means; which we say was more from necessity, than from all instituted things in the world. If you would make laws against the things that God may dispose, to meet with everything that may happen, yea, make a law in the face of God, and you tell God you will meet with all his dispensations, and you will stay things whether he will or no. But if you make laws of good government, that men may know how to obey and do, for government, you may make laws that have frailty and weakness, aye, and good laws that may be observed. But if nothing should be done but what is according to law, the throat of the nation may be cut, till we send for some to make a law. Therefore certainly it is a pitiful, beastly notion, to think that though it be for ordinary government to live by law and rule, yet I think him

["blanks for 2 lynes"]

yet to be clamoured at and blottered at,—when matters of necessity come, inviolably, then extraordinary remedies may not be applied. Who can be so pitiful a person? I confess if necessity be pretended, there is so much the more sin by laying the irregularity of men's actions upon God, as if it were he who sent the necessity, who doth indeed send a necessity but to prevent the end. For as to an appeal to God, I own it conscientiously to God, and the principles of Nature dictate the thing, if there be a supposition, I say, of that which is not, every act at that time hath the more sin. This perhaps is rather to be disputed than otherwise, but I must say, I do not know one action, no, not one, but it hath been in order to the peace and safety of the nation. And the keeping of some in prison hath been upon such clear and just grounds, that no man can except against it. I know there are some imprisoned in the Isle of Wight, Cornwall, and elsewhere, and the cause of their imprisonment was, they were all found acting things that tended to the disturbance of the peace of the nation. Now these principles made us say to them, pray live quietly in your own counties, you shall not be urged with bonds or engagements, or to subscribe to the government. Yet they would not so much as say, we will promise to live peaceably. If others be imprisoned, it is because they have done such things; and if other particulars strike, we know what to say, as having endeavoured to walk as those that would not only give an account to God, another Magistrate, but as to give an account to mem.

I confess I have digressed much to let you know that you would not be discouraged in this war. If you judge it truly necessary, that you cannot avoid it, I would not have you to be discouraged, if you think the State is exceeding poor. Give me leave to tell you, we have managed the Treasury not unthriftily, nor to private uses, but for the use of the nation and government, and shall give you this short account. When their Long Parliament sat, this nation owed 700,000*l*. We examined it; it was brought unto that. In that short meeting that was within half a year after the government came to our hands, I believe there was rather more, than less. They had 120,000*l*. a month; they had the King's, Queen's, Prince's, Bishops' lands, all delinquents' estates, and the Dean and Chapters' lands, which was a very rich treasure. As soon as ever we came to the government, we abated 30,000*l*. the first half year, and 60,000*l*. after. We had no benefit of those estates at all considerable, I do not think the fiftieth part of what they had, and give me leave to tell you, you are not so much in debt as we found you. We know it hath been maliciously dispersed, as if we had set the nation into 2,500,000*l*. debt; but I tell you, you are not so much in debt by some thousands, I think I may say, by some hundreds of thousands. This is true that I tell you. We have honestly, it may be not so wisely as some others would have done, but with honest and plain hearts laboured and endeavoured the disposal of treasure to public uses, and laboured to pull off the common charge, as you see, 60,000*l*. a month. And if we had continued that charge that was left upon the nation, perhaps we could have had as much money, as now we are in debt. These things being thus, I did think it my duty to give you this account, though it be wearisomeness to yourselves and me.

Now if I had the tongue of an angel, if I were so certainly inspired as the holy men of God have been, I could rejoice for your sakes and for these nations' sakes, and for the sake of God, and of this cause that we have been engaged in, that I could move affections in you to that, which if you do it will save this nation. If not, you plunge it, in all human appearance, and all interests, yea, and all the Protestants in the world, to irrecoverable ruin. Therefore I pray, aye, and beseech you in the name of Christ, shew yourselves to be men, quit yourselves like men. It doth not infer any reproach, if you do shew yourselves to be men, Christian men, which will only make you quit yourselves. I do not think that, to that work you have in hand, a neutral spirit will do it. It is a Laodicean spirit, and we know what God said of that Church; it was lukewarm, and therefore he would spew it out of his mouth. It is not a neutral spirit that is incumbent upon you; and if not a neutral spirit, it is much less a stupefied, inclining you in the least disposition the wrong way. They are, in their private consciences, every day making shipwrack, and it is no wonder, if these can shake hands with men of reprobate interests; such, give me leave to think, are the Popish interests, because the Apostle brands them so, having seared consciences, though I do not judge every man, but the ringleaders are such, the Scriptures foretold they should be such. It is not such a spirit will carry the work on. It is men that have works with faith, that know how to lay hold on Christ for remission of a Christian State, till a man be brought to glory in hope. Such an hope kindled in men's spirits will act them to such ends as you are tending to, and so many as are partakers of this, and own your standings wherein the Providence of God hath set and called you to this work, will carry it on. If men through scruple be opposite, you cannot take them by the hand to carry them, because it were absurd; for if a man be scrupling the plain truth before him, it is in vain to meddle with him. He hath placed another image of the business in his own mind; and to say, "Oh! if we could but exercise wisdom to gain civil liberty, religion would follow," that's as common as can be in the world. Certainly there

are such men, who are not maliciously blind; may be, it is that
blindness which God for some causes exercises. It cannot be
expected that they should do anything these men, without they
must demonstrate that they are in bonds. Could we have carried it
hitherto, if we had disputed these things? I must confess, I reckon
that difficulty more than all the wrestling with flesh and blood.
Doubting, hesitating men, they are not fit for your work. You
must not expect that men of hesitating spirits, under the bondage
of scruples, will be able to carry on this work, much less such as
are mere carnal, natural, and such as having an outward
profession of Godliness, which the Apostle speaks of often, are
the enemies of the cross of Christ, whose God is their belly, and
whose glory is their shame, who mind earthly things. Do you
think these men will rise to such a spiritual heat for the nation,
that shall carry you to such a thing as this, that will meet with all
the oppositions that the Devil and wicked men can make? Give me
leave to tell you, those that are called to this work, it will not
depend upon formalities, nor notions, nor speeches. I do not look
the work should be done by these, but by men of honest hearts,
engaged to God, strengthened by providence, enlightened in his
words to know his word; to which he hath set his seal, sealed with
the blood of his Son in the blood of his servants. It is such a spirit
as will carry on this work.

Therefore I beseech you, do not dispute of unnecessary or
unprofitable things, that may divert you from the carrying on of
so glorious a work as this is. I think every objection that ariseth, is
not to be answered; nor have I time for it. I say, look up to God!
Have peace amongst yourselves! Know assuredly, that, if I have
interest, I am by the voice of the people the Supreme Magistrate,
and, it may be, know somewhat that may satisfy my conscience if I
stood in doubt. But it is an union, really it is an union, between
you and me, and both of us united in faith and love to Jesus Christ,
and to his peculiar interest in the world, that must ground this
work. And in that, if I have any peculiar interest that is personal to
myself, that is not subservient to the public end, it were no
extravagant thing for me to curse myself, because I know God will
curse me, if I have. And I have learned too much of God, not to
dally with him and to be bold with him in these things; and I never
was, and I hope I never shall be, bold with him, though I can be

bold with men, if Christ be pleased to assist. I say, if there be love between us,—that the nations may say, these are knit together in one bond to promote the glory of God against the common enemy, to suppress everything that is evil, and encourage whatsoever is of godliness,—yea, the nation will bless you. And really, really, that and nothing else will work off these disaffections from the minds of men, which are as great, if not greater than all the oppositions you can meet with. I do know what I say. When I speak these things, I speak my heart before God; and as I said before, I dare not be bold before him. I have a little faith. I have a little lived by faith, and therein I may be bold. If I should not speak the affections and secrets of my heart, I know he would not bear it at my hands. Therefore in the fear and name of God, go on with love and integrity against whatsoever arises contrary to these ends, which you have known and been told of; and the blessing of God go with you. The blessing of God will go with you.

I have but this one thing to say more. I know it is troublesome, but I did read a Psalm yesterday, which truly may not unbecome me both to tell you of, and you to observe. It is the eighty-fifth Psalm, that is very instructive and significant; and though I do but a little touch upon it, I desire your perusal at your pleasure. It begins, "Lord, thou hast been favourable to thy land: thou hast brought back the captivity of Jacob. Thou hast forgiven the iniquity of thy people, thou hast covered all their sins. Thou hast taken away all thy wrath, thou hast turned thyself from the fierceness of thine anger. Turn us, O God of our salvation, and cause thine anger towards us to cease. Wilt thou be angry with us for ever? Wilt thou draw out thine anger to all generations? Wilt thou revive us again, that thy people may rejoice in thee?" Then he calls upon God as the God of his salvation, and then saith he, "I will hear what the Lord will speak: for he will speak peace unto his people and to his saints: but let them not turn again to folly. Surely his salvation is nigh them that fear him, Oh, that glory may dwell in our land. Mercy and truth are met together: righteousness and peace have kissed each other. Truth shall spring out of the earth, and righteousness shall look down from heaven. Yea, the Lord shall give that which is good, and our land shall yield its increase. Righteousness shall go before him, and shall set us in the way of his steps." Truly I wish that this Psalm, as it is written in the book, might be better written in our hearts, that we may say as David, thou hast done this, and thou hast done that; thou hast pardoned our sins, thou hast taken away our iniquities. Whither can we go to a better God, for he hath done it? It is to him any nation may come in their extremity for the taking away of his wrath. How did he do it? By pardoning their sins and taking away their iniquities. If we can but cry unto him, he will turn and take away our sins. Then let us listen to him, and then consult and meet in Parliament, and ask him counsel, and hear what he saith, for he will speak peace to his people. If you be the people of God, and be for the people of God, he will speak peace, and we will not again return to folly, as to which there is a great deal of grudging in the nation, that we cannot have our horse-races, cock-fightings, and the like. I do not think these are unlawful, but to make them recreations, that they will not endure to be abridged of them, is folly. Till God hath brought us to this spirit, he will not bear with us. Aye, but he bears with them in France; they are so and so. Have they the gospel as we have? They have seen the sun but a little; we have great lights. If God give you a spirit of reformation, you will preserve this nation from turning again to these fooleries. And what will the end be? Comfort and blessing. Then mercy and truth shall meet together. Here is a great deal of truth among professors, but very little mercy. They are ready to cut the throats of one another; but when we are brought unto the right way, we shall be merciful as well as orthodox, and we know who it is that saith, that if a man could speak with the tongue of men and angels, and yet want that, he is but sounding brass and a tinkling cymbal. Therefore I beseech you in the name of God, set your hearts to this, and if you give your hearts to it, then you will sing Luther's Psalm. That is a rare Psalm for a Christian, and if he set his heart open and can approve it to God, we shall hear him say, "God is our refuge and strength, a very present help in trouble." If Pope, and Spaniard, and Devil, and all, set themselves against us, though they should compass us about like bees, as it is in the hundred and eighteenth Psalm, yet in the name of the Lord we should destroy them. And as it is in this Psalm of Luther's, "we will not fear though the earth be removed, and though the mountains be carried into the middle of the sea, though the waters thereof roar and be troubled, though the mountains shake with the swelling thereof. There is a river, the streams whereof shall make glad the city of God. God is in the midst of her, she shall not be moved." Then he repeats, two or three times, "The Lord of Hosts is with us, the God of Jacob is our refuge."

I have done. All that I have to say, is to pray God, that he will bless you with his presence, and that he that hath your hearts and mine would shew his presence in the midst of us. I desire you will go together and choose your Speaker.'

8.

27 November 1656 – Speech in the Painted Chamber to the Parliament there assembled

The friendly relations of Protector and parliament are indicated in the early passage of and assent to a fair number of bills. Here the Commons was fulfilling at least one main function of a 'normal' seventeenth-century parliament – a good augury for a life span beyond five months. 'Great debates' on matters large and small encouraged the civilian Cromwellians and Cromwell himself, increasingly anxious to be less a general and more 'a good constable', to contemplate constitutional change.

'Mr Speaker,

I had some doubt in myself whether I should have spoken or no at this time, but from something you delivered I think myself concerned to speak a little.

Mr Speaker, this is the first time we have met together, and it is with great joy of heart to me to meet you here. I do now receive a return from God in some measure of my prayers for you, and though you have sat but a little time, that you have made many good laws, the effects whereof the people of this Commonwealth will with comfort find hereafter. Therefore, Mr Speaker, you might have spared the excuse you made concerning your time, and as you have so well proceeded hitherto I doubt not but you will make a good progress. And I shall be always ready to assist you and join with you in anything for the being and well being of these nations, and continue my prayers for you.'

9.

23 January 1656/7 – Speech in answer to the congratulations of Parliament

Although the Protectorate was making headway both in and out of parliament, opposition continued among royalists at home and abroad, embittered republicans, and frustrated radicals, both civilian and military. Some plotted the assassination of Cromwell, believing that without him the régime would collapse ignominiously. In January 1656/7 a particularly inept attempt was made by Miles Sindercombe. A Commons resolution congratulating the Protector on his escape underlines the pleasant atmosphere at Westminster and Whitehall. But 'imagination' of the death of Oliver continued as in the tract *Killing No Murder* written by a former Leveller.

'Mr Speaker,

I confess with much respect that you have put this trouble on yourselves upon this occasion; but I perceive there be two things that fill me full of sense. One is, the mercy on a poor unworthy creature; the second is, this great, and as I said, unexpected kindness of Parliament in manifesting such a sense thereof, as this is which you have now expressed: I speak not this with compliment.

That that detracts from the thing in some sense is, the inconsiderableness and unworthiness of the person that hath been the object and subject of this deliverance, to wit, myself. I confess ingenuously to you, I do lie under the daily sense of my unworthiness and unprofitableness, as I have expressed to you. And if there be, as I must readily acknowledge there is, a mercy in it to me, I wish I may never reckon it on any other account than this, that the life that is lengthened may be spent and improved to

His honour that hath vouchsafed the mercy, and to the service of you and those you represent.

I do not know, nor did I think it would be very seasonable for me to say much to you upon this occasion, being a thing that ariseth from yourselves. Yet methinks the kindness you bear forth should kindle a little desire in me even at this present to make a short return. And as you have been disposed hither by the providence of God to congratulate my mercy, so give me leave in a very word or two to congratulate with you. Congratulations are ever conversant about good bestowed upon men, or possessed by them. Truly I shall in a word or two congratulate you with good you are in possession of, and in some respect I also with you.

God hath bestowed upon you, and you are in possession of it, three nations and all that appertains to them, which in either a geographical or topical consideration are nations. In which also there are places of honour and consideration, not inferior to any in the known world. Without vanity it may be spoken, truly God hath not made so much soil, furnished with so many blessings, in vain. But it is a goodly sight, if a man behold it *uno intuito*, and therefore this is a possession of yours worthy [of] congratulation. This is furnished, give me leave to say, for I believe it is true, with the best people in the world possessing so much soil; a people in civil rights, in respect of their rights and privileges, very ancient and honourable. And in this people, in the midst of this people, a people, I know every one will hear it, that are to God as the apple of his eye; and he says so of them, be they many or be they few. But they are many, a people of the blessing of God, a people under his safety and protection; a people calling upon the name of the Lord, which the heathen do not; a people knowing God, and a people, according to the ordinary expressions, fearing God. And you have of this no parallel, no, not in all the world. You have in the midst of you glorious things, glorious things. For you have laws and statutes and ordinances, which, though not so all of them conformable as were to be wished to the law of God, yet on all hands pretend not to be long rested in, further than as they are conformable to the just and righteous laws of God. Therefore I am persuaded there is a heart and spirit in every good man to wish they did all of them answer the pattern. I cannot doubt but that which is in the heart will in due time break forth. That endeavours will be that way, is another of your good things, with which in my heart you are worthily to be congratulated. And you have a magistracy that in outward profession, in pretence, in endeavour, doth desire to put life into these laws. And I am confident that among you will rest nothing, but a desire to promote every desire in others and every endeavour that hath tended or shall tend to the putting of these laws in execution. I do for this congratulate you. You have a gospel-ministry amongst you; that have you. Such a one as without vanity I speak it, or without caring at all for any favour or respect from them, save what I have upon an account above flattery or good words, such an one as hath excelled itself, and I am persuaded, to speak with confidence before the Lord, is the most growing blessing, one of them, on the face of this nation. You have a good eye, and in that I will share with your favours, a good God, a God that hath watched over you and us. A God that hath visited these nations with a stretched out arm and bore his witness against the unrighteousness and ungodliness of men, against those that have abused such nations, such mercies throughout, as I have reckoned up to you. A God that hath not only withstood such to the face, but a God that hath abundantly blessed you with the evidences of his goodness and presence. And he hath done things wonderful amongst us by terrible things in righteousness, he has visited us by wonderful things; in mercy and compassion hath he given us this day of freedom and liberty to speak this, one to another, and to speak of his mercies as he had been pleased to put into our hearts.

Truly, this word of conclusion. If this be so, give me leave to remember you but one word, which I offered to you with great love and affection the first day of meeting with you, this Parliament. It pleased God to put into my heart then to mention a Scripture to you, which would be a good conclusion of my speech now at this time to you. It was, that we being met to seek the good of so great an interest, as I have mentioned, and the glory of that God who is both yours and mine, how could we better do it than by thinking of such words as these, "His salvation is nigh them that fear him; that glory may dwell in our land"! I would not comment upon it. I hope I fear him, and let us more fear him. If this mercy at all doth concern you, as I see it doth, let me, and I hope you will with me, labour more to fear him than we have done, seeing such a blessing as his salvation is nigh them that fear him, seeing we are all of us the representatives of all the good of all these lands, that glory may dwell in our land. If this be so, mercy and truth shall meet together, righteousness and peace shall kiss each other. We shall know, you and I, as the father of this family, how to dispose our mercies to God's glory, how to dispose our severity, how to distinguish betwixt obedient and rebellious children, and not to do as Eli did, who told his sons he did not hear well of them, when perhaps he saw ill by them; and we know the severity of that. And therefore let me say that, though I would not descant upon the words, mercy must be joined with truth, truth in that respect that we think it our duty to exercise a just severity, as well as to apply kindness and mercy. And truly, righteousness and peace must kiss each other. If we will have peace without a worm in it, lay we foundations of justice and righteousness. And if it shall please God so to move you, as that you marry this double couple together, mercy and truth, righteousness and peace, you will, if I may be free to say so, be blessed whether you will or no.

And that you and I may, for the time the Lord shall continue us together, set our hearts upon this, is that which shall be my daily prayer; and I heartily and humbly acknowledge my thankfulness to you.'

10.

28 February 1656/7 – Speech to the Officers, concerning their address as to a Bill for Kingship, now before the House

On 23 February Sir Christopher Packe, a City MP, presented 'a paper' (referred to as a Remonstrance) 'somewhat come to his hand', providing for major constitutional changes, including a second chamber (suggested by the constitutional issues raised by the Commons' prosecution, trial and judgment upon Nayler) and the offer to the Protector of the title and status of king. Cromwell's failure to support the Major-Generals' Decimation Bill (thrown out in January), together with his growing propensity to seek civilian backing, excited suspicions among Army officers that a 'sell-out' was in the offing. To head off restlessness Cromwell met about a hundred leading officers to explain the situation. As this abstract of what must have been a long and very circumstantial speech indicates, their General was by no means apologetic, reviewing past, present and future development in self-justification. He was only partially successful in preventing army 'distempers'.

7 March 1656/7. Passages between the Protector and the hundred officers of the army, touching Kingship.

I suppose you have heard of the address made by one hundred officers to his Highness yesterday seven-night, that his Highness would not hearken to the title [of King] because it was not pleasing to his army and was matter of scandal to the people of God, of great rejoicing to the enemy; that it was hazardous to his own person and of great danger to the three nations; such an assumption making way for Charles Stuart to come in again.

His Highness returned answer presently to this effect, That the first man that told him of it was he, the mouth of the officers then present, (meaning Colonel Mills); that for his part he had never been at any cabal about the same, (hinting by that the frequent cabals that were against Kingship by certain officers).

He said the time was when they boggled not at the word (King), for the Instrument by which the government now stands was presented to his Highness with the title (King) in it, as some there present could witness, (pointing at a principal officer then in his eye,) and he refused to accept of the title. But how it comes to pass that they now startle at title, they best knew. That for his part he loved not the title, a feather in a hat, as little as they did.

That they had made him their drudge upon all occasions. To dissolve the Long Parliament, who had contracted evil enough by long sitting. To call a Parliament, or Convention, of their naming; who met, and what did they? Fly at liberty and property, in so much as if one man had twelve cows, they held another that wanted cows ought to take a share with his neighbour. Who could have said anything was their own, if they had gone on? After their dissolution, how was I pressed by you (said he) for the rooting out of the ministry, nay rather than fail, to starve them out!

A Parliament was afterwards called; they sat five months; it's true we hardly heard of them in all that time. They took the Instrument into debate, and they must needs be dissolved; and yet stood not the Instrument in need of mending? Was not the case hard with me, to be put upon to swear to that which was so hard to be kept?

Some time after that, you thought it was necessary to have Major-Generals, and the first rise to that motion then was the late general insurrections, and was justifiable, and your Major-Generals did your parts well; you might have gone on. Who bid you go to the House with a Bill and there receive a foil?

After you had exercised this power a while, impatient were you till a Parliament was called. I gave my vote against it, but you were confident by your own strength and interest to get men chosen to your hearts and desires. How you have failed therein and how much the country hath been disobliged is well known.

That it is time to come to a settlement, and lay aside arbitrary proceedings so unacceptable to the nation. And by the proceedings of this Parliament you see they stand in need of a check or balancing power, (meaning the House of Lords, or a house so constituted) for the case of James Naylor might happen to be your own case. By their judicial power they fall upon life and member, and doth the Instrument in being enable me to control it?

These were some of the heads insisted on in his speech, though perhaps not the same words yet the full sense, and the officers since that time are quieted and many fallen from the rest. Three Major-Generals are come about for a second House and a successor . . . &c.

II.

31 March 1657 – 'The Humble Petition and Advice.' Speech to the House of Commons at Whitehall on their presenting the Bill

The following speeches (11–17), some to the Commons and some to its committee, waiting upon Cromwell to urge acceptance of what had become the Humble Petition and Advice, a new structured written constitution, may be taken together. The new 'Government' envisaged reductions of the role of the Council (significantly renamed 'Privy Council'), limitations upon religious toleration, and the establishment of a second chamber ('the Other House'), and saw the acceptance of 'the title' of king as a *sine qua non*. Presented with the Petition on 31 March the Protector asked time to consider its content and implications. A Commons Committee (including lawyers like Bulstrode Whitelocke and Nathaniel Fiennes, 'kinglings' to a man) waited on Cromwell during April pushing the necessity and advantages of acceptance. Cromwell characteristically delayed, while sounding out opinions in the army and elsewhere, probing his own conscience and inclinations, and consulting Providence, which he customarily put forward as the instigator of many of his actions (and inactions).

'Mr Speaker,

This frame of government, that it hath pleased the Parliament by your hand to offer to me, truly I should have a very brazen forehead if it should not beget in me a great deal of consternation of spirit, it being of so high and great importance, as by your opening of it, and by the reading of it, is manifest to all men to be. The welfare, the peace and settlement of three nations, and all that rich treasure of the best people in the world being involved therein, I say, this consideration alone ought to beget in me the greatest reverence and fear of God, that ever possessed a man in this world.

I rather truly study to say no more at this time than is necessary to give a brief and short answer, suitable to the nature of the thing. The thing is of weight, the greatest weight of anything that was ever laid before a man. And therefore it being of that weight, and consisting of so many parts as it doth,—in each of which much more than my life is concerned,—truly I think I have no more to desire of you at this time, but that you would give me time to deliberate and consider what particular answer I may return to so great a business as this is.

I have lived the latter part of my life in, if I may say so, the fire, in the midst of trouble. And all things, all the things that hath befallen me since I was first engaged in the affairs of this Commonwealth, truly if it could be supposed they should be brought into a narrow compass that I could take a view of them at once, I do not think they would, nor do I think they ought to, move my heart and spirit with that fear and reverence of God that becomes a Christian, as this thing that hath been now offered by you to me. And truly my comfort in all my life hath been, that the burdens that have lain heavy upon me, they have been laid upon me by the hand of God. And I have not known, and have been many times at a loss, which way to stand under the weight of what hath lain upon me, but by looking at the candour and pleasure of God in it, which hitherto I have found to be a good pleasure towards me. And should I give any resolution in anything suddenly, without seeking to have an answer put into my heart, and so into my mouth, by him that hath been my God and my guide hitherto, it would give you very little cause of comfort in such a choice, as you have made in such a business as this is. Because, it would savour more to be of the flesh, to proceed from lust, to arise from arguments of self-love; and if, whatsoever the issue of this business shall be, it should have such motives in me, and such a rise in me, it may prove even a curse to you and to these three nations, who I verily believe have intended well in this business, and have had those honest and sincere aims to the glory of God, the good of his people, and the rights of the nation. I verily believe these have been your aims, and God forbid that so good aims should suffer by any dishonesty or indirectness on my part. For although in the affairs that are in the world things may be intended well,—as they are always, or for the most part, by such as love God and fear God and make him their aim; and such honest ends and purposes as these are I believe yours to be,—yet if these considerations fall upon a person or persons that God takes no pleasure in, that perhaps may be at the end of this work, that to please any of those humours or considerations that are of this world shall run upon such a rock as this is without due consideration, without integrity, without sincerity, without approving the heart to God, and seeking an answer from him, and putting things as for life and death to him, that such an answer may be received as may be a blessing to the person to be used to answer these noble and worthy and honest intentions of those that have prepared and perfected this work, it would be like a match, where a good and worthy and virtuous man mistakes in the person that he makes love to, and it after proves a very great curse to the man and to the family. And if this should be so to you, and to these nations, whose good I cannot be persuaded but you have in your thoughts aimed at, why then it had been better, I am sure of it, that I had never been born.

I have therefore but this one word to say to you, that seeing you have made this progress in this business, and completed the work on your part, I may have some short time to ask counsel of God and of my own heart. And I hope that neither the humour of any weak or unwise people, nor yet the desires of any that may have lusting after things that are not good, shall steer me to give other than such an answer as may be ingenuous and thankful, thankfully acknowledging your care and integrity, and such an answer as shall be for the good of those, that I presume you and I serve, and are ready to serve. And truly I may say this also, that as the thing will deserve deliberation, the utmost deliberation and consideration on my part, so I shall think myself bound to give as speedy an answer to these things as I can.'

12.

3 April 1657 – 'The Humble Petition and Advice.' Speech at Whitehall to Lord Whitelocke and the Committee appointed to attend his Highness

'My Lord,

This paper in my hand is a copy of the Petition and Advice, which it pleased the Parliament to present unto me in the Banqueting-House on Tuesday last.

I am very heartily sorry that I did not make this desire of mine known to the Parliament before this time, which was that I acquainted them with by letter this day. The reason was, because some infirmity of body had seized upon me before these two last days of yesterday and Wednesday.

I have as well as I could taken consideration of the things contained in it, and sought of God that I might return such an answer as might become me and be worthy of the Parliament.

I must needs bear this testimony for you, that you have been zealous of the two greatest concernments that God has in the world. The one is that of religion and the preservation of the professors thereof, to give them all due and just liberty, and to assert the truths of God, which you have done in part in this paper, and referred to be done more fully by yourselves and me hereafter. And as to the liberties of men professing godliness under a variety of forms amongst us, you have done that which never was done before, and I pray God it may not fall upon the people of God, or any sort of them, as a fault if they do not put such a value upon what is done as never was put upon anything since Christ's time for such a Catholic interest for the people of God.

The other thing cared for is the civil liberties and interests of the nations, which although it be, and indeed ought to be subordinate to a more peculiar interest of God, yet it is the next best God hath given men in the world, and better than any words, if well cared for, to fence the people of God in their interest. And if any one whatsoever think that the interest of God's people and the civil interest are inconsistent, I wish my soul may not enter into his or their secret.

These are things, I must acknowledge, Christian and honourable, and are provided for by you, both like Christians, men of honour, and Englishmen: and to this I must and shall bear my testimony, while I live, against all gainsayers whatsoever. And upon these two interests I shall, if God account me worthy, live and die. And I must say, that if I were to give an account before a greater tribunal than any that's earthly, and if I were asked why I engaged all along in the late wars, I could give no account but it would be wicked, if it did not comprehend these two ends.

Only you will give me leave to say, and to say it seriously, the issue will prove it so, that you have one or two considerations that do stick with me. The one is that you have named me by another title than that I now bear; you do necessitate my answer to be categorical, and you leave me without a liberty of choice save as to all.

I question not your wisdom in doing of it, but think myself obliged to acquiesce in your determinations. Knowing you are men of wisdom, and considering the trust you are under, it is a duty not to question the reasons of anything you have done. I should be very brutish should I not acknowledge the exceeding high honour and respect you have had for me in this paper. Truly, according to what the world calls good,—it has all good in it according to worldly apprehension, to wit, sovereign power ,—you have testified your value and affection as to my person as high as you could; for more you could not do. I shall always keep a grateful memory of that in my heart, and by you I give the Parliament this my grateful acknowledgment. Whatever other men's thoughts may be, I shall not own ingratitude.

But I must needs say that that may be fit for you to do, which may not be fit for me to undertake. As I should reckon it a very great presumption should I ask you the reason of your doing any one thing in this paper,—except very few things the Instrument bears testimony to itself,—so you will not take it unkindly if I ask you this addition of the Parliament's favour, love and indulgence towards me, that it be taken in tender part if I give such an answer, as I find in my heart to give in this business, without urging many reasons for it, save such as are most obvious and most for my advantage and purpose in answering, to wit, that I am unable for such a trust and charge. And if the answer of the tongue as well as the preparation of the heart be from God, I must say my heart and thoughts, ever since I heard the Parliament were upon this business,—though I could not take notice of your proceedings therein without breach of your privileges, yet as a common person I confess I heard of it, as in common with others,—I must say I have been unable to attain no further than this, that seeing the way is hedged up as it is to me, (I cannot accept the things offered unless I accept all,) I have not been able to find it my duty to God and to you to undertake this charge under that title. The most I said in commendation of this Instrument may be returned upon me thus, Are there such good things so well provided for, why cannot you accept them without such an ingredient? Nothing must make a man's conscience his servant, and really and sincerely it is my conscience that guides me to this answer. And if Parliament be so resolved to necessitate my answer to be categorical it will not be fit for me to use any inducements by you to alter their resolutions.

This is all I have to say. I desire it may be, and I do not doubt but it will be, with candour and ingenuity represented to them by you.'

13.

8 April 1657 – 'The Humble Petition and Advice.' Speech in the Banqueting-House at Whitehall to the House of Commons

'Mr Speaker,

No man can put a greater value than I hope I do, and shall do, upon the desires and advices of the Parliament. I could in my own heart aggravate both concerning the persons advising, and concerning the advice, readily acknowledging that it is the advice of the Parliament of these three nations. And if a man could suppose it were not a Parliament to some, yet doubtless it should be so to me, and to us all that are engaged in this common cause, wherein we have been engaged. I say, surely it ought to be a Parliament to us, because it arises as a result of those issues and determination of settlement that we have laboured to arrive at: and therefore I do most readily acknowledge the Authority advising these things.

I can aggravate also to myself the general notion of the things advised to, as being things tending to the settlement of the chiefest things that can fall into the hearts of men to desire or to endeavour after: and this at such a time when truly I may think the nation is big with expectation of anything that may add to their better being. I therefore must needs put a very high esteem upon, and have a very reverent opinion of anything that comes from you: and so I have had of this Instrument, and I hope, so I have already expressed myself. And what I have expressed hath been, if I flatter not myself, from a very honest heart towards the Parliament and the public. I say not these things to compliment you, for we are past all those things, all considerations of that kind. We must all be very real now, if ever we will be so.

Howbeit, your title and name you give to this paper makes me to think you intended advice, and I should transgress against all reason should I make any other construction than that you did intend advice. I would not lay a burden on any beast, but I would consider his strength to bear it: and if you will lay a burden upon a man that is conscious to his own infirmities and disabilities, and doth make some measure of counsel that may seem to come from heaven,—counsel in the word of God, who leaves a room for charity, and for men to consider their own strength,—I hope it will be no evil in me to measure your advice and mine own infirmity together. And truly those will have some influence upon conscience, conscience in him that hath received talents to know how he may answer the trust of them: and such a conscience have I had, and still have. And therefore when I thought I had an opportunity to make answer, I made that answer; and am a person, and have been, before and then and since, lifting up my heart to God, to know what might be my duty at such a time as this, and upon such an occasion and trial as this was to me.

Truly, Mr Speaker, it has been heretofore a matter of, I think, but a philosophical discourse, that a great place, great authority, is a great burden. I know it is so, and I know a man that is convinced in his conscience, that nothing less will enable him to the discharge of it than to have assistance from above; that it may very well require him, in such a subject so convinced and so persuaded, to be right with the Lord in such undertakings. And therefore to speak very clearly and plainly to you, I had, and I have, hesitation as to that individual thing. If I undertake anything not in faith, I shall serve you in mine own unbelief, and I shall then be the unprofitablest servant that ever a people or nation had.

Give me leave therefore to ask counsel. I am ready to render a reason of my apprehension, which happily may be overswayed by better apprehension. I think so far I have deserved no blame, nor do I take it that you lay any upon me, only you mind me of the duty that is incumbent upon me. Truly the same answer that I have as to this point of duty one way, the same consideration have I as to duty another way. I would not urge to you the point of liberty surely you have provided for liberty. I have borne my witness to it, civil and spiritual; the greatest provision that ever was made have you made, and I know you do not intend to exclude me. The liberty I ask is to vent my own doubts, and mine own fears and mine own scruples, though happily, in such cases as these are, the Word hath judged that a man's conscience ought to know no scruples. Surely mine doth, and I dare not dissemble: and therefore they that are knowing in the ground of their own actions will be best able to measure advice to others.

There are many things in this Government besides that one of the name and title, that deserve very much information as to my judgment. It is you, and none but you, that can capacitate me to receive satisfaction in them. Otherwise, I say truly, I must say that I am not persuaded to the performance of my trust and duty, nor informed, and so not acted as I know you intend I should, and every man in the nation should,—and you have provided for them,—as a free man, as a man that doth possibly, rationally, and conscientiously. And therefore I cannot tell what other return to make to you than this. I am ready to give you a reason if you will, I say, capacitate me to give it, and yourselves to receive it, and to do that in the other things, that may inform me a little more particularly than this Vote, that you have expressed yesterday, and hath been now read by you to me.

And truly I hope when I understand the ground of these things, the whole neither being for your good nor mine, but for the good of the nations, there will be no doubt but we may even in these particulars find out those things that may answer our duty, mine and all our duties, to those nations whom we serve.

And this is that, that I do, with a great deal of affection and honour, and respect, offer now to you.'

14.

11 April 1657 – 'The Humble Petition and Advice.' Speeches to the Committee.

Lord Whitelocke. 'I only understand, that by order of the Parliament, this Committee are tied up to receive what your

Highness shall be pleased to offer, as to your doubts or scruples
upon this paper: the very words of the Order are, *That the
Committee have power to attend your Highness, to receive from
your Highness your doubts and scruples, touching any the
particulars contained in the humble Petition and Advice, formerly
presented; and in answer thereunto, to offer to your Highness
reasons for your satisfaction, and for the maintenance of the
Resolutions of the House; and such particulars as we cannot
satisfy your Highness in, that we may report the same to the
Parliament what particulars your Highness shall think fit to object.*
Your Highness is pleased to mention the government, as it now is,
and it seems to some of our apprehensions as if your Highness did
make that an objection, *If the government be well, why do you
change it?* If that be intended by your Highness as an objection in
the general, I suppose the Committee will give you satisfaction.'

Lord Protector. 'Sir, I think that neither you nor I, but meet
with a very good heart to come to some issue of this great
business. And truly that is, that I cannot assure you I have all the
reason and argument in the world to move me to it, and am
exceeding ready to be ordered by you in the way of proceeding.
Only I confess, according to those thoughts I have, as I have
answered my own thoughts in preparing for such a work as this is,
I have made this notion of it to myself, that having met you
twice,—at the Committee first, and returned you that answer that
I gave you then, and the House a second time,—I do perceive that
the favour and the indulgence that the House shews me in this, is,
that I might receive satisfaction. I know they might have been
positive in the thing, and said they had done enough. If they had
only made such an address to me, they might have insisted upon it,
only to offer it. Yet I could plainly see it was my satisfaction they
aimed at. I think really and sincerely it is my satisfaction they
intend, and truly I think there is one clause in the Paper that doth a
little warrant that, "to offer such reasons for his satisfaction, and
for the maintenance of the Resolutions of the House".
Now Sir, it is true the occasion of all this is the answer that I
made. That occasions a Committee to come hither in order to my
satisfaction. And truly, Sir, I doubt,—if you will draw out those
reasons from me, I will offer them to you,—but I doubt on my
own part if you should proceed that way. It would put me a little
out of the method of my own thoughts; and it being mutual

122 *Speeches*

satisfaction that is endeavoured, if you will do me the favour, it will more agree with my method. I shall take it as a favour, and if it please you, I will leave you to consider together your own thoughts of it.'

Lord Whitelocke. 'The Committee that are commanded by the Parliament, and are here present to wait upon your Highness, I do suppose cannot undertake to give the Reasons of the Parliament, for that they have done; but any Gentleman here can give his own particular apprehension for your Highness' satisfaction; and if you will be pleased to go in the way which you have propounded, and either in general or in particular to require a satisfaction from the Committee, I suppose we shall be ready to do the best we can to give you satisfaction.'

Lord Protector. 'I think if this be so, then I suppose nothing can be said by you, but what the Parliament hath dictated to you, and I think that is clearly expressed, that the Parliament intends satisfaction: then is it as clear, that there must be reasons and arguments, that have light and conviction in them, in order to satisfaction.

I speak for myself in this, I hope you will think it not otherwise. I say it doth appear so to me, that you have the liberty of your own reasons. I think if I should write any of them, I cannot call this the "reason" of the Parliament. The Parliament in determinations and conclusions, by votes of the several particulars of the government, that reason is dilated and diffused, and every man hath a share of it. And therefore when they have determined such a thing, certainly it was reason that led them up into it; and if you shall be pleased to make me partaker of some of that reason, I do very respectfully represent to you, that I have a general dissatisfaction at the thing. And I do desire that I may be informed in the grounds that lead you, whom I presume are all satisfied persons to the thing and every part of it. And if you will be pleased to think so fit, I will not farther urge it upon you. To proceed that way, it will be a favour to me, otherwise, I shall deal plainly with you, it doth put me out of the method of my own conceptions; and then I shall beg that I may have an hour's deliberation, and that we might meet again in the afternoon.'

Lord Chief Justice. 'The Parliament sent us to wait upon your Highness, to give your Highness any satisfaction that is in our understandings to give. The whole paper consists of many heads, and if your Highness intend satisfaction, the propositions being general, we can give but general satisfaction, and therein we are ready. If that be your Highness' meaning, I think we shall be ready to give satisfaction as far as our understandings.'

Lord Protector. 'If you will please to give me leave, I do agree. Truly the thing is general as it is; either falling under the notion of settlement, that is a general that consists of many particulars, and truly if you call it by that it is tituled, there it is general, it is advice, desires and advice. And that, the truth is, that I have made my objection in, is but to one thing as yet; only the last time I had the honour to meet the Parliament, I did offer to them that they would put me into a condition to receive satisfaction as to all the particulars. No question, I might easily offer something particular for debate, if I thought that that would answer the end; for truly I know my end and yours is the same, that is, to bring things to an issue one way or other, that we may know where we are, that we may attain that general end, and that is settlement. The end is in us both, and I durst contend with any one person in the world, that it is not more in his heart than in mine. I could go to some particulars to ask a question, or ask a reason of the alteration, which would well enough let you into the business, that it might; yet I say, it doth not answer me. I confess I did not so strictly examine that Order of Reference, or whether I read it or no I cannot tell you. If you will have it that way, I shall, as well as I can, make such an objection as may occasion some answer to it, and though perhaps I shall object weak enough, I shall very freely submit it to you.'

Lord Chief Justice. 'The Parliament hath commanded us for that end, to give your Highness satisfaction.'

Lord Commissioner Fiennes. 'May it please your Highness, looking upon the Order, I find that we are empowered to offer any reasons that we think fit, either for the satisfaction of your Highness, or maintenance of what the Parliament hath given you their advice in; and I think we are rather to offer to your Highness the Reasons of the Parliament, if your Highness' dissatisfaction be to the alteration of the government in general, or in particular.'

Lord Protector. 'I am very ready to say I have no dissatisfaction that it hath pleased the Parliament to find out a way, though of alteration, to bring these nations into a good settlement; and perhaps you may have judged the settlement we were in, was not so much for the great end of government, the liberty and good of the nations, and the preservation of all those honest interests that have been engaged in this cause. I say I have no objection to the general, that the Parliament hath thought fit to take consideration of a new settlement or government. But you having done it as you have, and made me so far interested in the business as to make such an overture to me, I shall be very glad, if you so please to let me know it, that besides the pleasure of Parliament I may be told somewhat of the reason of Parliament for interesting me in this thing and for making the alteration such as it is. Truly I think I shall as to the other particulars swallow this procedure. I shall be very ready to assign particular objections to clear that to you, that it may be either better to clear, or to help me at least to a clearer understanding of the things for better good,—for that I know is in your hearts as well as mine,—though I cannot presume that I have anything to offer you that may convince you. But if you will take it in good part, I shall offer somewhat to every particular.

If you please. As to the first of the thing, I am clear as to the ground of the thing, being so put to me as it hath been put. I think that some of the grounds upon which it is done will very well lead into such objections or doubts as I may offer, and will be a very great help to me in it, and if you will have me discuss this, or that, or the other doubt that may arise methodically, I shall do it.'

Lord Whitelocke, giving the reason for the alteration of the present settlement, says 'that it will not be so clear a settlement and foundation for the preservation of the Rights and Liberties of the Nation, as if we came to a settlement by the Supreme Legislative power; upon that ground it was taken into consideration . . .' and, referring to the alteration of title, remarks, 'it was thought that the title which is known by the Law of England for many ages, many hundreds of years together received, and the Law fitted to it, and that to the Law, that it might be of more certainty and clear establishment, and more comformable to the laws of the nation, that that title should be that of *King*, rather than that other of *Protector*.

The *Master of the Rolls* thought his Highness mistaken in

thinking it a mere difference of name, 'as if it were a bare title . . .
for upon due consideration you shall find that the whole body of
the Law is carried upon this wheel . . .' i.e. Kingship. The title of
Protector was based on the Instrument only, and 'it hath no limit at
all'; there was a great prejudice against change of names, witness
the failure of the King to call himself King of Great Britain instead
of King of England, and the unwillingness of Parliament to be
called 'The Representative of the People.' The Parliament having
voted to restore the title of King, 'this is vox populi,' and he hoped
his Highness would agree to it.

Lord Protector. 'I cannot deny but the things that have been
spoken have been spoken with a great deal of weight. And it is not
fit for me to ask any of you, if you have a mind to speak further of
this! But if it had been so your pleasure, truly then I think it would
have put me in, according to the method and way I have conceived
to myself, to the more preparedness to have returned some
answer. And if it had not been to you a trouble, I am sure the
business requires it from any man in the world if he were, in any
case much more from me, to make serious and true answers. I
mean such as are not feigned in my own thoughts, but such
wherein I express the truth and honesty of my heart: I mean that
by true answers.

I did hope that when I had heard you, so far as it is your pleasure
to speak to this head, I should have then, taking some short notice
as I did, have been in a condition this afternoon, if it had not been
a trouble to you, to have returned my answer upon a little
advisement with myself. But seeing you have not thought it
convenient to proceed this way, truly I think I may well say that I
had need have a little thoughts of the thing to return an answer to
it, lest your debates should end on my part with a very vain
discourse and with lightness, which it is very like to do. I say
therefore, if you think to proceed further to speak to these things, I
should have made my own short animadversions on the whole
this afternoon, and made some short reply, and this would have
ushered me in, not only to have given the best answer I could, but
to have made my own objections.'

The *Lord Chief Justice* then spoke, 'since it is your Highness'
pleasure, that it should be spoken now altogether, by those that
have anything to say.' It was proposed to set up Kingship, because

it was approved of by the word of God, ancient, and well known to the Law; whereas the other title was not upon a sure establishment. 'If so be your Highness should do any act, and one should come and say, *My Lord Protector, why are you sworn to govern by the Law, and you do thus and thus, as you are Lord Protector? Do I?* Why, how am I bound to do? *Why, the King could not have done so!* Why, but I am not King, I am not bound to do as the King, I am Lord Protector; shew me that the Law doth require me to do it as Protector; if I have not acted as Protector, shew me where the Law is! Why you put any one to a stumble in that case, . . .' *Sir Charles Wolseley* repeated the argument, 'that the Law knows not a Protector'; 'this nation hath ever been a lover of Monarchy, and of Monarchy under the title of King'; 'your Highness hath been pleased to call yourself, as when you speak to the Parliament, a servant; you are so indeed to the people, and 'tis your greatest honour so to be. I hope then, Sir, you will give the people leave to name their own servant; that is a due you cannot, you will not certainly deny them.' *Lord Commissioner Fiennes, Lord Commissioner Lisle,* and *Lord Broghill* made similar speeches.

Lord Protector. 'I have very little to say to you at this time. I confess I shall never be willing to deny or defer those things that come from the Parliament to the supreme Magistrate, if they come in the bare and naked authority of such an assembly as known by that name, and are really the representation of so many people as a Parliament of England, Scotland, and Ireland, is. I say it ought to have its weight, and it hath so, and ever will have with me. In all things a man is free to answer desires as coming from Parliaments; I may say that. But in as much as the Parliament hath been pleased to condescend to me so far, to do me this honour, a very great one added to the rest, to give me the advantage of so many Members of theirs, so able, so understanding the grounds of things, it is, I say, a very singular honour and favour to me. And I confess, I wish I may, and I hope I shall, do that that becomes an honest man to do, in giving an answer to these things, according to the desire, that either I have, or God shall give me, or I may be helped by reasoning with you unto. And I did not indeed in vain allege conscience in the first answer I gave; but I must say, I must be a very unworthy person to receive such favour, if I should prevaricate when I said things did stick upon my conscience, which I must still say they do. Only I must say I am in the best way that I can be for information, and I shall gladly receive it.

Here have been divers things spoken by you today, with a great deal of judgment, and ability, and knowledge. And I think the things, or the arguments, or reasonings that have been used, have been upon these three accounts; to speak to the thing simply, or in the abstract notion of the title, and the positive reasons upon which it stands; and then comparatively both in the thing and in the foundation of it, which,—what it is to shew the goodness of it comparatively,—it is alleged to be so much better than what is, and that is so much short of doing the work that this will do; and thirdly, some things have been said by way of precaution, upon arguments that are a little from the thing in the nature of it, but are considerations from the temper of the people of the nation, what will gratify them, which surely is considerable, as also by way of anticipation of me in my answer, by speaking to some objections that others have made against this thing. These are things in themselves each of them considerable. To answer to objections, I know it is a very weighty thing; and to make objections is very easy, and that will fall to my part. And I am sure I shall, if I make them to men that know so well how to answer them, because they have in part received them from others upon the debates already had. But upon the whole matter, I having as well as I could taken these things that have been spoken, which truly are to be acknowledged by me to be very learnedly spoken, I hope therefore you will give me a little time to consider of them, and tell me when it may be your best time for me to return to you to meet you again.'

Lord Whitelocke. 'Your Highness will be pleased to appoint your own time.'

Lord Protector. 'On Monday at nine of the clock, I will be ready to wait upon you.'

15.

13 April 1657 – 'The Humble Petition and Advice.' Speech to the Committee

'My Lord,

I think I have a very hard task upon my hand. Though it be but to give an account of myself, yet I see I am beset on all hand here. I say, but to give an account of myself, but it is in a business that is, in a business that is very comprehensive of others, in some sense to us, and, as the Parliament have been pleased to make it, of all the interests of these three nations.

I confess I consider two things. First, to return some very weak answer to the things that were so ably and well said the other day on behalf of the Parliament's putting the title in the Instrument of Settlement. I hope it will not be expected that I should answer to everything that was then said, because I suppose the main things that were spoken were arguments from ancient constitutions and settlements by the laws, of which I am sure I could never be well skilled, and therefore must ask the more pardon in what I have transgressed in my practice, or shall now trangress through my ignorance of them in my answer to you. Your arguments I say, which were chiefly founded upon the law, seem to carry with them a great deal of necessary conclusion to enforce that one thing of Kingship; and if the argument come upon me to enforce upon the ground of necessity, why then I have no room to answer, for what must be, must be. And therefore I did reckon it much of my business to consider, whether there was such a necessity, or would arise such a necessity from those arguments.

It was said that Kingship was not a title but an office, so interwoven with the fundamental laws of this nation, as if they could not, or well could not, be executed and exercised without it: partly, if I may say so, upon a supposed ignorance of the law that it hath of any other title; it knows no other, neither does any other know it, the reciprocation is such. This title or name, or office as you pleased to say, is understood in the dimensions of it, in the powers and prerogatives of it, which are by the law made certain. And the law can tell when it keeps within compass, and when it exceeds its limits. And the law knowing this, the people can know it also, and the people do love what they know: and it will be neither *pro salute populi*, nor for safety, to obtrude upon them names that they do not nor cannot understand. It is said also, that the people have been always, by their representatives in Parliament, unwilling to vary names; forasmuch as hath been said before, they love settlement. And there were two good instances given of that. The one, in King James his time, about his desire to alter somewhat of the title; and another, in the Long Parliament, wherein they being otherwise rationally moved to admit of the word "Representative" instead of "Parliament", they refused it for the same reason. It hath been said also, that the holding to this word King doth strengthen the settlement, because it doth not do anything *de novo* but resolves things into their old current. It is said, it is the security of the chief magistrate, and that it secures all that act under him. Truly these are the principal grounds that were offered the last day, so far as I do recollect.

I cannot take upon me to refel those grounds, for they are strong and rational, but if I shall be able to make any answer unto them, I must not grant that they are necessarily concluding, but take them only as arguments that have perhaps much of conveniency and probability towards concluding. For if a remedy or expedient may be found, then they are not necessary, they are not inevitable grounds. And if not necessary and concluding, why then, they will hang upon the reason of expediency or conveniency: and if so, I shall have a little liberty to speak, otherwise I am concluded before I speak. And therefore it will behove me to say what reasons I have why they are not, why they are not absolute and necessary conclusions, nor that they are,—nor that it is, I should say,—so interwoven in the laws, but that the laws may not possibly be administered and executed to equal justice and equal satisfaction of the people, and equally to answer all objections, as well without it, as with it. And then, when I have done that, I shall only take the liberty to say a word or two for my own grounds, and when I have said what I can say as to that, I hope you will think a great deal more than I say.

Truly though Kingship be not a title, but a name of office that runs through the law, yet it is not so *ratione nominis*, from the reason of the name, but from what is signified. It is a name of office plainly implying the supreme authority; it is no more, nor can it be stretched to more. I say it is a name of office plainly implying the supreme authority, and if it be so, why then I would suppose,—I am not peremptory in anything that is a matter of deduction and inference of my own,—why then I would suppose, whatsoever hath been or shall be the name in which the supreme authority shall act, why I say, if it had been these four or five letters, or whatsoever else it had been, that signification goes to the thing signified, and not the thing to the name; certainly it does, and not the thing to the name. Why then there can be no more said but this. Why, this hath been said, This hath been the name fixed, under which the supreme authority has been known. Happily as it hath been fixed, so it may be unfixed. And certainly if fixed in the right of authority, I mean as a legislative power, in the right of a legislative power, I think the authority that could christen it with such a name could have called it by another name. And therefore if it was but derived from that, and certainly they had the disposal of it and might have had it, they might have detracted or changed. And I hope it will be no offence to you to say, as the case now stands, so may you. And if it be so that you may, why then, I say there is nothing of necessity in the argument, but consideration of the expedience of it. I had rather if I were to choose, if it were the natural question, which I hope is altogether out of the question, but I had rather have any name from this Parliament, than any name without it; so much do I think of the authority of Parliament. And I believe all men are of my mind, in that I think the nation is very much of that mind; though that be an uncertain way of arguing, what mind they are of. I think we may say that without offence, for I would give none, though the Parliament be the truest way to know what the mind of the nation is. Yet, if the Parliament will be pleased to give me a liberty to reason for myself, and that that be made one argument, I hope I may urge against that, else I cannot freely give a reason for my own mind. But I say undoubtedly, let us think what we will, what the Parliament settles is that which will run through the law, and will lead the thread of government through the land, as well as what has been; considering that what hath been, hath been but upon the same account, save that there has been some long continuance of the thing. It is but upon the same account; it had its original somewhere, and it was in consent, in consent of the whole, there was the original of it. And consent of the whole will I say be the needle that will lead the thread through all, and I think no man will pretend right against it or wrong. And if so, then, under favour to me, I think all these arguments from the law are, as I said before, not necessary, but are to be understood upon the account of conveniency. It is in your power to dispose and settle as before, and we can have confidence that what you do settle will be as authentic as those things that were before, especially as to this individual thing, the name or title upon Parliamentry account, upon Parliamentary authority. Why then, I say, there will be way made, with leave, for me to offer a reason or two to all that has elsewhere been said: otherwise I say my mouth is stopt.

There are many enforcements to carry on this thing [i.e. the Protectorship]. I supposing it will stand upon a way of expediency and fitness, truly I should have urged one consideration more that I had forgotten; and that is, not only to urge from reason but from experience. Perhaps it is a short one, but it is a true one, under favour, and is known to you all in the fact of it, although there has been no Parliamentary declaration. That the supreme authority going in another name and under another title than King, why it has been complied with twice without it: that is, under the *Custodes Libertatum Angliae*, and it has since I exercised the place. And truly I may say that almost universal obedience has been given from all ranks and sort of men to both.

And to begin with the highest degree of majesty, the Law. At the first alteration, and when that was the name, though it was the name of an invisible thing, yet the very name, though a new name, was obeyed, did pass for current and was received, and did carry on the justice of the nation. I do very well remember that my Lords the Judges were somewhat startled, and yet upon consideration, if I mistake not, I believe so,—there being of them without reflection as able and as learned as have sat there,—though they did I confess at first demur a little, yet they did receive satisfaction and did act as I said before. I profess it, for my own part I think I may say it, since the beginning of that change, I would be loth to speak anything vainly, but since the beginning of that change unto this day I do not think that in so many years, in those that were called, and worthily so accounted, halcyon days of peace, in Queen

Elizabeth's, and King James's, and Charles's time, I do not think but that the laws did proceed with as much freedom and justice, with less private solicitation, either from that time that was called then so, or since I came to the government. I do not think under favour that the laws have had a more free exercise, uninterrupted by any hand of power, the judges less solicited by letters or private interpositions either of my own or other men's, in double so many years, in all those times of peace.

And if more of my Lords the Judges were here, than now are, they could tell what to say to what has been done since. And therefore I say, under favour, these two experiences do manifestly shew, that it is not a title, though so interwoven with the laws, that makes the law to have its free passage and do its office without interruption as we think, but that if a Parliament shall determine that another name shall run through the laws, I believe it may run with as free a passage as this; which is all that I have to say upon that head. And if this be so, then truly other things may fall under a more indifferent consideration, and then I shall arrive at some issue to answer for myself in this great matter.

And all this while nothing that I shall say does anyway determine anything against any resolution or thoughts of the Parliament. But really and honestly and plainly considering what is fit for me to answer; the Parliament desires me to have this title, it hath stuck with me, and doth yet stick. And truly although I hinted the other day that I thought that your arguments to me did partly give positive grounds for what was to be done, and comparative grounds,—saying that which you were pleased to do, and I gave no cause for that I know of,—that is, to compare the effects of Kingship with such a name as I for the present bear with Protectorship, I say, I hope it will not be understood that I contend for the name, or any name, or anything. But truly and plainly, if I speak as in the Lord's presence, I in all things wait as a person under the disposition of the providence of God, neither naming one thing nor another, but only answering to this name or title. For I hope I do not desire to give a rule to anybody, because I have not professed, I have not professed, I have not been able, and I have said truly, I have not been able to give one to myself. But I would be understood in this. I am a man standing in the place I am in, which place I undertook not so much out of the hope of doing any good, as out of a desire to prevent mischief and evil, which I did see was imminent upon the nation. I saw we were running headlong into confusion and disorder, and would necessarily run into blood, and I was passive to those that desired me to undertake the place that now I have. I say, not so much out of the hope of doing good, for which a man may lawfully,—if he deal deliberately with God and his own conscience,—a man may lawfully, as the case may be, though the case is very fickle, desire a great place to do good. But I profess I had not that apprehension when I undertook this place, that I could do much good; but I did think I might prevent imminent evil. And therefore I am not contending with one name compared with another, and therefore have nothing to answer to any arguments that were used in giving preference to Kingship or Protectorship. For I should almost think that any name were better than my name, and I should altogether think any person fitter than I am for any such business, and I compliment not, God knows it. But this I would say, that I think from my very heart that in your settling of the peace and liberties of this nation, which cries as loud upon you as ever nation did, you should labour for somewhat that may beget a consistency, otherwise this nation will fall to pieces. And in that, as far as I can, I am ready to serve not as a King, but as a constable. For truly I have as before God thought it often, that I could not tell what my business was, nor what I was in the place I stood, save by comparing it with a good constable to keep the peace of the parish. And truly this has been my content and satisfaction in the troubles that I have undergone, that yet you have peace. Why now truly, if I may advise, I wish to God you may be but so happy as to keep peace still, if you cannot, attain to those perfections as to do this. I wish to God we may have peace though: I do. But the fruits of righteousness are sown in meekness, a better thing than we are aware of. I say therefore,—I do judge for myself,—there is no such necessity of the thing, for other names may do as well. I judge for myself.

I must say a little,—I think I have somewhat of conscience to answer as to this matter,—why I cannot undertake this name. Why truly, truly I must go a little out of the way to come to my reasons, and you will be able to judge of them when I have told you them; and I shall deal seriously, as before God. If you do not all of you know them, I am sure some of you do, and it behoves me to say, I know my calling from the first to this day. I was a person that from my first employment was suddenly preferred and lifted up from lesser trusts to greater, from my first being a captain of a troop of horse. And I did labour as well as I could to discharge my trust, and God blessed me as it pleased him. And I did truly and plainly,—and then in the way of a foolish simplicity, as it was judged by many great and wise men, and good men too,—desire to make use of my instruments to help in this work. And I will deal plainly with you, I had a very worthy friend then, and he was a very noble person, and I know his memory is grateful to you all, Mr John Hampden. At my first going out to the engagement I saw these men were beaten, and at every hand, I did indeed. And I desired him too, that he would make some addition to my Lord of Essex's army of some new regiments, and I told him I would be serviceable to him in bringing such men in as I thought had a spirit that would do something in the work. This is very true that I tell you, God knows I lie not. Your troopers, said I, are most of them old decayed serving men and tapsters, and such kind of fellows, and, said I, their troopers are gentlemen's sons, younger sons, persons of quality: do you think that the spirits of such base and mean fellows will ever be able to encounter gentlemen that have honour, courage and resolution in them? Truly I pressed him in this manner conscientiously, and truly I did tell him, You must get men of a spirit,—and take it not ill what I say, I know you will not,—of a spirit that is like to go as far as a gentleman will go, or else I am sure you will be beaten still. I told him so, I did truly. He was a wise and worthy person, and he did think that I talked a good notion but an impracticable one. Truly I told him I could do somewhat in it. I did so. And truly I must needs say that to you, impute it to what you please, I raised such men as had the fear of God before them, and made some conscience of what they did. And from that day forward I must say to you they were never beaten; wherever they engaged the enemy they beat them continually.

And truly this is a matter of praise to God; and it has some instruction in it,—to own men that are religious and godly, and so many of them that are honestly and peaceably and quietly disposed to live within government, and will be subject to those gospel rules of obeying magistrates and living under authority. I reckon no godliness without this circle, but of this spirit. Let it pretend what it will, it is diabolical, it is devilish, it is from a diabolical spirit, from the height of Satan's wickedness. Why, truly I need not say more than to apply it thus. I will be bold to apply it thus to this purpose, because it is my all. I could say as all the world say, and run headily upon anything, but I must tender this unto you as a thing that sways with my conscience, or else I were a knave and a deceiver. I tell you there are such men in the nation that are godly, men of the same spirit, men that will not be beaten down with a carnal or worldly spirit while they keep their integrity. I deal plainly and faithfully with you, I cannot think that God would bless me in the undertaking of anything, that would justly and with cause grieve them. That they will be troubled without cause, I must be a slave if I should comply with any such humours. I say, that there are honest men and faithful men and true to the great things of our government, to wit, the liberty of the people, giving them that that is due to them and protecting their interest. I think verily God will bless you for what you have done in that, and what you have a desire to do in that, and they that are truly honest will bless you for it. But if that I know, as indeed I do, that very generally good men do not swallow this title, though really it is no part of their goodness to be unwilling to submit to what a Parliament shall settle over them, yet I must say that it is my duty and my conscience to beg of you, that there may be no hard thing put upon me, things I mean hard to them, that they cannot swallow. If the nation may as well be provided for without these things, by some of these things I have hinted unto you,—as according to my poor apprehension it may,—I think truly it will be no sin to you to seek their favour, as it was to David in another case, no grief of heart to yours that you have a tenderness, even possibly if it be to their weakness, to the weakness of those that have integrity and uprightness, and are not carried away with the hurries that I see some are, who think that their virtue lies in despising authority, opposing of it. I think you will be better able to root out of this nation that spirit and principle,—and it is as desirable as anything in the world,—by complying, indulging, and being patient unto the weaknesses and infirmities of men that have been faithful, and have bled all along in this cause, and are faithful and will oppose all oppositions, I am confident of it, to the things that are fundamental in your Government, in your settlement for civil and gospel liberties. I confess, for it behoves me to deal plainly with you, I must confess I would say,—I hope I may be understood in this, for indeed I must be tender in what I say to such an audience as this is,—I say I would be understood, that in this argument I do not make a parallel between men of a different mind and the Parliament, which shall have their desires; I know there is no comparison, nor can it be urged upon me. That my words have the least colour that way may be because the Parliament seems to give liberty to me to say anything to you as that that is a tender of my humble reasons and judgments and opinions unto you. And if I think they are such and will be such to them, and that they are faithful servants and will be so to the supreme authority and the legislative wherever it is, if I say I should not tell you, knowing their mind to be so, I should not be faithful, if I should not tell you so, to the end you may report it to the Parliament.

And truly I would say something for myself, for my own mind. I do profess it, I am not a man scrupulous about words or names or such things, I am not: but as I have the Word of God, and I hope I shall ever have, for the rule of my conscience, for my information, so truly that men have been led in the dark paths through the providence and dispensations of God. Why surely it is not to be objected to a man, for who can love to walk in the dark? But providence does oftentimes so dispose, and though a man may impute his own blindness and folly and blindness to providence sinfully, yet that must be at my peril. The case may be, that it is the providence of God that does lead men in darkness. I must needs say I have had a great deal of experience of providence, and though it is no rule without or against the Word, yet it is a very good exposition of the Word in many cases. Truly the providence of God has laid this title aside providentially. *De facto* it is laid as aside and this not by sudden humour or passion, but it has been the issue of a great deliberation as ever was in a nation; it has been the issue of ten or twelve years' civil war, wherein much blood has been shed. I will not dispute the justice of it when it was done, nor need I now tell you what my opinion is in the case if it were *de novo* to be done. But if it be at all disputable,—and that a man

comes and finds that God in his severity has not only eradicated a
whole family and thrust them out of the land for reasons best
known to himself, but has made the issue and close of it to be the
very eradication of a name or title, which *de facto* is the case,—it
was not done by me, nor by them that tendered me the
government I now act in. It was done by the Long Parliament, that
was it. And God has seemed providentially not only to strike at
the family but at the name. And as I said before, *de facto* it is
blotted out, it is a thing cast out by Act of Parliament, it's a thing
has been kept out to this day. And as Jude saith in another case,
speaking of abominable sins that should be in the later times, he
doth likewise when he comes to exhort the saints tell them they
should *hate even the garment spotted with the flesh*. I beseech you
think not I bring it as an argument to prove anything, or to make
any comparison, I have no such thoughts. God hath seemed to
deal so. He hath not only dealt so with the persons and the family,
but he hath blasted the title. And you know, when a man comes *a
parte post* to reflect and to see that this is done and laid in the dust,
I can make no conclusion but this,—they may have strong
impressions upon such weak men as I am, and perhaps if there be
any such, upon weaker men it will be stronger,—I would not seek
to set up that that providence hath destroyed and laid in the dust,
and I would not build Jericho again. And this is somewhat to me,
and to my judgment and conscience: that it is truly. It is that which
hath an awe upon my spirit.

And I must confess as times are, they are very fickle, very
uncertain. Nay, God knows, you had need have a great deal of
faith to strengthen you in your work, and all assistance. You had
need to look at settlement. I would rather I were in my grave than
hinder you in anything that may be for settlement, for the nation
needs it and never needed it more. And therefore out of the love
and honour I bear you,—which I am for ever bound to do:
whatever becomes of me, I am for ever bound to acknowledge
that you have dealt most honourably and worthily with me, and
lovingly, and have had respect for one that deserves nothing,—
indeed out of the love and faithfulness I bear you, and out of the
sense I have of the difficulty of your work, I would not have you
lose any help that might serve you, that may stand in stead to you,
but would be a sacrifice that there might be, so long as God shall

please to let the Parliament sit, a harmony, a better understanding and good understanding between all of you. And whatsoever any man thinks, it equally concerns one man as another to go on to a settlement: and where I meet any that are of another mind, indeed I could almost curse him in my heart. And therefore, to the end I might deal faithfully and freely, I would have you lose nothing that might stand you in stead this way. I would not that you should lose any servant or friend that may help on this work, or that if there should be any of an unmanly or womanish spirit they should be offended by that that signifies no more to me than as I have told you, that is I do not think the thing necessary: I would not that you should lose a friend for it. If I could help you to many and multiply myself into many I would be to serve you in settlement, and therefore would not that any ,—especially any of those that indeed perhaps are men, that do think themselves engaged to continue to you and to serve you,—should be anyways disobliged from you. The truth is I did make that my conclusion to you at the first, when I told you what method I would speak to you in. I may say that I cannot with conveniency to myself, nor good to this service that I wish so well to, speak out all my arguments in order to safety, and in order to tendency to an effectual carrying on of the work. I say I do not think it fit to urge all the thoughts I have in my mind as to that point of safety, but I pray to God Almighty, that he would direct you to do according to his will: and this is that poor account I am able to give you of myself in this thing.'

16.

20 April 1657 – 'The Humble Petition and Advice.' Speech to the Committee

'My Lord,
  I have, as well as I could, considered the arguments used by you the other day to enforce the conclusion that refers to the name and

title, that was the subject-matter of the debates and conferences that have been between us.

I shall not now spend your time, nor mine own much, in repeating those arguments and in giving answers to them: indeed, I think they are but the same that they were formerly, only there were some additional enforcements of those arguments by new instances. I think truly, after the rate of this debate, I may spend your time, which I know is very precious: and unless I were a satisfied person, the time would spin out and be very unprofitably spent; so it would. I only must say a word or two as to that I think was new.

It was said, that what comes from the Parliament in the exercise of the legislative power, which this [present title of "Protector"] is,—I understand it to be an exercise of the legislative power, and the laws were always formerly passed this way [i.e. by Ordinance], and that of Bills was of a newer date, I understand that I say,—but it is said, that what was, what is done by the Parliament now, and simply hangs upon their legislative, seems to be a thing that is *ex dono*, and not *de jure*; not a thing that is of so good weight and so strong, as what refers from them to the law that is already in being. I confess there is some argument in that; that there is. But if the strength will be as good without it, though it comes as a gift from you,—I mean as a thing that you provide for them, or else it will never come at them: so in a sense it comes from you. It is that that they otherwise come by, therefore in a sense it is *ex dono*. For he that helps a man to what he cannot otherwise come by, he doth an act that is very near a gift. And you helping them to it, it is a kind of gift to them, otherwise they could not have it. But if you do it simply by your legislative power, the question is not what makes this title more firm,—whether the manner of your settling of it, or the manner of your doing it, it is always as great a labour,—but yet the question lies in the acception of them who are concerned to yield obedience, and accept this. And therefore if this title of "Protector" is a thing that hath for its root and foundation but your legislative in an act of yours, if I may put a but to it, I do not do so, for I say it is on as good a foundation as that other title is: and if it be as well accepted, and that the other be less than truly it is, I should think it the better.

And then, all that argument on behalf of the title of "Kingship", I say is founded upon the law. I say all those arguments that are founded in the law are for it; because it hath been said it doth agree with the law, the law knows the office, the law knows the people know it, and the people are likelier to receive satisfaction that way. Those have been arguments that have been already, and truly I know nothing that I have to add to them. And therefore I say all those arguments may stand as we found them, and left them already.

Only this I think truly, as it hath been said to me, I am a person that have done that, that never any that were actually Kings of England did, refused the advice of Parliament. I confess that runs to all, and that may be accounted a very great fault in me, and may arise up in judgment against me another time, if my case be not different from any man's that was in the chief command and government of these nations that ever was before. And truly I think it is. They are men that have been in, and owned to have been in the right of the law, as inheritors coming to it by birthright; and when otherwise, as by the authority of Parliament, by the confirmation of Parliament, they are men who yet have had some previous pretence of title, or claim to it. I think, under favour, I deserve less blame than another doth, if I cannot so well comply with the title, and with the desires of Parliament in it, as others do. For they that are in would take it for an injury to be outed of it. Truly these arguments are very strong to them, why they should not refuse that, that is intended to them by the Parliament.

But,—I have dealt plainly with you, and I have not complimented with you,—I have not desired, I have no title to the government of these nations, but what was taken up in a case of necessity, and temporary, to supply the present emergency. Without which we must needs,—I say we had been all after the rate of the printed book, and after the rate of those men that have been taken going into arms, if the government had not been taken up by me. It was as visible to me as the day, if I had not undertaken it. And so it being put upon me, I being then General, as I was General by Act of Parliament, it being put upon me to take the power in my hand, after the assembly of men that was called together had been dissolved,—really the thing would have issued itself in this book, for as I am informed the book knows an author, that was a leading principal person in that assembly,—when now I say, I speak in the plainness and simplicity of my heart as before Almighty God, I did out of necessity undertake that, that no man I think would have undertaken but myself. It hath pleased God that I have been instrumental to keep the peace of the nation to this day, and to keep it under a title that some say signifies but a keeping it to another's use. To a better use, that may improve it to a better use? And this I may say, I have not desired the continuance of my power or place, either under one title or an other: that I have not. And I say it, if the wisdom of Parliament could find where to place things so as they might save this nation and the interests of it,—the interest of the people of God in the first place, of those Godly honest men, for such a character I reckon them by, and of those who live in the fear of God, and desire to hold forth the excellency and virtue of a Christian course in their life and conversation, for I reckon that also proceeds from faith and love,—looking to their duties towards Christians and to the humanity, to men as men, and to such liberties and interests, as the people of this nation are of, (and I look upon that duty as a standing truth of the Gospel, and who lives up to that, according to that, is a Godly man in my apprehension, and therefore I say,) if the wisdom of this Parliament, I speak not this vainly nor like a fool, but as to God, and if the wisdom of this Parliament should have found a way to settle the interests of this nation, upon the foundations of justice and truth and liberty to the people of God, and to the concernments of men as Englishmen, I would have lain down at their feet, or any body's feet else, that this might have run in such a current. And therefore I say, I have no pretensions to these things for myself, or to ask this or that, or to avoid this or that.

I know the censures of the world may quickly pass upon me, but I thank God I know not where to lay the weight, that is laid upon me. I mean the weight of reproach and contempt and scorn, that hath been cast upon me, because I have not offered you any name in competition with Kingship. I know the evil spirits of men may easily obtrude upon a man, that he would have a name that the law knows not, and that is boundless, and is that under which a man exercises more arbitrariness. I know there is nothing in that argument, and if it were in your thoughts to limit my Title, or to do anything of that kind, aye whatsoever it was, it would bound it and limit it sufficiently. I wish it were come to that, that no favour should be shewed to me, but that the good of these nations might be consulted, as I am confident they will be by you in whatsoever you do. But I may say this in answer to that, that doth a little pinch upon me, and the more so when I am told it is my duty.

I think it can be no man's duty, nor obligation, but it is between God and himself, if he be conscious of his own infirmities, disabilities, and weaknesses, and that he is not able to encounter with them, although he may have a little faith too for a little exercise. I say I do not know which way it can be imputed to me for a fault or laid upon me as a duty, except I meant to gripe at the government of the nations without a legal consent: which I say I have done in times past upon the principles of necessity. And I promise you, I shall think whatever is done without authority of Parliament in order to settlement, will neither be very honest, nor yet that that I understand. I think we have fought for the liberties of the nation, as well as for other interests.

You will pardon me that I speak these things in such a way as this is. I may be borne withal; because, I have not truly well borne the exercise that hath been upon me now, these three or four days: I have not, I say. I have told you my thoughts and have laid them before you. You have been pleased to give me your grounds, and I have told you mine. And truly I do purposely refuse to mention those arguments that were used when you were last here, but rather tell you what since I tell you lies upon my heart out of the abundance of difficulty and trouble that lies upon me. And therefore, you having urged me, I mean, offered reasons to me, and urged them with such grounds as did occur to you,—and having told you the last time I met you that the satisfaction of them did not reach to me, so as wholly to convince my judgment of what was my duty,—I have thought rather to answer you with telling you my grief, and the trouble I am under. And truly my intentions and purposes they are honest to the nation, and shall be by the grace of God. And I cannot tell how upon collateral pretences to cut towards things that will be destructive to the liberties of this nation. Any man may give me leave to die, and everybody may give me leave to be as a dead man, when God takes away the spirit and life and activity that is necessary for the carrying on such a work.

And therefore I do leave the former debates as they were, and as we had them, letting you know that I have looked a little upon the Paper, the Instrument I would say, in the other parts of it. And considering that there are many particulars in the Instrument, some of general reference, others specified, and all of weight, let the title be what it will, of weight to the concernment of the nations, I think I may desire that those may be such, as whatever they be applied to, either to one thing or another, they might be such as the people have no cause to regret, as I am confident your care and faithfulness needs neither a spur, nor any admonition to that. I say, reading in your Order, by order of Parliament, for the Committee, that there are divers particulars that are, that if I do make any scruple of them I should have the freedom with this committee to cast my doubts, the truth of it is I have a Paper here in my hand, that doth contain divers things with relation to the Instrument, that I hope have a public aspect with them. Therefore I cannot presume but they will be very welcome to you: therefore I shall desire that you will receive them. I should desire, if it please you, that liberty,—which I submit to your judgment whether you think I should have it or no,—that I might tender these few things and some others that I have in preparation. And truly I shall reduce them to as much brevity as I can: they are too large here. And if it please you, tomorrow in the afternoon at three of the clock I shall meet you again, and I hope we shall come to know one another's minds, and shall agree to that that shall be to the glory of God, and the good of these nations.'

17.

21 April 1657 – 'The Humble Petition and Advice.' Speech to the Committee

'My Lord,

I think you may well remember what the issue was of the last conference I had with you, and what the stick was then. I confess I took occasion from the Order of the Parliament, in which they gave you power to speak with me about those things that were in the body of that Instrument and desire. That which you have been pleased to speak with me about is the title, but I did offer to you that I might confer with you about those other particulars, and might receive satisfaction from you as to them. Whether a good issue will be to all these affairs or no is only in the hands of God; that is a great secret, and secrets belong to God and things revealed to us. And such things as are the subject-matter of this Instrument of yours, and as far as they may have relation to me, that you and I may consider, what may be for the public good, that so they may receive such an impression as can humanly be given to them.

I would be well understood, that I say the former debate and conferences have been upon the title, and that rests as it did. And now seeing that, as I said before, your Order of Commitment doth as well reach to the particulars contained in the Instrument as to that of the title, I did offer to you that I should desire to speak with you about them also, that so we may come to an understanding one with another, not what the thing is in parts, but what it is in the whole conduceable to that end that we all ought to aim at, which is a general settlement upon good foundations. And truly as I have often said even to the Parliament itself, when it gave me the honour to meet me in the Banqueting-House, so I must say to you that are a Committee, a very considerable representation of them, that I am hugely taken with the word settlement, with the thing and with the notion of it. I think he is not worthy to live in England that is not. I will do my part so far as I am able to expel that man out of the nation, that doth not affect of that in the general, to come to a settlement. Because indeed it is the great misery and unhappiness of a nation to be without it; and it is like a house, and much worse than a house divided against itself, it cannot stand without settlement. And therefore I hope we are all so far at a good point, and the spirit of the nation, I hope in the generality of it, is so far at a good point. We are all contending for a settlement, that is sure, but the question is *de modo* and of those things that will make it a good one, if it be possible. That is no fault to aim at perfection in settlement. Truly I have said, and I say it again, that I think that is it that tends to the making of the nation to enjoy the things we have declared for,—and I would come upon that issue with all men or any man,—the things we have declared for, that have been the ground of our quarrelling and fighting all along, is that that will accomplish our general work. Settlement is the general work now, that which will give the nation to enjoy their civil and religious liberties, that will conserve the liberty of every man and not rob any man of what is justly his. I think, I hope those two things make up settlement. I am sure they acquit us before God and man, who have endeavoured, as we have done, through some streamings of blood to attain that end.

If I may tell you my experiences in this business and offend no good man that loves the public before that which is personal, truly I shall a little briefly recapitulate to you what my observation, and endeavour, and interest, hath been to this end. And I hope no man, that hath been interested in transactions all along, will blame me if I speak a little plainly; and he shall have no cause to blame me, because I will take myself into the number of culpable persons, if there be any such, though perhaps apt enough out of the self-love I have to be willing to be innocent where I am so, and yet to be as willing to take my reproach if anybody will lay it upon me where I am culpable. And truly I have through the providence of God endeavoured to discharge a poor duty, having had, as I conceive, a clear call to the station I have acted in, in all these affairs; and I believe very many are sufficiently satisfied in that. I shall not go about to say anything to clear it to you, but must exercise myself in a little short chronology to come to that, that I say is really all our business at this time, and the business of this nation.

To come upon clear grounds and to consider the providences of God, how they have led us hitherunto. After it pleased God to put an end to the war of this nation,—a final end which was done at Worcester, in the determination and decision that was there by the hand of God, for other war we have had none, that perhaps deserves the name of war since that time, which is now six years,—I came in September up to the Parliament that then was, and truly I found the Parliament, as I thought, very well disposed to put a good issue to all these transactions that had been in the nation, and I rejoiced at it. And though I had not been well skilled in parliamentary affairs, having been near ten years in the field, yet in my poor measure my desires did tend to some issue, believing verily that all the blood that had been shed and all that distemper that God had suffered to be amongst us, and in some sense God hath raised among us, that surely fighting was not the end but the means that had an end, and was in order to somewhat. Truly it was then I thought upon settlement, that is that men might come to some consistency, and to that end I did endeavour to add my mite, which was no more than the interest of any one Member, I am sure not of better right than any one Member that was there, after I was returned again to that capacity. And I did,—I shall tell you no fable, but the things that diverse persons here can tell, whether I say true or no,—I did endeavour it. I would make the best interpretation of this, but yet this is truth and nothing of discovery on my part, but that which everybody knows to be true, that the Parliament having done these memorable things that they had done, things of honour and things of necessity, things that if at this day you have any judgment that there lies a possibility upon you to do any good, to bring this nation to any foot of settlement, I may say you are all along beholding to them in good measure for. But yet truly as men that contend for public interest are not like to have the applause of all men, nor justification from all hands, so it was with them. And truly when they had made preparation that might lead to the issuing in some good for the settlement of these nations in point of liberty and freedom from tyranny and oppression, from the hazard of our religion to throw it away upon men that designed by innovations to introduce Popery and by complying with some notions introduce arbitrariness upon a civil account, why they had more enemies than friends. They had so all along, and this made them careful out of principles of Nature, that do sometimes suggest best. And upon the utmost undeniable grounds they did think that it was not fit for them presently to go and throw themselves and all this cause into hands, that perhaps had no heart nor principle with them to accomplish the end that they aimed at. I say perhaps through infirmity they did desire to have continued themselves and to have perpetuated themselves upon that Act, which was perhaps justly enough obtained and necessarily enough obtained when they got it from the King; and though truly it was good in the first obtaining of it, yet it was by most men, who had ventured their lives in this cause, judged not fit to be perpetuated, but rather as a thing that was to have an end when it had finished its course; which was certainly the true way of it, in subserviency to the bringing in that which might be a good and honest settlement to the nation. I must say to you, I found them very willing to perpetuate themselves. And truly this is not a thing of reflection upon all, for perhaps some were not so. I can say so of some of them; the sober men that I had converse with, they would not have had it perpetual, but the major part I think over-ruled in that they would have continued. This is true that I say to you, I was entreated to it and advised to it, and it was by this medium they thought to have accomplished it, that is to have sent into the country to have reinforced their number, and by new elections to have filled them up. And this excuse it had, it would not be against the liberty of the people, nor against the succession of men to come into rule and government, because as men died out of the House so they should be supplied. And this was the best answer that could be given to that objection that was then made, that the best way to govern is to have men successive and in such great bodies as Parliaments, to have men to learn to know how to obey as well as to govern. And truly the best expedient that we then had was this that I tell you. The truth of it is, this answer did not satisfy a company of poor men that had thought they had ventured their lives, and had some thoughts that they had a little interest to inquire after the things, and the rather because really they were invited out upon principles of honesty, conscience, and religion, for spiritual liberties as many as would come. Where the cause was a little doubtful, there was a Declaration that was very inviting, and men did come in upon that invitation, and did thereby think themselves not to be mercenary men, but men that had wives and children in the nation and therefore might a little look after satisfaction in what would be the issue of the business.

And when this thing was thus pressed, and it may be overpressed, that a period might be put, and that that might be ascertained and a time fixed, why truly then the extremity ran another way. This is very true that I tell you, though it shame me. I do not say it shames all that were of the House, for I know all were not of that mind. Why truly when this was urged, they ran into another extremity. What was that? Why truly then it was, seeing a Parliament might not be perpetual, the Parliament might be always sitting; and to that end was there a Bill framed, that Parliaments might always be sitting, that as soon as one Parliament went out of their place, another might leap in. And when we saw this, truly we thought we did but make a change in pretence and did not remedy the thing. And then when that was pursued with that great heat, that I dare say there was more progress made in it in a month, than was with the like business in four, to hasten it to an issue that such a Parliament might be brought in as would bring the state of this nation into a continual sitting of Parliaments, we did think, who are plain men, and I do think it still, that it had been according to the foolish proverb, out of the frying-pan into the fire. For looking at the government they would then have, it was a Commonwealth's government, why, we should have had fine work then, we should have had a Council of State and a Parliament of four hundred men executing arbitrary government without intermission, saving of one company, one Parliament, leaping into the seat of another while they left them warm. The same day that one left, the other was to leap in. Truly I did think, and I do think this a foolish remedy, however some are very much enamoured with that kind of government. Why this design of theirs, it was no more but this, that Committees of Parliament should take upon them, and be instead of, the Courts of Westminster,—perhaps some will think there had been no hurt in that,—and arbitrariness would have been in Committees, where a man can neither come to prove nor defend, nor know his judges, because there are one sort of men that judge him today and another sort of men tomorrow. This should have been the Law of England; this should have been the way of judging this nation. And truly I thought that that was an ill way of judging, for I may say to you with truth to that, after it pleased God your poor army, these poor contemptible men, came up hither, it was so,—an outcry here in this place to see a cause heard, determined, and judged, and Committees erected to fetch men from the extremest parts of the nation to London to attend Committees, to determine all things and without any manner of satisfaction. Whether a man travel never so right or wrong, he must come and he must go back again as wise as he came.

This truly was the case and our condition, and truly I must needs say, take all in that was in the practices, I am sorry to tell the story of it, though there was indeed some necessity of the business, a necessity of some Committees to look to indemnity, but no necessity of Committees instead of Courts of Justice. But it was so, and this was the case of the people of England at that time. And the Parliament assuming to itself the authority of the Three Estates that were before,—it was so assuming that authority,—and if any man would have come and said, What are the rules you judge by? the answer would have been, Why! we have none, but we are supreme in Legislative and in Judicature! This was the state of the case, and I thought, and we thought, and I think so still, that this was a pitiful remedy, and it will be so when and while the Legislative is perpetually exercised, when the Legislative and Executive powers are always the same. And truly I think the Legislative would be almost as well in the four Courts of Westminster-Hall, and if they could make laws and judge too, you would have excellent laws, and the lawyers would be able to give you excellent counsel. And so it was then; this was our condition without scruple and doubt, and I shall say no more to it. But truly it was offered then, truly and honestly, and we did desire and beg that we might have a settlement, and that that now is here, that is there proposed a settlement. It was desired then, it was offered and desired, that the Parliament would be pleased, either of their own number or any else, to choose a certain number of men to settle the nation. This method of theirs is unsettlement; this is confusion. For give me leave, if anybody now have the face to say, and I would die upon this, if any man in England have the impudence or the face to say, that the exceptions of the Parliament was the fear of their hasty throwing of the liberties of the people of God and the nation into a bare representative of the people,—

which was then the business we opposed,—if any man have that face to say it now that did then, or I will say more, ought then to judge it had been a confounding of the whole cause we had fought for, which it was, I would look upon that man's face, I would be glad to see such a man. I do not say there is any such here, but if any such should come to me, see if I would not look upon him and tell him he is an hypocrite. I dare say it, and I dare to die for it, knowing the spirit that hath been in some men to me. They come and tell me, they do not like my being Protector! Why do you not? Why? Because you will exercise arbitrary government. Why, what would you have me do? Pray turn General again, and we will like you exceeding well? I was a child in its swaddling clouts. I cannot transgress by the Government. I can do nothing but in ordination with the Council. They fear arbitrary government by me upon that account; but if it turned to be a General, they were not afraid of arbitrary government? Such as these are, such hypocrisies as these are, should they enter into the heart of any man that hath any truth or honesty in him?

And truly that is our case, and finding our case to be thus, we did press the Parliament, as I told you, that they would be pleased to select some worthy persons that had loved this cause and the liberties of England and the interests of it, and we told them we would acquiesce and lie at their feet. But to be thrown into Parliaments that should sit perpetually, though but for three years, they had had too much experience of it; the experience of which may remain to this day to give satisfaction to honest and sober men. Why truly we did think it might satisfy, but it did not, and thereupon we did think that it was the greatest of dangers to be overwhelmed and brought under a slavery by our own consent, and iniquity to become a law; and there was our ground we acted upon at that time. And truly they had perfected the Bill for the perpetuating of Parliaments to the last clause, and were resolved to pass it as a Bill *in paper* rather than comply with any expedient. If your own experience add anything to you in this, in this point, whether or no in cases civil and criminal, if a Parliament should assume an absolute power without any control, to determine the interests of men in property and liberty, whether or no this be desirable in a nation, if you have any sense, as I believe you have, yea more than I have, I believe you will take it for a mercy that that did not befall England at that time; and that is all I will say of it.

Truly I will now come and tell you a story of my own weakness and folly, and yet it was done in my simplicity, I dare vow it was thought, and some of my companions did urge it upon me. And truly this is a story that would not be recorded, a story that would not be told but when good use may be made of it. I say it was thought then that men of our judgment that had fought in the wars and were all of a piece upon that account, why surely these men will hit it, and these men will do to the purpose whatsoever can be desired! Truly we did think, and I did think so; the more to blame. And such a company of men were chosen and did proceed into action. And truly this was the naked truth, that the issue was not answerable to the simplicity and honesty of the design. What the issue of that meeting would have been, and was feared, you all know; upon which sober men of that meeting did withdraw and came and returned my power as far as they could, they did actually the greater part of them, into my own hands, professing and believing that the issue of that meeting would have been the subversion of the laws and of all the liberties of this nation, the destruction of the Ministry of this nation, in a word the confusion of all things and instead of order to set up the judicial law of Moses in abrogation of all our administrations, to have been administered the judicial law of Moses, *pro hic et nunc*, according to the wisdom of any man that would have interpreted the text this way or that way. And if you do not believe that they were sent home by the major part, who were judicious and sober, and feared the worst upon this account, and with my consent also, *a parte post* you will believe nothing. For the persons that led in the meeting were Mr Feak and his meeting in Blackfriars, Major-General Harrison and those that associated with him at one Mr Squibb's house; and there were all the resolutions taken that were acted in that House day by day; and this was so *de facto*, I know it to be true. And that this must be the product of it, I do but appeal to that book I told you of the other day, that all Magistracy and Ministry is Antichristian, and therefore all these things ought to be abolished; which we are certain must have been the issue of that meeting.

So that you have been delivered, if I think right, from two evils. The one evil a secular evil, that would have swallowed up all civil interest and put us under the most horrid arbitrariness that ever was exercised in the world, that we might have had five hundred or six hundred friends, with their friends, to have had a judgment of all causes, and to have judged without a rule, thinking that the power that swallowed up all the other lawful powers in the nation, hath all the power that ever they had, both a Legislative and a Judiciary. This, I say, would have swallowed up the civil interest. And the other, merely under a spiritual interest, had swallowed up again in another extreme all our religious interest, all our Ministry, and all the things we are beholden to God for. Truly we think we ought to value this interest above all the interests in the world; but if this latter had not been as sure destroyed as the former, I understand nothing. And having told you these two things, truly I must needs say it makes me in love with this Paper and with all things in it, and with these additions that I have to tender to you, and with settlement above all things in the world, except that where I left you the last time; and for that I think we have debated. I have heard your mind and you have heard mine. I have told you my heart and my judgment, and the Lord bring forth his own issue. I think we are not now to consider what we are on the foot of government which called this Parliament, which, till there be an end put to it, is that that hath existence. And I shall say nothing to that. If that accomplisheth the end of our fighting and all these blessed and goods ends that we should aim at, if it do, I would we might have that and remain where we are; if it do not, I would we might have that which is better. Why truly I now come out of myself to tell you, that as to the substance and body of your Instrument I do look upon it as having things in it, if I may speak freely and plainly,—I may, and we all may,—I say the things that are provided for in this Instrument have the liberty of the people of God so as they have never had it, and he must be a pitiful man that thinks the people of God ever had that liberty, either *de facto* or *de jure*. That is to say, *de jure* from God I think they have had it from the beginning of the world to this day, and have it still; but asserted by a *jus humanum*, I say they never had it so, as they have it now. And I think you have provided for the liberty of the people of God and of the nation; and I say, he sings sweetly that sings a song of reconciliation betwixt these two interests, and it is a pitiful fancy, and wild and ignorant, to think they are inconsistent. They may consist, and I speak my conscience, I think in this government you have made them to consist, and therefore I must say in that and in other things, you have provided well; that you have. And because I see the Vote of the Parliament gives you leave to speak with me about the particulars, I think the Parliament doth think that any Member they have is not to be neglected in offering of anything that may be of additional good, and upon that accompt I have a little surveyed the Instrument. I have a Paper here to offer you upon that account, and truly I must needs say and think, that in such a case as this is, in so new a work and so strange a work as this is that is before you, it will not be thought ill of. I do with a little earnestness press you to some explanations that may help to complete and leave me satisfied; for it is only handled with me, this transaction is only handled with me at this time, and with you and the Parliament, whom you represent. I say, I would be glad that you might leave me and all opposers without excuse, as well as that I could wish that you should settle this nation to the uttermost good of it in all things. The things I have to offer you, they are not very weighty, they may tend to the completion of the business, and therefore I shall take the freedom to read them to you.

In the fourth Article and second paragraph, you have something under that head that respects the calling of Members of Parliament. You would not exclude those that were under Duke Hamilton in that invasion because it hath been said to you perhaps, that if you exclude all those, you shall have no Members from Scotland. I hope there be persons of that nation that will be ready to give a better testimony of their country than to admit of that argument; and I hope it is none. But if it be one, then truly to meet with the least upon that uncertainty of the qualifications you should indeed not exclude men of your own country perhaps upon lesser crimes, and hold them off upon stricter characters, if it is thought that that qualification suffices, that saith that the testimony that they shall have is that they are men that have given good testimony in their peaceable and quiet living. Why truly for diverse years they have not been willing to do other; they have not had an easy possibility to do otherwise, to live unquietly; though perhaps they have been the same men many of them, that have borne arms against us, and though I know many of them are good men and worthy men. And therefore whether it be not fit in that place to explain somewhat else, and put some other character upon it, that may be accounted a good testimony of their being otherwise minded and of their being of another judgment. I confess I have not anything here to supply it with, but certainly if it should be so, as it is in your Article, though they be never so indisposed and enemies, and remain so, yet if they have lived peaceably where they could neither will nor choose, they are to be admitted. I only tell you so, being without any amendment for it, and when I have done I shall offer the whole to you. This is the second paragraph.

In the third paragraph of the same Article, whereas it is said that no persons in Ireland be made uncapable to elect or be elected that, before the first of March, 1649, have borne arms for the Parliament or otherwise given testimony of their good affections and continued faithful to the Parliament whether it be not necessary that it be more clearly expressed, it seeming to capacitate all those who have revolted from the Parliament, if they have borne arms for the State before the first of March, 1649. It seems to restore them, but if since then they have revolted, as many of our English-Irish I doubt have done, why then the question is, whether these men, who have very lately been angry and fled to arms, whether you will think their having borne arms formerly on the Parliament's side should be an exemption to them. That is but tendered to you, that some worthy person here will give an answer unto.

In the fifth paragraph of the same Article, you have incapacitated public preachers from sitting in Parliament, and truly I think that your intention is, that such as have a Pastoral function, such as are actually and really Ministers. For I must say to you in the behalf of our Army, in their next place to their fighting they have been very good preachers, and I should be sorry they should be excluded from serving the Commonwealth because they have been accustomed to preach to their troops, companies, and regiments, which I think have been one of the best blessings upon them to the carrying on of the great work. I think you do not mean so, but I tender it to you, that if you think fit there may be a consideration had of it. There may be some of us, it may be, that have been a little guilty of that, who would be loth to be excluded from sitting in Parliament.

In the same paragraph there is care taken for the nominating the Commissioners to try the Members which are chosen to sit in Parliament; and truly those Commissioners are uncertain persons and it is hard to say what may happen. I hope they will always be good men, but if they should be bad, then perhaps they will keep out good men. Besides we think truly, if you will give us leave to help, as to the freedom of Parliament it will be something that will go rather harshly down, rather than otherwise. Very many reasons might be given, but I do but tender it to you. I think if there be no Commissioners, it would be never a whit the worse, but if you make qualifications, if any man will presume to sit without those qualifications, you may deal with them. A man without his qualifications sitting there, is as if he be not chosen; and if he sit without being chosen, and so without a qualification, I am sure the old custom was to send him to the Tower, to imprison such a one, if any man sit there that have not right to sit there. If any stranger come in upon a pretended title of election, then perhaps it was a different case, if any sit there upon pretence of a qualification upon him, you may send him to prison without any more ado. Whether you think fit to do so or no, it is a Parliamentary business; I do but hint it to you. I believe if any man had sat in former Parliaments, that had not taken the oaths prescribed, it would have been fault enough. I believe something of that kind would be equivalent to any other way, if not better.

In that Article, which I think is the fifth Article, which concerns the nomination of the other House, it is in the beginning of that Article, that the House is to be nominated, as you design it, by his Highness and the approbation is to be from this House, I would say to be from the Parliament; is it not so? But then now, if any shall be subsequently named by his Highness, after this House is sat, upon any acccidental removal or death, you do not say. Though it seems to refer to the same method that the paragraph as to the first election doth, yet it doth not refer clearly to this, that the nomination shall be where it was, in the Chief Officer, and the approbation in the other House. If I do not express it clearly, I hope you will pardon me, but I think that is the aim of it; it is not clearly expressed there as I think. You will be able to judge whether it be or no.

In the seventh Article, that which concerns the revenue, that is the revenue that you have appointed to the government, you have distributed 300,000 pounds of it to the maintenance of the civil authority, 1,000,000 pounds to be distributed to the maintenance of your forces by sea and land. You have indeed said it in your Instrument, and we cannot doubt of it, but yet you have not made it certain, nor yet of temporary supplies which are intended for the peace and safety of the nations. It is desired that you would take it into your thoughts, and make both those certain both as to the sum and time, that those supplies shall be continued. And truly I hope I do not curry favour with you, but it is desired, and I may very reasonably desire, that these monies, whatever they are, that they may not,—if God shall bring me to any interest in this business, which lieth in his own power,—that these monies may not be issued out by the authority of the Chief Magistrate, but by the advice of his Council; seeing you have in your Instrument made a co-ordination in general terms, I desire that this might be a reserved thing, that the monies might not be distributed save in this manner. It will be a safety to whomsoever is your supreme Magistrate, as well as security to the public, that the monies might be issued out by the advice of the Council; and that the Treasurers that receive the money may be accountable every Parliament, within a certain time limited by yourselves, that every new Parliament the Treasurer may be accountable to the Parliament for the disposing of the treasure.

And there is mention made of the Judges in the ninth Article. It is mentioned that the Officers of State and the Judges are to be chosen by the approbation of the Parliament. If there be no Parliament sitting, if there be never so great loss of Judges, it cannot be supplied. And whether you do not intend, that it should be by the choice of the Chief Magistrate with the consent of Council, in the intervals of Parliament, to be afterwards approved by Parliament.

The thirteenth Article relates to several qualifications that persons must be qualified with, that are put into places of public office and trust. Now if men shall step into public places and trust, that are not so qualified, they may not execute it; and an "office of trust" is a very large word, it goeth almost to a constable; if not altogether, it goeth far. Now if any shall come that are not so qualified, they certainly do commit a breach upon your rule, and whether you will not think in this case, that if any shall take upon them an office of trust, that a penalty shall be put upon them. Where he is excepted by the general rule, whether you will not think it fitting, in that respect, to deter men from accepting of offices and places of trust contrary to that Article.

The next thing I shall speak to is fetched in I may say in some respects by head and shoulders in your Instrument, yet in some respects it hath affinity with it. I may say I think it is within your Order to confer upon this account; I am sure of it. There is a mention, in the last part of your Instrument, of your purpose to do many good things, I am confident not like the gentleman that made his last will and set down a great number of the names of men that should receive benefit by him, and there was no sum at the latter end. I am confident that you are resolved to deal effectually in the thing at the latter end, and I should wrong my own conscience, if I should think otherwise. I hope you will think sincerely as before God, that the laws must be regulated; I hope you will. We have been often talking of them, and I remember well, in the old Parliament, that we were more than three months and could not get over the word "incumbrances". And then we thought there was little hope of regulating the Law, when there was such a difficulty as that. But surely the laws need to be regulated? And I must needs say, I think it is a sacrifice acceptable to God upon many accounts, and I am persuaded it is one thing that God looks for and would have. I confess, if any man would ask me, Why, how would you have it done? I confess I do not know how. But I think verily at the least, the delays in suits and the excessiveness in fees, and the costliness of suits, and those various things, that I do not know what names they bear,—I have heard talk of "demurrers" and such like things as I scarce know,—but I say certainly, that the people are greatly suffering in this respect; they are so. And truly if this whole business of settlement, whatsoever the issue of it shall be, if it comes, as I am persuaded that it doth, as a thing that would please God by a sacrifice in, or rather as an expression of our thankfulness to God, I am persuaded that this will be the one thing that will be upon your hearts, to do something that is honourable and effectual in it.

That truly, I say, that is not in your Instrument is somewhat that relates to the reformation of manners. You will pardon me my fellow soldiers that were raised upon the just occasion of the insurrection, not only to secure the peace of the nation, but to see that persons, that were least likely to help on peace or continue it but rather to break it, were careful of their behaviour, dissolute and loose persons that can go up and down from house to house; and they are gentlemen's sons that have nothing to live on, and cannot be supposed to live to the profit of the Commonwealth. Which I think had a good course taken with them; and I think that which was done to them was honourably, and honestly, and profitably done. And for my own part, I must needs say it shewed the dissoluteness that was then in the nation; as indeed it springs most from that part of the Cavaliers, it shewed what was like to happen should that party run on, and no care be taken to reform the nation, to prevent abuses that will not perhaps fall under this consideration. We can send our children into France before they know God or good manners, and return with all the licentiousness of that nation; neither care taken to educate them before they go, nor to keep them in good order when they come home. Indeed this makes the nation, not only to commit those abominable things among us, inhuman things, but hardens men to justify those things, and, as the Apostle saith, not only to do wickedness themselves, but take pleasure in them that do so. And truly if something be not done in this kind, without sparing any condition of men, without sparing men's sons though they be noblemen's sons, let them be who they will, if debauched it is for the glory of God that nothing of outward consideration should save them in their debauchery from a just punishment and reformation. And truly I must needs say it, I would as much bless God to see something done as to that heartily, upon this account, not only to those persons mentioned but to all the nation, that some course might be taken for reformation, that there might be some stop put to such a current of wickedness and evil as that is. And truly, to do it heartily, and nobly, and worthily, the nobility of this nation especially, and the gentry, will have cause to bless you. And likewise I would that some care might be taken, that those good laws already made for the punishing of vice may be effectually put in execution. This I must needs say for our Major-Generals that do you service, I think it was excellent good service, I profess I do. And I hope you will not think it unworthy of you to consider that, when you have seen that though you have good laws against the common country disorders that are everywhere, who is there to execute them? Really a Justice of Peace shall from the most be wondered at as an owl, if he go but one step out of the ordinary course of his fellow Justices in the reformation of these things. And therefore I hope I may represent that to you, as a thing worthy of your consideration, that something may be found out to suppress such things. I am persuaded you would glorify God in it, as much as any one thing you can do, and so I think; you will pardon me.

I cannot tell in this Article, that I am now to speak unto, whether I speak to anything or nothing. There is a desire that the Public Revenue be not alienated, but by the consent of Parliament. I doubt Public Revenue is like *Custodes Libertatis Angliae*; that is a notion only, and not to be found that I know of. But if there be any, and God bless us in our settlement, there will be Public Revenue accruing, and whether you will subject this to any alienation without the consent of Parliament, is that which is offered to you.

Truly a thing that I have further to offer to you, it is last in this paper, and that is a thing that is mentioned in the sixteenth Article, that you would have those Acts and Ordinances that have been made since the late troubles, during the time of them, that they should, if they be not contrary to this Advice, remain in such force and manner, as if this Advice had not been given. Why that that is doubted is, whether or no this will be sufficient to keep things in a settled condition; because it is but an implication, it is not determined, but you do pass by the thing without such a foundation as will keep those people which are now in possession of estates upon this account, that their titles may be questioned and shaken if it be not explained. And truly I do believe you intended very fully in this business. If the words already do not suffice, that I submit to your own advisement, but there is in this a very great consideration. There have been since the government several Acts and Ordinances, that have been made by the exercise of that legislative power that was exercised since we undertook this government, and I think your Instrument speaks a little more faintly to these and dubiously than to the other. And truly I will not apologize for anything but surely two persons, two sorts of men, will be nearly concerned upon this account, that is, those who have exercised that power, and the persons who are the objects of that exercise. It dissettles them wholly, if you be not clear in your expressions in this business, and it will dissettle us very much to think that the Parliament doth not approve well of what hath been done upon a true ground of necessity, as far as it hath saved this nation from running into total arbitrariness, or from being subjected to any sort of men that would perhaps have lorded it too much over their brethren. We think we have in that thing deserved well of the State. If any man will ask me, But ah! sir, what have you done since? Why ah! as I will confess my fault where I am guilty, so I think, taking the things as they were, I think we did the Commonwealth service! And we have in that made great settlements; that we have! We have settled almost the whole affairs of Ireland, the rights and interest of the soldiers there, and of the planters and adventurers. And truly we have settled very much of the business of the ministry, and I could wish that that be not to some the *gravamen*, I wish it be not. But I must needs say, if I have anything to rejoice before the Lord in this world as having done any good or service, I can say it from my heart, and I know I say the truth, that it hath been,—let any man say what he will to the contrary, he will give me leave to enjoy my own opinion in it, and conscience, and heart,—I dare bear my testimony to it, there hath not been such a service to England since the Christian religion was professed in England. I dare be bold to say it, however here and there there may have been passion and mistakes. And the ministers themselves, take the generality of them, they will tell you it is the Institution of Triers that hath done this. And we did take to it upon that account, and we did not think to do that which we did *virtute Instituti*, as *jure divino*, but as a civil good; so we did in this thing. We know not better how to keep the Ministry good and to augment it to goodness, than to put such men to be Triers, men of known integrity and piety, orthodox men and faithful; we know not how better to answer our duty to God and the nation, and the people of God in that respect, than in doing what we did. And I dare say, if the grounds upon which we went will not justify us, the issue and event of it doth abundantly justify us; God having had exceeding glory by it, in the generality of it, I am confident fortyfold. For as heretofore the men that have been admitted into the ministry in times of Episcopacy,—alas, what pitiful certificates served to make a man a minister! If any man could understand Latin and Greek, it was as if he spake Welsh, he was sure to be admitted, which I think in those days went for Hebrew with a great many. But certainly the poorest thing in the world would serve the turn, and a man was admitted upon such an account; aye, and upon a less! I am sure the admission that hath been to those places since, hath been under this character as the rule, that they must not admit a man unless they be able to discern some of the grace of God in him; a qualification which was so put too, as that it was not foolishly or senselessly enforced, but so far as men could judge according to the rules of charity; but such a man whose good life and conversation they could have a very good testimony of, four or five of the neighbour ministers who knew him, they would try, nor would they admit him unless he could give a very good testimony of the grace of God in him. And to this I say, I must speak my conscience in it, it was an excellent good thing, though a great many are angry at it. And how shall you please everybody? Then say some, none must be admitted except perhaps he will be baptized. This is their opinion, they will not admit a man into a congregation except he be so, much less to be a minister. The Presbyterian, he will not admit him except he will be ordained. Generally they will not go to the Independents. Truly I think, if I may not be thought partial, I think if there be a freedom of judgment, it is there. Here are three sorts of godly men that you are to take care for, and that you have provided for in your settlement; and how could you now put it to the Presbyterian, but you must have done it with a possibility of the exclusion of all those of Anabaptism, and of the Independents. And now we have put it into the way, that if a man be of any of these judgments, if he have the root of the matter in him, he may be admitted. This hath been our care and work by some ordinances of ours, both laying the foundations of it, and many hundreds of ministers being in upon it; and if this be a time of settlement, then I hope it is not a time of shaking. And therefore I hope you will be pleased to settle this business, that you will neither shake the persons that have been poorly instrumental to call you to this opportunity of settling this nation and doing good to it, nor shake those honest men's interests that have been thus settled, considering so much good hath been wrought by them. And so I have done with the offers to you.

But here is somewhat that is indeed exceedingly past my understanding, for I have as little skill in Arithmetic as I have in the Law. There are great sums; it is well if I can count them to you. The present charge of the forces both by sea and land, including the government, will be 2,426,989 pounds. The whole present revenue in England, Scotland, and Ireland is 1,900,000 pounds; I think this was reckoned at the most, as now the revenue stands. Why now towards this, you settle by your Instrument 1,300,000 pounds for the government, and upon that account to maintain the force by land and sea; and this without Land Tax, I think. And this is short of the revenue that now may be raised by the present Government, 600,000 pounds. I hope you will so far remedy this, because you see even now the present government is 1,900,000 pounds, and the whole sum which now may be raised comes short of the present charge, 542,689 pounds! And although an end should be put to the Spanish war, yet there will be a necessity for the preservation of the peace of the three nations, to keep up the present established Army in England, Scotland, and Ireland, and also a considerable fleet for some good time, until it shall please God to quiet and compose men's minds and bring the nation to some better consistency. So that considering the pay of the Army, coming to upwards 1,000,000 pounds, and the government 300,000 pounds, it will be necessary that for some convenient time, seeing you find things as you do,—and it is not good to think a wound healed, before it be,—that there should be raised over and above 1,300,000 pounds, the sum of 600,000 pounds per annum, which makes up the sum of 1,900,000 pounds; and that likewise the Parliament declare how far they will carry on the Spanish war, and for what time, and what further sum they will raise for the carrying on the same, and for what time. And if these things be not ascertained, as one saith, money is the cause, certainly whatever the cause is, if money be wanting the business will fall to the ground and all our labours will be lost. And therefore I hope you will have an especial care of this particular. And indeed having received such large expressions from you, we may believe, we need but offer these things to you, that these things will be cared for. And these things have all of them been made overture of to you and are before you, and so hath likewise the consideration of the debts, which truly I think are apparent.

And so I have done with what I have to offer to you, I think I have truly on my part, until I shall understand wherein it is in me to do further, and when I shall understand your pleasure in these things a little further. We have answered the order of Parliament in considering and debating of those things, that were the subject-matter of debate and consideration; and when you will be pleased to let me hear further of your thoughts in these things, then I suppose I shall be in a condition to discharge myself as God shall enable me. And I speak not this to evade, but I speak it in the fear and reverence of God, and I say plainly and clearly I hope, when you shall have been pleased among yourselves to take consideration of these things, that I may hear what your thoughts are of them. I do not say it as a condition to anything, but I shall be very ready, freely, and honestly and plainly, to discharge myself of what in the whole, upon the whole, may reasonably be expected from me, as God shall set me free to answer you in.

18.

8 May 1657 – 'The Humble Petition and Advice.' Speech in the Banqueting-House at Whitehall to the House of Commons

The next three speeches (18–20) can again be taken together. Cromwell eventually firmly rejected the title of king, but was ready to accept the bulk of the Petition while suggesting 'improvements' upon it. It was a traumatic experience for the Commons. Many original supporters of the Petition fell away while former opponents began to see advantages in it. During May it was further amended and an Additional Petition drafted. Some kinglings

hoped that the Protector would be led eventually by the logic of
events to monarchy – others feared it. Major-General Lambert,
author of the Instrument, gave up his commission. On 9 June
(Speech 20) Cromwell sealed the new constitution by assenting to a
large body of bills. On 25 June Parliament was adjourned until
January 1657/8. On 26 June there was a second Protectoral
installation in an emphatically civilian, almost a royal, ceremony.

'Mr Speaker,

I come hither to answer that that was in your last Paper to your
Committee you sent to me: which was in relation to the desires
which were offered to me by the House, in that they called their
Petition.

I confess, that business hath put the House, the Parliament, to a
great deal of trouble, and spent much time. I am very sorry for
that. It hath cost me some, and some thoughts: and because I have
been the unhappy occasion of the expense of so much time, I shall
spend little of it now.

I have, the best I can, resolved the whole business in my
thoughts: and I have said so much already in testimony to the
whole, that I think I shall not need to repeat anything that I have
said. I think it is a government that, in the aim of it is for the
settling of the nation on a good foot, in relation to civil rights and
liberties, which are the rights of the nation. And I hope I shall
never be found to be one of them that go about to rob the nation of
those rights, but shall ever be found to serve them, what I can, to
the attaining of them. It is also exceeding well provided there for
the safety and security of honest men, in that great, natural, and
religious liberty, which is liberty of conscience. These are the great
fundamentals: and I must bear my testimony to them,—as I have,
and shall do so still, so long as God lets me live in this world,—
that the intentions of the things are very honourable and honest,
and the product worthy of a Parliament.

I have only had the unhappiness,—both in my conferences with
your Committees, and in the best thoughts I could take to
myself,—not to be convinced of the necessity of that thing, that
hath been so often insisted on by you, to wit, the title of King, as in
itself so necessary, as it seemed to be apprehended by yourselves.
And yet I do, with all honour and respect to the judgment of a
Parliament, testify that, *caeteris paribus*, no private judgment is to

lie in the balance with the judgment of Parliament. But, in things that respect particular persons, every man that is to give an account to God of his actions, he must, in some measure, be able to prove his own work, and to have an approbation in his own conscience of that, that he is to do, or to forbear. And, whilst you are granting others liberties, surely you will not deny me this? It being not only a liberty, but a duty,—and such a duty as I cannot, without sinning, forbear,—to examine mine own heart, and thoughts, and judgment, in every work which I am to set my hand to, or to appear in, or for. I must confess therefore, that though I do acknowledge all the other particulars, yet I must be a little confident in this, that, what with the circumstances that accompany human actions,—whether they be circumstances of time or persons, whether circumstances that relate to the whole, or private or particular circumstances, that compass any person that is to render an account of his own actions,—I have truly thought, and do still think, that if I should at the best do anything on this account, to answer your expectation, at the best I should do it doubtingly. And certainly what is so done, is not of faith; and whatsoever is not so,—whatsoever is not of faith,—is sin to him that doth it. Whether it be with relation to the substance of the action about which that consideration is conversant, or whether to circumstances about it, it is that consideration which makes all indifferent actions good or evil,—I say in whatever circumstances,—and truly I mean good or evil to him that doth them. I lying under this consideration, think it my duty to let you know,—only I could have wished I had done it sooner, for the sake of the House, who hath laid so infinite obligations on me, I wish I had done it sooner for their sake, and for saving time and trouble; and indeed, for the Committee's sake, to whom I must acknowledge publicly I have been unreasonably troublesome, I say I could have wished I had given it sooner,—but truly this is my answer, that, although I think the Government propounded doth consist of very excellent parts, in all but that very thing, the title, as to me, I should not be an honest man if I should not tell you, that I cannot accept of the government, nor undertake the trouble and charge of it: which I have a little more experimented than everybody, what troubles and difficulties do befall men under such trusts, and in such undertakings. I say, I am persuaded therefore to return this answer to you, that I cannot undertake this government with that title of King. And that is my answer to this great weighty business.'

19.

25 May 1657 – 'The Humble Petition and Advice.' Speech in the Painted Chamber to the House of Commons, after giving consent

'Mr Speaker,

I desire to offer a word or two unto you: which shall be but a word.

I did well bethink myself, before I came hither this day, that I came not as to a triumph, but, with the most serious thoughts that ever I had in all my life, to undertake one of the greatest tasks that ever was laid upon the back of a human creature. And I make no question, but you will, and so will all men, readily agree with me, that, without the support of the Almighty, I shall necessarily sink under the burden of it; not only with shame and reproach to myself, but,—with that that is more a thousand times, and in comparison of which I and my family are not worthy to be mentioned,—with the loss and prejudice of these three nations. And that being so, I must ask your help, and the help of all those that fear God, that, by their prayers, I may receive assistance from the hand of God. His presence, going along, will enable to the discharge of so great a duty and trust as this is, and nothing else.

Howbeit I have some other things to desire of you, I mean of the Parliament: that, seeing this is but, as it were, an introduction to the carrying on of the government of these nations, and forasmuch as there are many things which cannot be supplied for the enabling to the carrying on of this work, without your help and assistance, I think it is my duty to ask your help in them. Not that I doubted; for I believe the same spirit that hath led you to this, will easily suggest the rest to you. The truth is,—and I can say it in the presence of God,—that nothing would have induced me to have undertaken this insupportable burden to flesh and blood, had it not been that I have seen in this Parliament all along, a care of doing all those things that might truly and really answer the ends that have been engaged for. You have testified your forwardness and readiness therein very fully already.

I thought it my duty,—when your Committee, which you were pleased to send to me, lately came to give the grounds and reasons of your proceedings, to satisfy my conscience and judgment,—I was then bold to offer to them several considerations, which were received by them, and hath been presented to you. In answer to which the Committee did bring several resolves of yours, which I have by me. I think those are not yet made so authentic and authoritative as was desired, and therefore though I cannot doubt it, yet I thought it my duty to ask it of you, that there may be a perfecting of those things. Indeed as I said before, I have my witness in the sight of God, that nothing would have been an argument to me,—how desirable soever great places may seem to be to other men,—I say nothing would have been an argument to me to have undertaken this, but, as I said before, I saw such things determined by you, as make clearly for the liberty of the nations, and for the liberty, and interest, and preservation of all such as fear God, of all that fear God under various forms. And if God make not these nations thankful to you for your care therein, it will fall as a sin on their heads. And therefore I say that hath been one main encouragement.

I confess there are other things that tend to reformation, to the discountenancing of vice, to the encouragement of good men, and virtue: and the completing of those things also I look forward to. Concerning some of which you have not yet resolved anything, save to let me know by your Committee, that you would not be wanting in anything that might make for the good of these nations. Nor do I speak it, as in the least doubting it, but I do earnestly and heartily desire,—to the end God may crown your work, and bless you, and this government,—that, in your own time, and with what speed you judge fit, these things may be provided for.'

20.

**9 June 1657 – Speech in the Painted Chamber to the House of
  Commons**

'Mr Speaker,

I perceive, that, among these many Acts of Parliament, there
hath been a very great care had by the Parliament to provide for
the just and necessary support of the Commonwealth, by those
Bills for the Levying of Money, now brought to me, which I have
given my consent unto.

Understanding it hath been the practice of those who have been
Chief Governors, to acknowledge with thanks to the Commons
their care and regard of the public, I do very heartily and
thankfully acknowledge their kindness herein.'

21.

**20 January 1657/8 – Speech in the House of Lords to the two
  Houses of Parliament**

When Parliament reassembled it had changed profoundly. During
the recess the Protector had nominated the membership of 'the
Other House', striving to give it the weight to be 'a screen or
balance' to the Commons. Not everyone named would actually
serve, e.g. some 'old' peers. Of necessity many experienced MPs
were transferred, leaving a vacuum filled by the excluded who were
allowed back under the terms of the new constitution. Cromwell's
speech was short and optimistic, leaving the government's views to
be elaborated upon by the Commissioner of the Great Seal,
Nathaniel Fiennes.

'My Lords, and Gentlemen of the House of Commons,

I meet you here in this capacity, by the Advice and Petition of
this present Parliament, after so much expense of blood and

treasure, to search and try what blessings God hath in store for these nations.

I cannot but with gladness of heart remember and acknowledge the labour and industry that is past, which hath been spent upon a business worthy of the best men, and the best Christians. It is very well known unto you all, what difficulties we have passed through, and what we are now arrived to. We hope we may say we have arrived at what we aimed at, if not at that which is much beyond our expectations.

The state of this cause, and the quarrel, what that was at the first, you all very well know: I am persuaded most of you have been actors in it. It was the maintaining of the liberty of these nations; our civil liberties, as men; our spiritual liberties, as Christians. I shall not much look back, but rather say one word concerning the state and condition we are all now in.

You know very well, the first Declaration after the beginning of this war, that spake to the life, was a sense held forth by the Parliament, that, for some succession of time, designs were laid to innovate upon the civil rights of the nations, to innovate in matters of religion. And those very persons, that a man would have thought should have had the least hand in the meddling with civil things, did justify them all; all irregular transactions that were in pulpits, in presses, and otherwise, which was verily thought would have been a very good shelter to them, to innovate upon us in matters of religion also; and so to innovate as to eat out the core, and power, and heart, and life of all religion, by bringing on us a company of poisonous Popish ceremonies, and imposing them upon those that were called and accounted the Puritans of the nation, and professors of religion amongst us; driving them to seek their bread in a howling wilderness, as was instanced to our friends, who were forced to fly for Holland, New-England, almost any-whither, to find liberty for their consciences.

You see that the Petition and Advice that brought me hither hath, not through a little difficulty, restored us both in point of civil liberty as we are men, and liberty for all those that are of the Protestant profession amongst us; who enjoy a freedom to worship God according to their consciences.

Now if this thing hath been the state and sum of our quarrel, and of those ten years' wars wherein we have been exercised, and that the good hand of God, for we are to attribute it to no other, hath brought this business thus home unto us, as it is stated in the Petition and Advice, then I think we have all cause to bless God, and the nations have cause to bless him.

I well remember I did a little touch upon the eighty-fifth Psalm, when I spake unto you in the beginning of this Parliament, which expresseth well that, that we may say as truly and as well, as it was said of old by the penman of that Psalm. The first verse is an acknowledgment to God, that he had been favourable unto his land, and had brought back the captivity of his people, and that he had pardoned all their iniquities, and covered all their sin, and taken away all his wrath. And indeed in these unspeakable mercies, blessings and deliverances out of captivity, pardoning national sins and national iniquities,—pardoning as God pardons the man whom he justifieth,—he breaks through and overlooks iniquity and pardoneth because he will pardon: and sometimes God pardoneth nations also. And if the enjoyment of our present peace and other mercies may be witnesses for God, we feel and we see them every day.

The greatest demonstration of his favour and love appears to us in this, that he hath given us peace, and the blessings of peace, to wit the enjoyments of our liberties, civil and spiritual. And I remember well the Church falls into prayer and into praises, great expectations of future mercies, and much thankfulness for the enjoyment of present mercies, and breaks into this expression, "Surely salvation is nigh unto them that fear him, that glory may dwell in our land." In the beginning he calls it his land, "Thou hast been favourable to thy land." Truly I hope this is his land: and in some sense it may be given out that it is God's land. And he that hath the weakest knowledge and the worst memory, can easily tell that we are a redeemed people. We were a redeemed people, when first God was pleased to look favourably upon us, and to bring us out of the hands of Popery in that never-to-be-forgotten reform-ation, that most significant and greatest the nation hath felt or tasted. I would but touch upon that, and but a touch, how hath God redeemed us as it is this day, not only from trouble and sorrow and anger, but unto a blessed and happy estate and condition, comprehensive of all the interests of every member, of every individual of these nations, as you very well see.

And then in what sense it is our land, through this grace and favour of God, that he hath vouchsafed unto us and bestowed upon us liberty with the gospel, with peace and rest out of ten years' war, and given us what we would desire. Nay, who would have fore-thought when we were plunged into the midst of our troubles, that ever the people of God should have had liberty to worship God without fear of enemies? Which is the very acknowledgement of the promise of Christ, that he would deliver his people from fear of enemies, that they might worship him in holiness and in righteousness all the days of their life. This is the portion that God hath given us, and I trust we shall for ever heartily acknowledge it.

The Church goes on there and makes her boast yet further, "His salvation is nigh them that fear him, that glory may dwell in our land." His glory, not carnal nor anything else, that accompanies this glory of a free possession of the gospel, this is that that we may glory in. And he says further, "Mercy and truth are met together, righteousness and peace have kissed each other." And it shall be such righteousness as comes down from heaven, "Truth shall grow out of the earth, and righteousness shall come down from heaven." Here is the truth of all, here is the righteousness of God, under the notion of righteousness, confirming our abilities, answerable to the truth that he hath in the gospel revealed towards us. And he closeth with this, "Righteousness shall go before him, and shall set us in the way of his steps." That righteousness, that mercy, that love and that kindness, which we have seen, and have been made partakers of from the Lord, it shall be our guide to teach us to know the right and the good way, which is to tread in the steps of mercy, righteousness, and goodness, that our God hath walked before us in.

We have a peace this day. I believe in my very heart you all think the things that I speak to you this day, I am sure you have cause to, and yet we are not without the murmurings of many people, who turn all this grace and goodness into wormwood, who indeed are disappointed by the works of God. And those men are of several ranks and conditions, great ones, lesser ones, men of all sorts, men that are of the episcopal spirit, with all the branches, the root and the branches: who gave themselves a fatal blow in this place, when they would needs make a Protestation, that no laws were good which were made by this House and the House of Commons in their absence: and so without injury to themselves they cut off themselves. Indeed, they are men that know not God, that know not how to account upon the works of God, how to measure them out, but will trouble nations for an interest that is but mixed at the best, made up of iron and clay like the feet of Nebuchadnezzar's image; whether they were more civil or spiritual was hard to say, but their continuance was like to be known beforehand, iron and clay make no good mixtures, they are not durable at all. You have now a godly ministry, you have a knowing ministry, such a one as, without vanity be it spoken, the world has not the like: men knowing the things of God, and able to search into the things of God, by that only that can fathom those things in some measure to wit the spirit of God. The spirit of a beast knows not the spirit of a man, nor doth the spirit of a man know the things of God: but the things of God are known by the spirit. Truly I will remember but this one thing of those; their greatest persecution hath been of the people of God, men of the spirit of God, as, I think, very experiences will sufficiently demonstrate.

Besides, what's the reason think you, that men slip in this age wherein we live? As I told you before, because they understand not the works of God: they consider not the operation of his laws, they consider not, that God resisted and broke in pieces the powers that were, that men might fear him, might have liberty to do and enjoy all that we have been speaking of, which certainly God has manifested that this was the end, and that he hath brought the things to pass. Therefore it is that men yet slip, and engage themselves against God. They engage themselves, I say, against God, and for that very cause in the twenty-eighth Psalm, saith David, He shall break them down, and not build them up. If therefore you would know upon what foundation you stand, own your foundation from God. He hath set you where you are: he hath set you in the enjoyment of your civil and spiritual liberties.

I deal clearly with you, I have been under some infirmity, therefore dare not speak further to you, but to let you know this much, that I have with truth and simplicity declared the state of our cause, and attainments in it, to you, by the industry and labour of this Parliament when they last met. Upon this foundation you shall find,—I mean the foundation of a cause and quarrel thus attained to, and wherein we are thus instated,—I should be very glad to lay my bones with yours, and would have done it with all heartiness and cheerfulness, in the meanest capacity that I was ever yet in, to serve the Parliament.

If God give you strength, as I trust he will,—he hath given it you, for what I have been speaking of but what you have done, he hath given you strength to do what hath been done,—and if God should bless you in this work, and make this meeting happy upon this account, you shall all be called the blessed of the Lord; the generations to come will bless us. "You shall be the repairers of breaches, and the restorers of paths to dwell in"; and if there be any work that mortals can attain to in the world beyond this, I acknowledge my ignorance.

As I told you, I have some infirmities upon me, I have not liberty to speak more unto you, but I have desired an honourable person here by me to discourse a little more particularly what may be more proper for this occasion and this meeting.'

22.

25 January 1657/8 – Speech in the Banqueting-House at White-hall to the two Houses of Parliament

This speech was a determined attempt to head the Commons off from constitutional niceties to consider wider issues affecting England, the British Isles and Europe – notably the whole of international Protestantism confronting aggressive popery – while at home civilian and military disunity and distemper prevailed. It failed. Experienced in parliamentary ways, the Commonwealths-men members and their allies continued their obstructive tactics, concentrating on assailing 'the Other House'.

'My Lords and Gentlemen of the Two Houses of Parliament, for so I must own you, in whom together with myself is vested the legislative power of these nations,

The impression of the weight of these affairs and interest for which we are met together is such, that I could not satisfy myself with a good conscience if I should not remonstrate to you somewhat of my apprehensions of the state of the affairs of these nations, together with the proposals of such remedies as may occur to those dangers that are imminent upon us.

I conceive the well-being, yea the being of these nations is now at stake, and if God bless this meeting our tranquillity and peace may be lengthened out to us; if otherwise, I shall offer it to your judgments and considerations, by that time I have done, whether there be, as to men, a possibility of discharging that trust that is incumbent upon us for the safety and preservation of these nations. And when I have told you what occurs to my thoughts, I shall leave it to such an operation on your hearts as it shall please God Almighty to work upon you. I look on this to be the great duty of my place, as being set on a watch-tower, to see what may be for the good of these nations and what may be for the preventing of evil, that so by the advice of so great and wise a Council as this is, that hath in it the life and spirit of these nations, that good may be attained and that evil, whatever it is, may be obviated. We shall hardly set our shoulders to this work, unless it shall please God to work some conviction upon our hearts that there is need of our most serious and best counsels at such a time as this is.

I have not prepared any such matter and rule of speech to deliver myself unto you, as perhaps might have been more fitter for me to have done and more serviceable for you to have understood me in, but shall only speak plainly and honestly to you out of such conceptions as it hath pleased God to set upon me. We have not been now four years and upwards in this government, to be totally ignorant of the things that may be of the greatest concernment to us. Your dangers, for that is the head of my speech, they are either with respect had to affairs abroad and their difficulties, or to affairs at home and their difficulties. You come, if I may say so now, in the end of as great difficulties and straits, as I think ever nation was engaged in. I had in my thoughts to have made this the method of my speech, to wit, to let you see the things that hazard your being and your well-being, but when I came seriously to consider better of it, I thought, as your affairs stand, that all things would resolve themselves into very being. You are

not a nation, you will not be a nation, if God strengthen you not to
meet with these evils that are upon us.

First, from abroad. What are the affairs, I beseech you, abroad?
I thought the profession of the Protestant religion was a thing of
well-being. And truly, in a good sense so it is, and it is no more;
though it be a very high thing, it is but a thing of well-being. But
take it with all the complications of it, with all the concomitants of
it, with respect had to the nations abroad, I do believe that he that
looks well about him and considereth the estate of the Protestant
affairs all Christendom over, he must needs say and acknowledge
that the greatest design now on foot, in comparison with which all
other designs are but low things, is, whether the Christian world
should be all Popery; or, whether God hath a love to, and we
ought to have a brotherly fellow-feeling of, the interest of all the
Protestant Christians in the world. And he that strikes at but one
species of a general to make it nothing, strikes at all. Is it not so
now, that the Protestant cause and interest abroad is struck at,
and is in opinion and apprehension quite underfoot, trodden
down? And judge with me, I beseech you, a little, whether it be so
or no; and then, I pray you, will you consider how far we are
concerned in that danger, as to being.

We have known very well that that which is accounted the
honest and religious interest of the nation, it was not trodden
down under foot all at once, but by degrees, that that interest
might be consumed as with a canker insensibly, as Jonah's gourd
was, till it was quite withered in a night. It is at another rate now,
for certainly this enmity is in the general; the Papacy, and those
that are the upholders of it, they have openly and avowedly trod
God's people under foot on that very notion and account, that
they were Protestants. The money that you parted with in that
noble charity that was exercised in this nation, and the just sense
that you had of those poor Piedmonts, was satisfaction enough to
yourselves of that as a precursory thing. If all the Protestants in
Europe had had but that head, that head had been cut off, and so
an end of all. Is this all? No! Look but how the House of Austria,
on both sides of Christendom, are armed and prepared to make
themselves able to destroy the whole Protestant interest. Is not, to
begin there, the King of Hungary prepared, who expecteth with
his partisans to make himself Emperor of Germany, and in the

judgment of all men not only in possibility but a certainty of the acquisition of it? Is not he, since he hath mastered the Duke of Brandenburg one of the Electors? And no doubt but he will have three of the Episcopal Electors, and the Duke of Bavaria. Who will he have to contest with him abroad, for taking the Empire of Germany out of his hands? And is not he the son of a father, whose principal interest and personal conscience guided him to exile all the Protestants out of his own patrimonial country, out of Bohemia,—got with the sword,—out of Moravia and Silesia? It is that which is in the daily complaints that come over to us, some of which we have but received within these two or three days, being conveyed by some godly Ministers in the city, that they are tossed out of Poland into the Empire, and out thence whither they can fly to get their bread, and are ready to perish for want of food. What think you of that other side of Europe, to wit, Italy,—if I may call it the other side of Europe, as I think I may,— Spain, and all those adjacent parts, with the Grisons, Piedmonts afore mentioned, the Switzers; they all, what are they but a prey of the Spanish power and interest? And look to that that calls itself the head of all this, a Pope fitted,—I hope indeed born not in, but out of due time,—to accomplish this bloody work, that so he may fill up his cup to the brim and make him ripe for judgment. He doth, as always he hath done. He hath influenced all the Powers and all the Princes in Europe to this very thing, and no man like this present man. So that I beseech you, what is there in all the parts of Europe, what is there I say is all the other parts of Europe, but a consent, co-operating at this very time and season to them, to suppress everything that stands in their way?

But it may be said, This is a great way off in the extremest parts of it; what is that to us? If it be nothing to you, let it be nothing to you. I have told you it is somewhat to you, and it concerns all your religion and all the good interest of Europe. I have, I thank God, considered. I would beg of you to consider a little more with me, what that resistance is that is likely to be made to this mighty current, that is like to be coming from all parts on all Protestants. Who is there that holdeth up his head to oppose this great design? A poor Prince! Indeed poor, but a man in his person as gallant, and truly I think I may say as good, as any these late ages have brought forth; a man that hath adventured his all against the Popish interest in Poland, and made his acquisition still good for the Protestant religion. He is now reduced into a corner, and that which addeth to the grief of all, and more than all that hath been spoken of before,—I wish it may not be too truly said,—is that men of our religion forget that, and seek his ruin. And I beseech you a little, consider the consequences of that. For what doth all this signify? Is it only a noise, or hath it an articulate sound with it? Men that are not true to that religion we profess,—I am persuaded with greater truth, uprightness and sincerity than it is by any collected body, so nearly gathered together as these nations are, in all the world,—God will find them out. I beseech you consider how things do co-operate, if this may seem but to be a design against your well-being. It is against your very being though, this artifice and this complex design against the Protestant interest, wherein so many Protestants are not so right as were to be wished. If they can shut us out of the Baltic Sea, and make themselves masters of that, where is your trade? Where are your materials to preserve your shipping, or where will you be able to challenge any right by sea, or justify yourselves against a foreign invasion in your own soil? Think upon it; this is in design. I do believe, if you will go to ask the poor mariner in his red-cap and coat, as he passeth from ship to ship, you will hardly find in any ship but they will tell you this is designed against you; so obvious is it, by this and other things, that you are the object. And, in my conscience, I know not for what else, but because of the purity of the Profession amongst you, who have not yet made it your trade to prefer your profit before your godliness, but reckon godliness the greater gain. But should it so happen that, as contrivances stand, you should not be able to vindicate yourselves against all whatsoever,—I name no one State upon this head, but I think all acknowledge that States are engaged in this combination,—judge you where you are!

You have accounted yourselves happy in being environed with a great ditch from all the world beside. Truly you will not be able to keep your ditch, nor your shipping, unless you turn your ships and your shipping into troops of horse and companies of foot, and fight to defend yourselves in *terra firma*. If these things succeed, *Liberavi animam meam*; I have told you of it. And if there be no danger in this, I have satisfied myself that I have told you. If you will judge it no danger, if you will think we may discourse of all things at pleasure, that it is a time of sleep and ease and rest, without a due sense of these things, I have this comfort to Godward, I have told you of it. And really, were it not that France, give me leave to say it, is a balance to this party at this time, should there be a peace made, that hath been and still is laboured and aimed at, a general peace, then will England be the general object of all the fury and wrath of all the enemies of God and our religion in the world. I have nobody to accuse, but do but look on the other side of the water. You have neighbours there, some that you are in amity with, some that have professed malice enough against you. I think you are fully satisfied in that. I had rather you would trust your enemy than some friends; that is, believe your enemy and trust him that he means your ruin, rather than have confidence in some that perhaps may be in some alliance with you. I perhaps could infer all this with some particulars, nay I could. For you know that your enemies be the same that have been accounted your enemies ever since Queen Elizabeth came to the Crown; an avowed, designed enemy, wanting nothing of counsel, wisdom and prudence to rout you out of the face of the earth. And when public attempts would not do, how have they, by the Jesuits and other their emissaries, laid foundations to perplex and trouble our government by taking away the lives of them that they judged to be of any use to preserve your peace! And at this time I ask you whether you do not think they are designing as busily as ever any people were to prosecute the same counsels and things to the uttermost?

The business was then, the Dutch needed Queen Elizabeth of famous memory for their protection. They had it. I hope they will never ill-requite it; for if they should forget either the kindness that was then shewed them, which was their real safety, or the desires this nation hath had to be at peace with them, truly I believe whoever exercises any ingratitude in this sort will hardly prosper in it. But this may awaken you; howsoever I hope, you will be awakened upon all these considerations. It is true, it is true they have professed a principle that, thanks be to God, we never knew. They will send arms to their enemies, and lend their ships to their enemies. They will do so, and truly that principle is not a matter in dispute at this time, only let everything weigh with your spirits as it ought, let it do so. And we must tell you, that we do know that this is true. I dare assure you of it, and that I think if your Exchange here were but resorted to, it would let you know as much as you can desire to know, that they have hired sloops, I think they call them or some other name, they have hired sloops to transport upon you four thousand foot and one thousand horse upon the pretended interest of that young man that was the late King's son. And this is I think a thing, so far from being reckoned a suggestion to any ill end or purpose, or to any other end than to awaken you to a just consideration of your danger and to unite you to a just and natural defence. Indeed I never did, and I hope I never shall, use any artifice with you to pray you to help us with money to defend ourselves, but if money be needful, I will tell you. I pray you help us with money, that the interest of the nation may be defended both abroad and at home. I will use no arguments, and thereby will disappoint the artifice of false men abroad that say it is for money that I say this. Whosoever shall think to put things out of frame upon such a suggestion, it will be in vain, for you will find I will be very plain with you before I have done, and that with all love and affection and faithfulness to you and these nations. If this be the condition of affairs abroad, I pray a little consider what is the estate of your affairs at home. And if both these considerations have but this effect, to get a consideration among you, a due and just consideration of our want, it is well. Let God move your hearts for the answering of anything that shall be due to the nation, as he shall please. And I hope I shall not be solicitous. I shall look up to him that hath been my God and my guide hitherto.

I say, I beseech you, look to your own affairs at home, how they stand. I am persuaded you are all, I apprehend you are all very honest and worthy good men, and that there is not a man of you but would desire to be found a good patriot. I know you would. We are apt to boast sometimes that we are Englishmen. And truly it is no shame to us that we are so, but it is a motive to us to do like Englishmen, and seek the real good of this nation and the interest of it. But I beseech you, what is our case at home? I profess I do not know well where to begin at this head or where to end, I do not, but I must needs say let a man begin where he will, he shall hardly be out of that drift I am speaking to you. We are as full of calamities and divisions among us in respect of the spirits of men, though, through a wonderful, admirable, and never to be sufficiently admired providence of God, in peace. And the fighting we have had and the success we have had, yea, we that are here, we are an astonishment to the world; and yet take us in that temper we are in, or rather distemper, it is the greatest miracle that ever befel the sons of men; and whosoever shall seek to break it, God Almighty rout that man out of this nation,—and he will do it, let the pretences be what they will. He that considereth not the woman with child, the sucking children of this nation that know not the right hand from the left, of whom, for aught I know, it may be said, this city is as full as it is said of Nineveh of old; he that considereth not these, and the fruit that is like to come out of the bodies of those now living added to these, he that considereth not these, must have a Cain's heart, who was marked and made to be an enemy to all men and all men enemies to him, for the wrath and justice of God will persecute such a man to his grave, if not to hell. I say, look on this nation. Look on it. Consider what are the varieties of interest in this nation, if they be worthy of the name of interests. If God did not hinder, all would but make up a confusion, and we shall find there will be more than a Cain in England, if God did not restrain, and we should have another more bloody civil war than ever we had in England. For I beseech you, what is the general spirit of this nation? Is it not that each sort of people, if I may call them sects, whether sects upon a religious account or upon a civil account, is not this nation miserable in that respect? What is that which possesses every sect? What is it? That every sect may be uppermost, that every sort of men may get the power into their hands,—and they would use it well,—that every sect may get the power into their hands. It were a happy thing if the nation would be content with rule, if it were but in civil things, with those that would rule worst; because misrule is better than no rule, and an ill government, a bad one, is better than none. It is not that only, but we have an appetite to variety, to be not only making wounds, but as if we should see one making wounds in a man's side and would desire nothing more than to be groping and grovelling with his fingers in those wounds. This is that men will be at; this is the spirit of those that would trample on men's liberties in spiritual respects. They will be making wounds, and rending and tearing, and making them wider than they are. Is not this the case? Doth there want anything,—I speak not of sects in an ill sense, but the nation is hugely made up of them,—and what is the want that these things are not done to the uttermost, but that men have more anger than strength? They have not power to attain their ends. And I beseech you judge what such a company of men of these sorts are doing while they are contesting one with another. They are contesting in the midst of a generation of men, a malignant Episcopal party, I mean contesting in the midst of these, all united. What must be the issue of such a thing as this? It is so. And do but judge what proofs have been made of the spirits of these men; summoning men together to take up arms, and to exhort each sort to fight for their notions, every sort thinking they are to try it out by the sword, every sort thinking that they are truly under the banner of Christ if they but come in and oblige upon this account. Now do but judge what a hard condition this poor nation is on. This is the state and condition we are in. Judge, I say, what a hard condition this poor nation is in, and the cause of God in the midst of such a party of men as the Cavaliers are and their participants, not only with respect to what these are like to do among themselves, but some of these, yea some of these, they care not who carry the goal; nay, some of these have invited the Spaniard himself to assist and carry on the Cavalier cause. And that this is true, and many other things that are not fit to be suggested to you because we should betray the interest of our intelligence, I dare assert.

I say, this is your condition. What is your defence? What hinders the eruption of all this upon you irresistibly, to your utter destruction? Truly you have an army in these parts, in Scotland, in England, and Ireland. Take them away tomorrow, would not all these interests run into one another? I know you are rational, prudent men; have you any frame or model of things that would satisfy the minds of men, if this be not the frame you are now called together upon and engaged in? I mean the two Houses of Parliament and myself. What hinders this nation from being made an Aceldama, if this do not? It is this without doubt; give the glory to God. Give the glory to God, for without this it would prove as great a plague as all that hath been spoken of. It is this without doubt that keeps this nation in peace and quietness. But what is the case of this army? a poor unpaid army, the soldiers going barefoot at this time, in this city, this weather, and yet a peaceable people, seeking to serve you with their lives, judging their pains and hazards, and all, well bestowed in obeying their officers and serving you to keep the peace of these nations. Yea, he must be a man that hath a heart as hard as the weather, that hath not a due sense of this. So that I say, that it is most plain and evident this is your outward and present defence. And yet at this day, do but you judge how it stands, the Cavalier party, the several humours of unreasonable men in these several ways having made batteries at this defence ever since you enjoyed your peace. What have they made their business but this, to spread libellous books, yea, and pretend the liberty of the people, which really wiser men than they may pretend. For let me say this to you at once, I never look to see the people of England come into a just liberty, if any other war should overtake us. I think, at least, that that is likely to bring us into our liberty, is a consistency and agreement within this meeting. Therefore all that I can say to you is this, it will be your wisdom, I do think truly, and your justice to keep this interest close to you, to uphold this settlement, which I have no cause to think but you are agreed to and that you like it. For I assure you, I am very greatly mistaken else to think that that which is now the settlement among us, is that which hath been my inducement to bear the burden I bear, and serve the Commonwealth in the place I am in.

And therefore if you should judge, that this be not argument enough to persuade you to be sensible of your danger, which besides good-nature and ingenuity would move a stone to be sensible of, therefore give us leave to consider a little what will become of us if our spirits should go otherwise. If our spirits be dissatisfied, what will become of things? Here is an army, five or six months behind in pay; yea, an army in Scotland near as much; an army in Ireland much more. And if these things be not considered,—I cannot doubt but that they will be considered,—I say judge what the case of Ireland is, should free quarter come upon the Irish people. You have a company of Scots in the north of Ireland that I hope are honest men; in the province of Galway almost all the Irish transported to the West. You have the interest of England newly begun to be planted. The people there are full of necessities and complaints. They bear to the uttermost, and should the soldiers run upon free quarter there upon your English planters as they must, the English planters must quit the country through mere beggary, and that which hath been the success of so much blood and treasure to get that country into your hands, what will be the consequence but that the English must needs run away for pure beggary and the Irish must possess the country for a receptacle to a Popish and Spanish interest? And hath Scotland been long settled? Have not they a like sense of poverty? I speak plainly, in good earnest I do think the Scots' nation have been under as great suffering in point of livelihood and substance outwardly as any people I have yet named to you. I do think truly, they are a very ruined nation, yet in a way,—I have spoken with some gentlemen come from thence,—hopeful enough yet. It hath pleased God to give that plentiful encouragement to the meaner sort, I must say the meaner sort, in Scotland. I must say, if it please God to encourage the meaner sort, the meaner sort live as well and are likely to come into as thriving a condition under your government, as when they were under their great Lords, who made them work for their living no better than the peasants of France. I am loth to speak anything which may reflect upon that nation, but the middle sort of this people grow up into such a substance, as makes their lives comfortable if not better than they were before. If now after all this, we shall not be sensible of all those designs which are in the midst of us, of the united Cavaliers, of the designs which are animated every day from Flanders and Spain, if we shall look upon ourselves as a divided people, a man cannot certainly tell where to find consistency anywhere in England. Certainly there is no consistency in anything, that may be worthy the name of the body of consistency, but in this company that are met here. How should that man lay his hand upon his heart and not talk of things, neither to be made out by the light of Scripture nor reason, and draw one another off from considering these things? I dare leave them with you and commit them to your bosom. They have a weight, a greater weight than any I have yet suggested to you from abroad or at home.

If this be our case abroad and at home, that our being and well-being,—our well-being is not worth the naming comparatively,—I say, if that be our case of our being abroad and at home that through want to bear up our honour at sea and for want to maintain that that is our defence at home we are in danger, and if that through our mistake we shall be led off our consideration of these things and talk of circumstantial things and quarrel about circumstances, and shall not with heart and soul intend and carry on these things, I confess I can look for nothing. I can say no more than what expresseth in print, of one that having consulted everything, he could hold to nothing like nothing, neither Fifth Monarchy nor Presbytery nor Independency, nothing, but at length concludes he was for nothing but an orderly confusion. And for men that have wonderfully lost their consciences and their wits, that suffices; I speak of men abroad that cannot tell what they would have, yet are willing to kindle coals to disturb others.

And now having said this, I have discharged my duty to God and to you in making this demonstration; and I profess to you not as a rhetorician. My business to you is to prove the verity of the designs from abroad and still unsatisfied spirits of Cavaliers at home, who from the first of our peace to this day have not been wanting to do what they could to kindle a fire at home in the midst of us. I say, if this be so the truth, I pray God affect your hearts with a due sense of it and give you one heart and mind to carry on this work for which we are met together. If these things be so, should you not meet tomorrow and accord in all things tending to the preservation of your rights and liberties, really it will be feared there is too much time elapsed to deliver yourselves from those dangers that hang upon you. We have had now six years' peace, and have had an interruption of ten years' war. We have seen and heard and felt the evils of it, and now God hath given us a new taste of the comfort and benefit of peace. Have you not had such a peace in England, Ireland and Scotland, that there is not a man to lift up his finger to put you into a distemper? Is not this a mighty blessing from the Lord of Heaven? Shall we now be prodigal of time? Should any man, shall we, listen to delusions to break and interrupt this peace? There is not any man that hath been true to this cause, as I believe you have been all, that can look for anything but the greatest rending and persecution that ever was in the world. I wonder then how it can enter into the heart of any man to undervalue these things, to slight peace and the Gospel, the greatest mercy of God. We have peace and the Gospel. Let us have one heart and soul, one mind to maintain the honest and just rights of this nation, not to pretend them to the destruction of our peace, to the destruction of the nation. Really, pretend what you will, if we run into another flood of blood and war, the sinews of this nation being wasted by the last, it must sink and perish utterly. I beseech you and charge you in the name and presence of God, and as before him, be sensible of these things and lay them to heart. You have a day of fasting coming on: I beseech God touch your hearts and open your ears to this truth, and that you may be as deaf adders to stop your ears to all dissension, and look upon them, whosoever they be. As Paul saith to the Church of Corinth, as I remember, "Mark such men as cause divisions and offences and would disturb you from that foundation of peace you are upon, upon any pretence whatsoever."

I shall conclude with this. I was free the last time of our meeting to tell you I would discourse upon a Psalm, and I did. I am not ashamed of it at any time, especially when I meet with men of such a consideration as you are. There you have one verse that I then forgat; "I will hear what the Lord will speak: he will speak peace to his people and to his saints, that they turn not again to folly." Dissension, division, destruction, in a poor nation under a civil war, having all the effects of a civil war upon it! Indeed if we return again to folly, let every man consider if it be not like to be our destruction. If God shall not unite your hearts and bless you, and give you the blessing of union and love to one another, and tread down everything that riseth up in your hearts or tendeth to deceive your own souls with pretences of this and that thing that we speak of, and if you do not prefer the keeping of peace, that we may see the fruits of righteousness in them that love peace and embrace peace, it will be said of this poor nation, *Actum est de Anglia*. But I trust God will never leave it to such a spirit. And while I live and am able, I shall be ready to stand and fall with you in this seeming promising union God hath wrought amongst you, which I hope neither the pride nor envy of men shall be able to dissipate and make void. I have taken my oath to govern according to the laws that are now made and to be made, and I trust I shall fully answer it. And know, I sought not this place, I speak it before God, angels and men, I did not. You sought me for it and you brought me to it, and I took my oath to be faithful to the interest of these nations, to be faithful to the government. All those things were implicit in my eye in that oath, to be faithful to this government upon which we are now met. And I trust, by the grace of God, as I have taken my oath to serve this Commonwealth on such an account, I shall, I must, see it done according to the articles of the government; that thereby liberty of conscience may be secured for honest people, that they may serve God without fear, that every just interest may be preserved, that a godly ministry may be upheld and not affronted by seducing and seduced spirits, that all men may be preserved in their just rights, whether civil or spiritual. Upon this account did I take oath and sware to this government. And so, having declared my heart and mind to you in this, I have nothing more to say but to pray God Almighty bless you.'

23.

28 January 1657/8 – Answer to the Committee of the House of Commons, which requested him to give directions for the printing of his speech of Monday 25 January

Cromwell followed the previous speech with a letter to the Speaker promising to send the Commons 'a paper which indeed I have forgot giving an account of the public moneys'. When this was reported to the House, a Committee was named to ask him for the paper and for the printing of his speech. His reply that he had no copy of it was an insight into his oratorical methods. The speech, as we know it, was in fact taken down by three shorthand writers. It survives only in a summary reported version. Note the concern Cromwell expressed about the privileges (in the technical parliamentary sense) of the Other House, which he obviously equated with those of the old House of Lords.

His Highness said, He could not have looked upon the Committee as a Committee of the House of Commons had he not seen the Paper and the persons of the Committee. That what he spake in the Banqueting-House was delivered to both Houses, the House of Lords and the House of Commons: And that he was exceeding tender of the breach of Privilege of either House, whereunto he had sworn, and by the blessing of God would maintain. And that he did not know, nor was satisfied, that it was not against the Privilege of either House for him to give an answer to either of the Houses apart. That he spake to the Houses those things that did lie upon his own heart; and that he did acquaint them honestly and plainly how things stood in matters of fact, but of particulars he doth not remember four lines. That he had considered with some persons about the papers relating to Money; and found some particulars short and some over; but he would take them into consideration and set them right, and would give a timely account thereof. He desired his affections might be presented to the House, and that he would be ready to serve them faithfully in that capacity he is in.

24.

4 February 1657/8 – Speech in the House of Lords, dissolving the two Houses

In spite of Cromwell's importunity and the efforts within the Commons by 'the court party', attention there was diverted by the opposition towards the Other House, while outside the restlessness among army and religious dissidents was positively encouraged by politicians. On the morning of 4 February, Cromwell, without consulting any one, came down to Westminster in a hired coach, summoned the Commons to come to 'the Lords House' where he harangued them, concluding with the dissolution, 'And let God be judge between you and me', to which it was reported 'many of the members cried out "Amen"'. The royalists hoped that the Protector had made a fatal blunder, which could only work in their favour. They were wrong. Although a period of difficulties ensued there were no signs of an imminent collapse of the regime.

'My Lords, and Gentlemen of the House of Commons,

The last time I met you here I had very comfortable expectations that God would make the calling of this parliament and the
meeting of it a blessing to ours and to these nations. And the Lord
is my witness, I desired the carrying on of the affairs of these
nations to those ends that I then expressed to you with so much
sincerity as satisfies my own conscience, and for which if I did deal
with you in hypocrisy, when I told you the blessing that we were
arrived at, if I did not with all my heart believe it and desire it with
my soul, then I most fear the uppermost Witness. And, as we told
you, we had attained mercy and truth, righteousness and peace, so
that we should go on to follow those footsteps that God had laid
for us, for the future improvement of them, improvement for
mercy and truth, and righteousness and peace.

I did think truly that that, that brought me into the capacity I
now stand in, and did then, was the Petition and Advice given me
by this Parliament, by you especially of the House of Commons,
who did in reference to the ancient Constitution frame your
Petition and advice by which you drew me to accept of the place I
now stand in. There is ne'er a man within these walls that can say,
Sir, you sought it! Nay, not a man nor woman treading upon
English ground. But contemplating, as well as I could, upon the
sad indisposition of these nations, broken almost in pieces with an
intestine war, recovered through the blessing of God unto a six or
seven years' peace, entire peace, having at the last arrived at an
opportunity of settlement, I did think us exceeding happy in that
progress that we had made. Being petitioned unto and advised by
you to undertake such a Government as this, of so great a weight
as this is, upon such conditions and with such considerations as
were not sudden to me but deliberated,—you know what your
Petition and Advice did offer me,—when I had conference with
you two or three times, I expostulated with you and dealt clearly
and candidly with you; I thought the burden too heavy for any
creature. And I told you that except there might be this and that
and the other thing, which you agreed to me, and upon which you
invited me to undertake this Government, I could not, I would not
undertake it. And when I had debated all those things with you,
everything in this Government, and you that were then in the
legislative capacity agreeing upon such a state of Government, as
that was which you brought to me and I sought not of you, I

looked that the same men that had made that frame would have
made it good to me when I came to act your Petition and Advice.
Give me leave to interpose this. No man, no man but a man
mistaken, and greatly mistaken, could think that I, that hath a
burden upon my back for the space of fifteen or sixteen years,
unless he would beforehand judge me an atheist, would seek such
a place as I bear. I can say it in the presence of God, in comparison
of which all we that are here are like poor creeping ants upon the
earth, that I would have been glad, as to my own conscience and
spirit, to have been living under a woodside to have kept a flock of
sheep, rather than to have undertaken such a place as this was. But
undertaking of it upon such terms as I did, known to you all that
did advise and petition, that I undertook it for the safety of the
nation, I did look that you, that did offer it unto me, should have
make it good. And I doubt if you had offered it to the meanest man
in this room, he would not have undertaken it really, if he had but
wisely considered his own person. But upon such terms really I
took it, and I am failed in these terms.

I did tell you at a conference concerning it, that I would not
undertake it without there might be some other body, that might
interpose between you and me, on the behalf of the Commonwealth to prevent a tumultuary and popular spirit. You granted it,
that I should name another House. And I named it with integrity, I
did. I named it of men that can meet you wheresoever you go and
shake hands with you, and tell you that it is not titles, it is not
lordship, it is not this nor that, that they value, but a Christian and
an English interest. Men of your own rank and qualities, and men
that I approved my heart to God in choosing; men that I hoped
would not only be a balance to a Commons' House of Parliament
but to themselves, having honest hearts, loving the same things
that you love, whilst you love England and whilst you love
Religion. And having proceeded upon these terms and finding
such a spirit as is too much predominant, everything is either too
high or too low, and when virtue and honesty and piety and
justice are aimed at, even in choosing in such a way as did satisfy
my conscience, then I was neither too high nor too low, but I
pitched upon men that I hope will be willing to sacrifice their lives
for these good interests. I thought in doing that, that was my duty
to God and satisfying my own conscience, I thought it would have

satisfied you. But if everything must be either too high or too low, you are not satisfiable, and I pray God misery be not found from the Lord,—I hope it will never be found from me,—a more necessary teacher than mercy. When I speak of mercy, I speak of the mercy that cometh from God to you. I take not myself to be able to dispense it as I would, but I say I did choose such a House as I thought I might answer for upon my life, that they would be true to those ends and those things that were the ground and state of our war with the Cavalier party all along. And what will satisfy, if this will not?

Again, I would not have accepted of this Government unless I knew that there would be a just reciprocation between the government and the governed, whether the governed representative or the whole collective body; those that were the representative of the whole body of the nation, unless they would take an oath to make good what the Parliament petitioned and advised me to. Upon that, the reciprocation of my part was the taking of an oath. I did take it. They that petitioned and advised me, know that I made everything in this Government a condition of my oath, and whosoever took the oath on their own part, took an oath answerable to mine. Did not every man that had a hand in the Petition and Advice, and drew me in,—I speak not in an ill sense, I would have amended that word,—and persuaded me to accept of their Petition and Advice, did not every man know upon what conditions I swore, and did not every man, that swore with reciprocation, know upon what conditions he swore? And what apprehension soever, what place soever, or sense soever this may have in your hearts, I tell you mine is different from yours, and I hope,—God knows upon what conditions I took that oath,—I took it upon the condition expressed in the Government. And I can say, with truth and uprightness, had that Government been settled, that we had been upon a foundation. I tell you what my understanding was of it. That when it was once agreed, we were upon a bottom. I thought myself bound to take the advice of the two Houses in anything, after that foundation was once agreed, in anything that might have been an emendation to it. But there was a supposition while we stood unsettled in anything till we knew what we should come at, the consequence whereof must necessarily have been absolute confusion. If you had once settled the

Government as it is,—not to make hereditary lords nor to make hereditary king or kings,—ye had had a basis to stand upon. The power of these nations consisting, as this Government, in the two Houses and myself, whatever had occurred to your judgment and your consciences had tended upon the same authority, to wit, the legislative power to have settled anything that might have been for further good. And therefore not to say what the meaning of your oath was to you,—that were a little to go against mine own principle to enter upon other men's consciences,—but I tell you what it was to me and in doing that I am satisfied enough. God will judge between me and you.

But alas! Is this the complaint that there hath been a misunderstanding in the way that things have been? There cannot be but misunderstanding, through the avoiding to do that that occurs to every man's reason. If there were an intention of settlement you would have settled upon this basis to have altered or allayed. Ye had the free exercise of a legislative power to have offered your judgment and opinion when you had pleased. But this hath not been done, it hath not. But what hath been done? Truly that that I cannot speak to you of but with shame, and with grief, and with sorrow. God is my witness, I speak it, it is evident to all the world, to all the town, to all the army, people living in the world, that a new business hath been seeking in the room of this, this actual settlement, settlement by your consent; and in this I do not speak to those gentlemen or lords, or whatever you will call them, I say not this to them, but I say it to you. You advised me to be where I am in this place, you, you did, for these persons were not in this capacity; but by you I am in this capacity and they are in this capacity, and yet instead of taken for agreed——. It was a stated business, the nation had time to look round about them. But if you must have and must have we know not what, you not only have disquieted yourselves, but the whole nation is disquieted; and give me leave to tell you what I think, running more in arrear of satisfaction, a likelihood of running into confusion in fifteen or sixteen days than really they have done from your last rising to this day, which was about the 26th of June and through these inventions of, really, designing a Commonwealth that some tribune of the people might be the man that might rule all. This hath been the business really. I am sorry to say it, but I think the meanest people that go about the streets take notice of it. This is the business; but is this all? They have engaged, or persuaded others to engage to carry that thing on; and hath that man been true to this nation, whosoever he be, that hath dared, especially if he hath taken an oath, thus to prevaricate? I tell you, you will not think us altogether asleep. We have known these things have been designed. We have known attempts have been made in the Army to seduce them, and almost the greatest confidence hath been in the Army to break us and divide us. I speak it in the presence of some of the Army, and I must tell you those things they have not been according to God nor according to truth, they have not. I do deal faithfully with you whilst I have seen the tendency of those things to be nothing else, pretend what you will, but the playing of the King of Scots his game, if I may so say, by beginning tumults and disturbances amongst us. I think myself bound as before God to do what I can to prevent it, that they go no further. I tell you, nay I thought it my duty in conscience to tell you what I told you at the last meeting in the Banqueting-House, when both the Houses met me there, I did tell you and I told you truly, and that which, God is my witness, is more confirmed to me since, more confirmed to me within a day or two than I knew of then, that the King of Scots hath an army at the waterside, drawn down towards the waterside, ready to be shipped for England. I tell you that I know this from their own mouths and from eye-witnesses of it, and that they are in a very great preparation to attempt upon us. And whilst that is doing, endeavours from some not far from this place to stir up the people of this town into tumulting, what if I said rebellion, and I hope I shall make it appear to be no better, if God assist me. It is not only that, but endeavours hath been to pervert the Army whilst you have been sitting, yea, and to draw the Army to the state of a question, a Commonwealth, a Commonwealth. If we have an enemy from the other side of the water ready to invade us, if we have men listing persons under Charles Stuart's commission, to cavalier, to join with any insurrection that may be here, and our Army endeavoured to be perverted, I beseech you all of you to judge with what hope, or comfort, or possibility of reason indeed, can it be expected that we must not presently run into blood and confusion.

And if this be so, and that I assign it to this cause, that which I do heartily and assuredly, even to the not assenting to that that you did invite me to, that Advice which might be the settling of the nation and might usher in any further advantages that might be for the public good of these nations; if I see this be the effect of your sitting under those carriages, I think it high time that an end be put to your sitting. And I do declare to you here, that I do dissolve this parliament. Let God judge between you and me.'

25.

6 February 1657/8 – Speech in the Banqueting-House at Whitehall to the Officers of the Army

To quieten the army the Protector called a meeting of a couple of hundred officers, making a long speech running over developments, especially his own role, since the early years of Charles I. Although some resignations and dismissals followed, he was assured of a general readiness 'to live and die with my Lord Protector'. This speech survives in a summary reported version only.

'Gentlemen, we have gone along together, and why we should now differ I know not. Let me now entreat you to deal plainly and freely with me, that if any of you cannot in conscience conform to the now Government, let him speak, for now it hath pleased God to put me in a capacity to protect you and I will protect you. And he drank to them, and many bottles of wine were then drunk but no reply made. There was one readable passage, that I omitted in his Highness' speech, that he did not doubt but it would be made out that some, if not some here present, have been tampering with the Army and the City, which if it shall be made to appear, he made no question but it was treason.'

26.

Summoned to Whitehall, the Lord Mayor and Aldermen of the City heard a two-hour speech in which the Protector set out dangers confronting his government, the nation generally, and themselves – notably a likely royalist invasion. The citizens are reported to have listened with cheerfulness and responded positively, presenting the Protector on 17 March with a loyal address, followed by a reorganization of their militia and defences. This speech survives in a summary reported version only.

The Lord Mayor, the Aldermen, and the Common Council of the City being come in a full number to attend his Highness at Whitehall on Friday, March the twelfth, they found there many of the commanders and officers of the Army, who were all admitted to his Highness's presence, who in a large speech did represent unto them the great deliverances which God hath vouchsafed to this nation, during the whole course and progress of the late wars, from the violence of their implacable enemies, and their combinations both public and domestic.

He represented unto them how eminently God had owned and prospered him in the great work in which he stood interested for the establishment of righteousness and peace. And at this present he could not but declare unto them the imminent danger in which both the City and the whole nation was like to be involved by reason of the contrivances of Charles Stuart and his party both at home and abroad, who secretly have used the utmost of their endeavours to embroil the nation and this City, the principal place at which they aim, in a new war, which suddenly would appear as soon as ever their intended invasion should take effect.

To make the truth of this discovery more apparent, his Highness insisted that he knew it to be true, and not only by letters of his and the City's adversaries which were intercepted, but by certain intelligence from several other hands beyond the seas of their proceedings, as also by information from the mouths of such persons who had promised to engage themselves to comply and act with them. And to make this yet more manifest, he informed that the Lord of Ormond,—whom by his own party is now called the Duke of Ormond,—had been in person in this city for three weeks together, being come out of Flanders on purpose to draw all unto him that possibly he could by encouraging and engaging them to forsake all other interests to adhere unto the cause of his master; his Highness did also acquaint them that he having used his uttermost endeavours to promote the cause for which he came, he departed privately from London on Tuesday, March the ninth.

But what was above all, he declared that in order to this invasion Charles Stuart was waiting in Flanders, having got together an army of about eight thousand horse and foot, whom he had quartered in several commodious places near unto the sea-side, as Bruges, Brussels, Ostend and other places; and that withal he had contracted for two and twenty ships, who were in readiness to transport his army, and only waited for the opportunity of some dark night to slip by the English fleet, when the mist had covered the face of the sea; and in being ships of no great burden, he represented that the ships of the enemy had some advantage over our ships, who were of a great burden and drawing much water and therefore not able to ride upon the Flats.

He concluded, that seeing the danger was so apparent and so near at hand, and that the safety and the peace of the city and the whole nation was highly concerned in it, he desired the City to be sensible of it, and laid open to them how deeply it concerned them to provide for their own security and the security of the whole nation. He therefore recommended to the Lord Mayor and Aldermen, and Common Council of the City, there assembled, the settling of their Militia, and that it might be established in the hands of faithful and pious men and such as were well affected to the present government, and such as are free from all discontent and faction; to put the City into a posture of defence that they may be ready to suppress all tumults and insurrections designed by the enemy against the peace and safety of the City.

This and much more to this effect his Highness represented as to the transaction of the affairs of State from the beginning of the wars unto this present, and the happy propagation of the gospel in these three nations.

The citizens departed with great cheerfulness and satisfaction . . . &c.

Oliver Cromwell died on 3 September 1658, the anniversary of his victories at Dunbar and Worcester. Distressed by family bereavements, he had been ailing for some time and rapidly ageing. Though there was great news from the Continent – notably victory in the Battle of the Dunes in June and the acquisition of Dunkirk – at home it was a period of oppression and depression, with rumours of plots and preventative arrests. Royalists (and others) expected the régime to collapse at his death. It did not. Nominated by him, his eldest son Richard succeeded quietly as Protector. Oliver had made more advances towards a settlement than might be supposed. Stuart Restoration was not inevitable. But less than two years later Charles II was back in England to apparent universal approval. Monarchy it seemed was once again – as to some it had seemed in 1657 – the best policy, this time best in the old line.

Conversations

In Committee, Whitehall, 24 June 1650

The Scots took amiss the abolition of the Stuart monarchy. In February 1648/9 the Prince of Wales was proclaimed King of Scotland on the understanding that he would take the National Covenant confirming presbyterianism. Commissioners were sent to treat with him in exile in Breda. By June 1650 Charles had cynically accepted and arrived in his northern kingdom intending to use the experienced Scots army to work his way back to England. To head off that possibility, the Rump's Council of State decided on a preventative invasion. The Commander-in-Chief, Thomas, Lord Fairfax, already unhappy about political developments, found his conscience too scrupulous to take that drastic step. Cromwell, who had returned from Ireland, and a Rump delegation attempted but failed to change his mind. The discussion like others here is recorded, probably authentically, by Bulstrode Whitelocke.

Cromwell. 'My Lord General, we are commanded by the Council of State to confer with your Excellency touching the present design (whereof you have heard some debate in the Council) of marching the army under your command into Scotland, and because there seemed to be some hesitation in yourself as to that journey, this committee were appointed to endeavour to give your Excellency satisfaction in any doubts of yours which may arise concerning that affair, and the grounds of that resolution of the Council for the journey into Scotland.'

Lord General. 'I am very glad of the opportunity of conferring with this committee, where I find so many of my particular friends, as well as of the Commonwealth, about this great business of our march into Scotland; wherein I do acknowledge myself not fully satisfied as to the grounds and justice of our invasion upon our brethren of Scotland, and I shall be glad to receive satisfaction therein by you.'

Lambert, Harrison, St John and Whitelocke each in turn asked Fairfax to indicate in detail his objections to the expedition.

Lord General. 'My Lords, you will give me leave then with all freeness to say to you that I think it doubtful whether we have a just cause to make an invasion upon Scotland. With them we are joined in the national League and Covenant; and now for us contrary thereunto, and without sufficient cause given us by them, to enter into their country with an army and to make war upon them, is that which I cannot see the justice of, nor how we shall be able to justify the lawfulness of it before God or Man.'

Cromwell. 'I confess (my Lord) that if they have given us no cause to invade them, it will not be justifiable for us to do it; and to make war upon them without a sufficient ground for it, will be contrary to that which in conscience we ought to do, and displeasing both to God and good men. But (my Lord) if they have invaded us, as your Lordship knows they have done, since the national Covenant, and contrary to it in that action of Duke Hamilton, which was by order and authority from the Parliament of that Kingdom, and so the act of the whole nation by their representatives. `And if they now give us too much cause of suspicion that they intend another invasion upon, joining with their king with whom they have made a full agreement, without the assent or privity of this Commonwealth, and are very busy at this present in raising forces and money to carry on their design.

If these things are not a sufficient ground and cause for us to endeavour to provide for the safety of our own country, and to prevent the miseries which an invasion of the Scots would bring upon us, I humbly submit it to your Excellency's judgment.

That they have formerly invaded us and brought a war into the bowels of our country, is known to all, wherein God was pleased to bless us with success against them and that they now intend a new invasion upon us I do as really believe, and have as good intelligence of it, as we can have of anything that is not yet acted.

Therefore I say (my Lord) that upon these grounds I think we have a most just cause to begin, or rather to return and requite their hostility first begun upon us, and thereby to free our country (if God shall be pleased to assist us, and I doubt not but He will) from the great misery and calamity of having an army of Scots within our country. That there will be war between us, I fear, is unavoidable. Your Excellency will soon determine whether it be better to have this war in the bowels of another country or of our own, and that it will be one of them, I think it without scruple.'

Lord General. 'It is probable there will be war between us, but whether we should begin this war and be on the offensive part, or only stand upon our own defence is that which I scruple. And although they invaded us under Duke Hamilton, who pretended the authority of the Parliament then sitting for it, yet their succeeding Parliament disowned that engagement, and punished some of the promoters of it.'. . .

St John. 'But (my Lord) that League and Covenant was first broken by themselves, and so dissolved as to us, and the disowning of Duke Hamilton's action by their latter Parliament cannot acquit the injury done to us before.'

Cromwell. 'I suppose your Excellency will be convinced of this clear truth, that we are no longer obliged by the League and Covenant which themselves did first break.'

Lord General. 'I am to answer only for my own conscience, and what that yields unto as just and lawful, I shall follow; and what seems to me or what I doubt to be otherwise I must not do.'

[Whitelocke put it that the known preparations for war being made in Scotland could only be directed against England.]

Lord General. 'I can but say as I said before, that everyone must stand or fall by his own conscience, those who are satisfied of the justice of this war, may cheerfully proceed in it, those who scruple it (as I confess I do) cannot undertake any service in it. I acknowledge that which hath been said to carry much weight and reason with it, and none can have more power upon me than this committee, nor none be more ready to serve the Parliament than myself in any one thing wherein my conscience shall be satisfied; in this it is not, and therefore that I may be no hinderance to the Parliament's designs, I shall willingly lay down my commission, that it may be in their hands to choose some worthier person than myself, and who may upon clear satisfaction of his conscience undertake this business, wherein I desire to be excused.'

Cromwell. 'I am very sorry your Lordship should have thought of laying down your commission, by which God hath blest you in the performance of so many eminent services for the Parliament. I pray, my Lord, consider all your faithful servants, us who are officers, who have served under you, and desire to serve under no other General. It would be a great discouragement to all of us, and a great discouragement to the affairs of the Parliament for our noble General to entertain any thoughts of laying down his commission. I hope your Lordship will never give so great an advantage to the public enemy, nor so much dishearten your friends as to think of laying down your commission.'

[Although the discussion went on for a good while longer, Fairfax was adamant in his decision.]

2.

Conversation with Ludlow, June 1650

On Fairfax's resignation, the Rump appointed Cromwell 'captain general and commander-in-chief'. Preparations went ahead for 'the marching of the army up to Scotland'. Cromwell, mindful of problems remaining in Ireland and anxious to improve a relationship with Edmund Ludlow lately gone sour, sounded him out about helping to achieve a settlement there. Ludlow's report of the conversation was written much later when he had turned utterly against 'the usurper'. At the time he accepted command of the Horse in Ireland while Cromwell went on to reduce Scotland to obedience at Dunbar (3 September 1650) and Worcester (3 September 1651), enhancing his own position of political indispensability.

Parliament voted Lieutenant-General Cromwell to be Captain-General of all their land forces, ordering a commission forthwith to be drawn up to that effect, and referred to the Council of State to hasten the preparations for the northern expedition. A little after, as I sat in the house near General Cromwell, he told me, that having observed an alteration in my looks and carriage towards him, he apprehended that I had entertained some suspicions of him; and that being persuaded of the tendency of the designs of us both to the advancement of the public service, he desired that a meeting might be appointed, wherein we might with freedom discover the grounds of our mistakes and misapprehensions, and create a good understanding between us for the future. I answered that he had discovered in me what I had never perceived in myself; and that if I troubled him not so frequently as formerly, it was either because I was conscious of that weight of business that lay upon him or that I had nothing to importune him withal upon my own or any other account; yet since he was pleased to do me the honour to desire a free conversation with me, I assured him of my readiness therein.

Whereupon we resolved to meet that afternoon in the Council of State, and from thence to withdraw to a private room, which we did accordingly in the Queen's guard-chamber, where he endeavoured to persuade me of the necessity incumbent upon him to do several things that appeared extraordinary in the judgment of some men, who in opposition to him took such courses as would bring ruin upon themselves, as well as him and the public cause, affirming his intentions to be directed entirely to the good of the people, and professing his readiness to sacrifice his life in their service.

I freely acknowledged my former dissatisfaction with him and the rest of the army, when they were in treaty with the King, whom I looked upon as the only obstruction to the settlement of the nation; and with their actions at the rendezvous at Ware, where they shot a soldier to death, and imprisoned divers others upon the account of that treaty, which I conceived to have been done without authority, and for sinister ends: yet since they had manifested themselves convinced of those errors, and declared their adherence to the Commonwealth, though too partial a hand was carried both by the Parliament and themselves in the distribution of preferments and gratuities, and too much severity exercised against some who had formerly been their friends, and as I hoped would be so still, with other things that I could not entirely approve, I was contented patiently to wait for the accomplishment of those good things which I expected, till they had overcome the difficulties they now laboured under, and suppressed their enemies that appeared both at home and abroad against them; hoping that then their principles and interest would lead them to do what was most agreeable to the constitution of a Commonwealth, and the good of mankind.

He owned my dissatisfaction with the army whilst they were in treaty with the King, to be founded upon good reasons, and excused the execution done upon the soldier at the rendezvous, as absolutely necessary to keep things from falling into confusion; which must have ensued upon that division, if it had not been timely prevented. He professed to desire nothing more than that the government of the nation might be settled in a free and equal Commonwealth, acknowledging that there was no other probable means to keep out the old family and government from returning upon us; declaring, that he looked upon the design of the Lord in this day to be the freeing of His people from every burden, and that He was now accomplishing what was prophesied in the 110th Psalm; from the consideration of which he was often encouraged to attend the affecting those ends, spending at least an hour in the exposition of that Psalm, adding to this, that it was his intention to contribute the utmost of his endeavours to make a thorough reformation of the Clergy and Law; but, said he, 'the sons of Zeruiah are yet too strong for us'; and we cannot mention the reformation of the law, but they presently cry out, we design to destroy property: whereas the law, as it is now constituted, serves only to maintain the lawyers, and to encourage the rich to oppress the poor; affirming that Mr Coke, then Justice in Ireland, by proceeding in a summary and expeditious way, determined more causes in a week, than Westminster-Hall in a year; saying farther, that Ireland was as a clean paper in that particular, and capable of being governed by such laws as should be found most agreeable to justice; which may be so impartially administered, as to be a good precedent even to England itself; where when they once perceive property preserved at an easy and cheap rate in Ireland, they will never permit themselves to be so cheated and abused as now they are. At last he fell into the consideration of the military government of Ireland, complaining that the whole weight of it lay upon Major-General Ireton; and that if he should by death or any other accident be removed from that station, the conduct of that part would probably fall into the hands of such men as either by principle or interest were not proper for that trust, and of whom he had no certain assurance. He therefore proposed that some person of reputation and known fidelity might be sent over to command the horse there, and to assist the Major-General in the service of the public, that employment being next in order to his own, desiring me to propose one whom I thought sufficiently qualified for that station.

3.

Conference at Lenthall's House, September 1651

The victory at Worcester (3 September 1651) was for Cromwell 'the crowning mercy' which, ensuring the Commonwealth's control over the whole of the British Isles, argued for moves towards 'a settlement of the nation', an essential feature of which would be a new representative, something for which there had been pressure from within the army since 1647. He requested 'a meeting of divers MPs and some chief officers at the Speaker's house'. Those present included Speaker Lenthall, Bulstrode Whitelocke, Chief Justice Oliver St John, and Generals Whalley, Fleetwood and Harrison, to whom Cromwell put the question, 'What was fit to be done and to be presented to Parliament?'

Speaker. 'My Lord, this company were very ready to attend your Excellence, and the business you are pleased to propound to us is very necessary to be considered. God hath given marvellous success to our forces under your command; and if we do not improve these mercies to some settlement, such as may be to God's honour, and the good of this Commonwealth, we shall be very much blameworthy.'

Harrison. 'I think that which my Lord General hath propounded is to advise as to a settlement both of our civil and spiritual liberties; and so that the mercies which the Lord hath given into us may not be cast away. How this may be done is the great question.'

Whitelocke. 'It is a great question indeed, and not suddenly to be resolved. Yet it were pity that a meeting of so many able and worthy persons as I see here, should be fruitless. I should humbly offer, in the first place, whether it be not requisite to be understood in what way this settlement is desired, whether of an absolute republic, or with any mixture of monarchy?'

Cromwell. 'My Lord Commissioner Whitelocke hath put us upon the right point: and indeed it is my meaning, that we should consider, whether a Republic, or a mixed monarchical government will be best to be settled? And if anything monarchical, then, in whom that power shall be placed?'

Sir Thomas Widdrington. 'I think a mixed monarchical government will be most suitable to the laws and people of this nation. And if any monarchical, I suppose we shall hold it most just to place that power in one of the sons of the late king.'

Colonel Fleetwood. 'I think that the question, whether an absolute republic, or a mixed monarchy, be best to be settled in this nation, will not be very easy to be determined!'

Lord Chief-Justice St John. 'It will be found that the government of this nation, without something of monarchical power, will be very difficult to be so settled as not to shake the foundation of our laws, and the liberties of the People.'

Speaker. 'It will breed a strange confusion to settle a government of this nation without something of monarchy.'

Colonel Desborow. 'I beseech you, my Lord, why may not this, as well as other nations, be governed in the way of a republic?'

Whitelocke. 'The laws of England are so interwoven with the power and practice of monarchy, that to settle a government without something of monarchy in it, would make so great an alteration in the proceedings of our law, that you have scarce time to rectify nor can we well foresee the inconveniences which will arise thereby.'

Colonel Whalley. 'I do not well understand matters of law: but it seems to me the best way, not to have anything of monarchical power in the settlement of our government. And if we should resolve upon any, whom have we to pitch upon? The king's eldest son hath been in arms against us, and his second son likewise is our enemy.'

Sir Thomas Widdrington. 'But the late king's third son, the duke of Gloucester, is still among us; and too young to have been in arms against us, or infected with the principles of our enemies.'

Whitelocke. 'There may be a day given for the king's eldest son, or for the duke of York his brother, to come in to the

Parliament. And upon such terms as shall be thought fit, and agreeable both to our civil and spiritual liberties, a settlement may be made with them.'

Cromwell. 'That will be a business of more than ordinary difficulty! But really I think, if it may be done with safety, and preservation of our rights, both as Englishmen and as Christians, that a settlement with somewhat of monarchical power in it would be very effectual.'

Whitelocke reports that the discussion continued with other participants making differing observations but that the military men were 'generally . . . against anything of monarchy' while the lawyers were for 'a mixed monarchical government and many were for the Duke of Gloucester to be made king'.

4.

Conversation with Whitelocke, November 1652

Whitelocke reports a conversation at a chance meeting with Cromwell in St James's Park during which the Lord General revealed with some frankness his doubts about the will and capacity of the Rump to achieve an acceptable settlement, and how his mind was working towards clarifying the role that he might himself play in determining developments. There is no inde-pendent confirmation of this record but it has a ring of truth.

It was about this time that the Lord General Cromwell, meeting with me in a fair evening walking in St James's Park . . . saluted me with more than ordinary courtesy, and desired me to walk aside with him, that we might have some private discourse together. I waited on him and he began the discourse betwixt us to this effect:

Cromwell. 'My Lord Whitelocke, I know your faithfulness and engagement in the same good cause with myself and the rest of our friends, and I know your ability and judgment, and your particular friendship and affection for me; indeed I am sufficiently satisfied in these things, and therefore I desire to advise with you in the main and most important affairs relating to our present condition.'

Whitelocke. 'Your Excellency hath known me long, and I think will say that you never knew any unfaithfulness or breach of trust by me; and for my particular affection to your person, your favours to me, and your public services, have deserved more than I can manifest; only there is, with your favour, a mistake in this one thing, touching my weak judgment, which is uncapable to do any considerable service for yourself or this Commonwealth; yet, to the utmost of my power, I shall be ready to serve you, and that with all diligence and faithfulness.'

Cromwell. 'I have cause to be, and am, without the least scruple of your faithfulness, and I know your kindness to me your old friend, and your abilities to serve the Commonwealth, and there are enough besides me that can testify it: And I believe our engagements for this Commonwealth have been, and are, as deep as most men's; and there never was more need of advice, and solid hearty counsel, than the present state of our affairs doth require.'

Whitelocke. 'I suppose no man will mention his particular engagement in this cause, at the same time when your Excellency's engagement is remembered; yet to my capacity, and in my station, few men have engaged further than I have done; and that (besides the goodness of your own nature and personal knowledge of me) will keep you from any jealousy of my faithfulness.'

Cromwell. 'I wish there were no more ground of suspicion of others, than of you. I can trust you with my life, and the most secret matters relating to our business; and to that end I have now desired a little private discourse with you; and really, my Lord, there is very great cause for us to consider the dangerous condition we are all in, and how to make good our station, to improve the mercies and successes which God hath given us; and not to be fooled out of them again, nor to be broken in pieces, by our particular jarrings and animosities one against another; but to unite our counsels, and hands and hearts, to make good what we have so dearly bought, with so much hazard, blood, and treasure; and that, the Lord having given us an entire conquest over our enemies, we should not now hazard all again by our private janglings, and bring those mischiefs upon ourselves, which our enemies could never do.'

Whitelocke. 'My Lord, I look upon our present danger as greater than ever it was in the field, and (as your Excellency truly observes) our proneness to destroy ourselves, when our enemies could not do it. It is no strange thing for a gallant army, as yours is, after full conquest of their enemies, to grow into factions and ambitious designs; and it is a wonder to me that they are not in high mutinies, their spirits being active, and few thinking their services to be duly rewarded, and the emulation of the officers breaking out daily more and more, in this time of their vacancy from their employment; besides, the private soldiers, it may be feared, will, in this time of their idleness, grow into disorder; and it is your excellent conduct which, under God, hath kept them so long in discipline, and free from mutinies.'

Cromwell. 'I have used, and shall use, the utmost of my poor endeavours to keep them all in order and obedience.'

Whitelocke. 'Your Excellency hath done it hitherto even to admiration.'

Cromwell. 'Truly God hath blessed me in it exceedingly, and I hope will do so still. Your Lordship hath observed most truly the inclinations of the officers of the army to particular factions, and to murmurings that they are not rewarded according to their deserts; that others, who have adventured least, have gained most; and they have neither profit, nor preferment, nor place in government, which others hold, who have undergone no hardships nor hazards for the Commonwealth; and herein they have too much of truth, yet their insolency is very great, and their influence upon the private soldiers works them to the like discontents and murmurings.

Then as for the Members of Parliament, the army begins to have a strange distaste against them, and I wish there were not too much cause for it; and really their pride, and ambition, and self-seeking, ingrossing all places of honour and profit to themselves and their friends, and their daily breaking forth into new and violent parties and factions; their delays of business, and designs to perpetuate themselves, and to continue the power in their own hands; their meddling in private matters between party and party, contrary to the institution of parliaments, and their injustice and partiality in those matters, and the scandalous lives of some of the chief of them; these things, my Lord, do give too much ground for people to open their mouths against them, and to dislike them. Nor can they be kept within the bounds of justice, law, or reason; they themselves being the supreme power of the nation, liable to no account to any, nor to be controlled or regulated by any other power, there being none superior, or co-ordinate with them. So that, unless there be some authority, and power so full and so high as to restrain and keep things in better order, and that may be a check to these exorbitancies, it will be impossible, in human reason to prevent our ruin.'

Whitelocke. 'I confess the danger we are in by these extravagances and inordinate powers is more than I doubt is generally apprehended; yet as to that part of it which concerns the Soldiery, your Excellency's power and commission is sufficient already to restrain and keep them in their due obedience; and, blessed be God, you have done it hitherto, and I doubt not but, by your wisdom, you will be able still to do it.

As to the Members of Parliament, I confess the greatest difficulty lies there; your commission being from them, and they being acknowledged the supreme power of the nation, subject to no controls, nor allowing any appeal from them. Yet I am sure your Excellency will not look upon them as generally depraved; too many of them are much to blame in those things you have mentioned, and many unfit things have passed among them; but I hope well of the major part of them, when great matters come to a decision.'

Cromwell. 'My Lord, there is little hopes of a good settlement to be made by them, really there is not; but a great deal of fear, that they will destroy again what the Lord hath done graciously for them and us; we all forget God, and God will forget us, and give us up to confusion; and these men will help it on, if they be suffered to proceed in their ways; some course must be thought on to curb and restrain them, or we shall be ruined by them.'

Whitelocke. 'We ourselves have acknowledged them the supreme power, and taken our commissions and authority in the highest concernments from them; and how to restrain and curb them after this, it will be hard to find out a way for it.'

Cromwell. 'What if a man should take upon him to be king?'

Whitelocke. 'I think that remedy would be worse than the disease.'

Cromwell. 'Why do you think so?'

Whitelocke. 'As to your own person the title of king would be of no advantage, because you have the full kingly power in you already, concerning the militia, as you are General. As to the nomination of civil officers, those whom you think fittest are seldom refused; and although you have no negative vote in the passing of laws, yet what you dislike will not easily be carried; and the taxes are already settled, and in your power to dispose the money raised. And as to foreign affairs, though the ceremonial application be made to the parliament, yet the expectation of good or bad success in it is from your Excellency; and particular solicitations of foreign ministers are made to you only. So that I apprehend, indeed, less envy and danger, and pomp, but not less power, and real opportunities of doing good in your being General than would be if you had assumed the title of king.'

Cromwell. 'I have heard some of your profession observe, that he who is actually king, all acts done by him as king are as lawful and justifiable as by any king who hath the crown by inheritance from his forefathers; and that by an act of parliament in Henry the Seventh's time it is safer for those who act under a king, be his title what it will, than for those who act under any other power. And surely the power of a king is so great and high, and so universally understood and reverenced by the people of this nation, that the title of it might not only indemnify, in a great measure, those that act under it, but likewise be of great use and advantage in such times as these, to curb the insolences of those whom the present powers cannot control, or at least are the persons themselves who are thus insolent.'

Whitelocke. 'I agree in general with what you are pleased to observe as to this title of king; but whether for your Excellency to take this title upon you as things now are, will be for the good and advantage either of yourself and friends, or of the commonwealth, I do very much doubt; notwithstanding that act of parliament, II Hen. VII which will be little regarded, or observed to us by our enemies, if they should come to get the upper hand of us.'

Cromwell. 'What do you apprehend would be the danger of taking this title?'

Whitelocke. 'The danger, I think, would be this: one of the main points of controversy betwixt us and our adversaries is whether the Government of this Nation shall be established in monarchy or in a Free State or Commonwealth; and most of our friends have engaged with us upon the hopes of having the government settled in a Free State, and to effect that have undergone all their hazards and difficulties, they being persuaded, though I think much mistaken, that under the government of a Commonwealth they shall enjoy more liberty and right, both as to their spiritual and civil concernments, than they shall under monarchy; the pressures and dislike whereof are so fresh in their memories and sufferings.

Now if your Excellency should take upon you the title of king, this state of your cause will be thereby wholly determined, and monarchy established in your person; and the question will be no more whether our government shall be by a monarch, or by a Free State, but whether Cromwell or Stuart shall be our king and monarch.

And that question, wherein before so great parties of the nation were engaged, and which was universal, will by this means become, in effect, a private controversy only. Before it was national, what kind of government we should have, now it will become particular, who shall be our governor, whether of the family of the Stuarts, or of the family of the Cromwells?

Thus the state of our controversy being totally changed, all those who were for a Commonwealth (and they are a very great and considerable party) having their hopes therein frustrated, will desert you; your hands will be weakened, your interest straitened and your cause in apparent danger to be ruined.'

Cromwell. 'I confess you speak reason in this; but what other thing can you propound that may obviate the present dangers and difficulties wherein we are all engaged.'

Whitelocke. 'It will be the greatest difficulty to find out such an expedient. I have had many things in my private thoughts upon this business, some which perhaps are not fit, or safe, for me to communicate.'

Cromwell. 'I pray, my Lord, what are they? You may trust me with them; there shall no prejudice come to you by any private discourse betwixt us; I shall never betray my friend; you may be as free with me as with your own heart, and shall never suffer by it.'

Whitelocke. 'I make no scruple to put my life and fortune into your Excellency's hand; and so I shall, if I impart these fancies to you, which are weak, and perhaps may prove offensive to your Excellency; therefore my best way will be to smother them.'

Cromwell. 'Nay, I prithee, my Lord Whitelocke, let me know them; be they what they will they cannot be offensive to me, but I shall take it kindly from you: therefore, I pray, do not conceal those thoughts of yours from your faithful friend.'

Whitelocke. 'Your Excellency honours me with a title far above me; and since you are pleased to command it, I shall discover to you my thoughts herein; and humbly desire you not to take in ill part what I shall say to you.'

Cromwell. 'Indeed I shall not; but I shall take it, as I said, very kindly from you.'

Whitelocke. 'Give me leave then, first, to consider your Excellency's condition. You are environed with secret enemies. Upon your subduing of the public enemy, the officers of your army account themselves all victors, and to have had an equal share in the conquest with you.

The success which God hath given us hath not a little elated their minds; and many of them are busy and of turbulent spirits, and are not without their designs how they may dismount your Excellency, and some of themselves get up into the saddle; how they may bring you down, and set up themselves.

They want not counsel and encouragement herein; it may be from some Members of the Parliament, who may be jealous of your power and greatness, lest you should grow too high for them, and in time overmaster them; and they will plot to bring you down first, or to clip your wings.'

Cromwell. 'I thank you that you so fully consider my condition; it is a testimony of your love to me, and care of me, and you have rightly considered it; and I may say without vanity, that in my condition yours is involved and all our friends; and those that plot my ruin will hardly bear your continuance in any condition worthy of you. Besides this, the cause itself may possibly receive some disadvantage by the strugglings and contentions among ourselves. But what, Sir, are your thoughts for prevention of those mischiefs that hang over our heads?'

Whitelocke. 'Pardon me, Sir, in the next place, a little to consider the condition of the King of Scots.

This prince being now by your valour, and the success which God hath given to the Parliament, and to the army under your command, reduced to a very low condition; both he and all about him cannot but be very inclineable to hearken to any terms, whereby their lost hopes may be revived of his being restored to the crown, and they to their fortunes and native country.

By a private treaty with him you may secure yourself, and your friends and their fortunes; you may make yourself and your posterity as great and permanent, to all human probability, as ever any subject was, and provide for your friends. You may put such limits to monarchical power, as will secure our spiritual and civil liberties, and you may secure the cause in which we are all engaged; and this may be effectually done, by having the power of the militia continued in yourself, and whom you shall agree upon after you.

I propound, therefore, for your Excellency to send to the King of Scots, and to have a private treaty with him for this purpose; and I beseech you to pardon what I have said upon the occasion. It is out of my affection and service to your Excellency, and to all honest men; and I humbly pray you not to have any jealousy thereupon of my approved faithfulness to your Excellency and to this Commonwealth.'

Cromwell. 'I have not, I assure you, the least distrust of your faithfulness and friendship to me, and to the cause of this Commonwealth; and I think you have much reason for what you propound; but it is a matter of so high importance and difficulty, that it deserves more time of consideration and debate than is at present allowed us. We shall therefore take a further time to discourse of it.'

With this the General brake off, and went to other company, and so into Whitehall; seeming, by his countenance and carriage, displeased with what had been said; yet he never objected it against me [Whitelocke] in any public meeting afterwards. Only his carriage towards me, from that time, was altered, and his advising with me not so frequent and intimate as before; and it was not long after that he found an occasion by honourable employment, to send me out of the way.

5.

Conversation with Whitelocke, 5 September 1653

The Long Parliament in its last months decided to send an embassy to the major Baltic Protestant power, Sweden, then ruled by Queen Christina. Their first nominee, confirmed by the Nominated Assembly, begged off. Others who were approached showed equal reluctance to go on an expedition that might well be as dangerous as it was fruitless. Royalists had assassinated other envoys. By late summer 1653 the matter, which had political, religious and economic implications, was urgent and a determined effort was made to get Bulstrode Whitelocke to go. On 5 September he was taken to see the Lord General Cromwell.

Whitelocke. 'My lord, I received your excellent letter but yesterday, and am now come to wait upon you to return my humble thanks for the great honour done me, in being judged worthy of so high a trust; but I beg your Excellency's consideration of my want of abilities, both of body and mind for this service, and the season of the year; besides, there are some things relating to my private family, wherewith I have acquainted Sir Gilbert Pickering, which are of no small concernment to me.'

Pickering. 'That is, my lord, that his lady is near her time of being brought to bed.'

Whitelocke. 'My lord, I am very free to serve the Commonwealth in anything within my capacity; and hope they will not expect from me what will be so great prejudice to me and my family, as this employment now would be.'

Cromwell. 'I am very sorry that the letter came no sooner to you.'

Pickering 'I confess it was my fault.'

Cromwell. 'Sir Gilbert Pickering would needs write a very fine letter; and when he had done it, did not like it himself. I then took pen and ink and straightway wrote that letter to you. And the business is of exceeding great importance to the Commonwealth, as any can be; that it is: and there is no prince or state in Christendom, with whom there is any probability for us to have a friendship, but only the queen of Sweden. She hath sent several times to us, but we have returned no embassy to her, only a letter by a young gentleman; she expects an ambassador from us, and if we should not send a man of eminency to her she would think herself slighted by us: and she is a lady of great honour, and stands much upon ceremonies.'

Whitelocke. 'The business being of so great concernment (as indeed it is) there is the more need of a person qualified with abilities for so great a charge which I have not, as your Excellency and all that know me will conclude; and I know best my own defects. I want experience in foreign affairs, and matters of state; in language and ceremony, of which the queen is so great a judge, and a lady that will soon discern my disabilities, and make advantage thereof; nor will she look upon me, as a person of eminency fit to be sent to her. So that (with submission to the judgment of your Excellency and the Council) I must conclude myself altogether unfit for this very weighty and high employment, whereof divers others in the nation are far more capable than I am.'

Cromwell. 'The Council have pitched upon you unanimously, as the fittest man in the nation for this service; we know your abilities, having long conversed with you; we know you have languages, and have travelled, and understand the interest of Christendom; and I have known you in the army, to endure hardships, and to be healthful and strong, and of mettle, discretion, and parts most fit for this employment: you are so indeed; really, no man is so fit for it as you are. We know you to be a gentleman of a good family, related to persons of honour; and your present office of Commissioner of the Seal will make you the more acceptable to her. I do earnestly desire you to undertake it, wherein you will do an act of great merit, and advantage to the Commonwealth, as great as any one member of it can perform; and which will be as well accepted by them: the business is very honourable, and exceeding likely to have a good success. Her public ministers here have already agreed upon most of the material and main points of the business; if it had not been such an employment, we would not have put you upon it: the business of trade, and of the funds, and touching the Dutch, are such as there cannot be any of greater consequence.'

Whitelocke. 'Your Excellency will pardon me if I cannot

subscribe to your favourable opinion of me; and I should be sorry, that a business of so great concernment should suffer under so weak a management as by my hand: besides, that which Sir Gilbert Pickering is pleased to tell you of my wife's condition, is, to my private comfort, of as high consequence as may be. I would not seem unkind or ungrateful to such a wife; and this time of the year, it is hard for me to be put upon so difficult and dangerous a journey.'

Cromwell. 'I know my lady is a good woman, and a religious woman, and will be contented to suffer a little absence of her husband for the public good; and for the time of year, really the life of the business consists in the dispatch of it at this time; the Dutch are tampering with the queen, but she holds them off, expecting to hear from us.'

Whitelocke. 'I see your Excellency is stayed for. I shall have some occasions into the country; and about a fortnight hence I will wait on you again, and in the meantime, you will give me leave to consider of this.'

Cromwell. 'I pray, my Lord Whitelocke, do not think of so long a time; but let me entreat you to accept of the employment, and to return your answer within a few days to me.'

Whitelocke. 'I shall attend your Excellency.'

6.

Conversation with Whitelocke, 13 September 1653

On 13 September Whitelocke met Cromwell again concerning the embassy to Sweden, but still hung back, pointing to his wife's qualms. He was finally persuaded by Cromwell's flattering importunity.

Whitelocke. 'I was to attend your Excellency, but missed of you.'

Cromwell. 'I knew not of it; you are always welcome to me. I hope you have considered the proposal I made to you, and are willing to serve the Commonwealth.'

Whitelocke. 'I have fully considered it; and with humble thanks acknowledge the honour intended me, and am most willing to serve your Excellency and the Commonwealth; but in this particular I humbly beg your excuse. I have endeavoured to satisfy my own judgment, and my nearest relations, but can do neither; nor gain a consent, and I should be very unworthy and ungrateful to go againt it.'

Cromwell. 'You know that no relations use to sway the balance in such matters as this. I know your lady very well, and that she is a good woman, and a religious woman; indeed I think she is: and I durst undertake, in a matter of this nature, wherein the interest of God and of his people is concerned, as they are in your undertaking of this business, I dare say my lady will not oppose it.'

Whitelocke. 'Truly, sir, I think there is no woman alive desires more the promoting of that interest; but she hopes it may be done as much, if not more, by some other person.'

Cromwell. 'Really I know not in England so fit a person as you are for it.'

Whitelocke. 'Your Excellency cannot but know my want of breeding and experience in matters of this nature, and of language.'

Cromwell. 'I know your education, travail, and language, and experience, have fitted you for it; you know the affairs of Christendom as well as most men, and of England, as well as any man, and can give as good an account of them. I think no man can serve his country more than you may herein; indeed I think so, and therefore I make it my particular suit, and earnest request to you to undertake it: and I hope you will show a little regard to me in it; and I assure you that you shall have no cause to repent it.'

Whitelocke. 'My lord, I am very ready to testify my duty to your Excellency. I acknowledge your many favours to me, and myself an officer under your command, and to owe you obedience. But your Excellency will not expect it from me in that wherein I am not capable to serve you: and, therefore, I make it my most humble suit to be excused from this service.'

Cromwell. 'For your abilities I am satisfied; I know no man so fit for it as yourself; and if you should decline it (as I hope you will not) the Commonwealth would suffer extremely by it, your own profession perhaps might suffer likewise, and the Protestant interest would suffer by it: indeed you cannot be excused, the hearts of all the good people in this nation are set upon it, to have you undertake this service, and if you should waive it, being thus, and at such a time when your going may be the most likely means to settle our business with the Dutch and Danes, and matter of trade, (and none, I say again, can do it better than you); the Commonwealth would be at an extreme prejudice by your refusal. But I hope you will hearken to my request, and let me prevail with you to undertake it: neither you nor yours, I hope, shall ever have any cause to wish you had not done it.'

Whitelocke. 'My lord, when a man is out of sight he is out of mind. Though your Excellency be just and honourable; yet your greater affairs calling you off, those to whom matters of correspondence and supplies must be referred, will perhaps forget one who is afar off, and not be so sensible of extremities in a foreign country as those who suffer under them.'

Cromwell. 'I will engage to take particular care of those matters myself, and that you shall neither want supplies nor anything that is fit for you: you shall be set out with as much honour as ever any ambassador was from England. I shall hold myself particularly obliged to you if you will undertake it; and will stick as close to you as your skin is to your flesh. You shall want nothing either for your honour and equipage, or for power and trust to be reposed in you, or for correspondence and supplies when you are abroad; I promise you, my lord, you shall not. I will make it my business to see it done. The Parliament and Council, as well as myself, will take it very well, and thankfully from you to accept of this employment; and all people, especially the good people of the nation, will be much satisfied with it: and, therefore, my lord, I make it again my earnest request to you to accept this honourable employment.'. . .

Whitelocke. 'I see your Excellency is inexorable for my excuse; and much set upon it, with more than ordinary earnestness, for me to undertake this service, for which, (though I judge myself insufficient) yet your judgment and the Council's is, that I am capable to do some service to the Commonwealth and to the Protestant interest herein, and to the honour of God, which is above all other motives: and hoping that it may be so; and to testify my regard and duty to your Excellency, who have honoured me with your personal request for it, and the Council having unanimously pitched upon me; and to manifest that I am not self-willed, and how much I value your Excellency's commands, and can submit my own to better judgments, I am resolved to lay aside further considerations of wife, children, friends, fortune, and all objections and fear of dangers, and to conform myself to your Excellency's desires, and to the votes of the Council, by accepting this difficult and hazardous employment; and do rest confident of your Excellency's care and favour towards me, who undertake it by your command: and hope that such allowances and supplies will be afforded me, and such memory had of me in my absence as shall be agreeable to the honour of the nation, and of yourself, and the business, as also of your servant.'

Cromwell. 'My lord, I do most heartily thank you for accepting the employment, whereby you have testified a very great respect and favour to me, and affection to the Commonwealth, which will be very well taken by them; and I assure you, that it is so grateful to me, who, upon my particular request have prevailed with you, that I shall never forget this favour, but endeavour to requite it to you and yours; really, my lord, I shall: and I will acquaint the Council with it, that we may desire further conference with you.'

7.

Conversation with Whitelocke, 30 October 1653

On 29 October 1653 Whitelocke was given his instructions for his embassy to Sweden. On the 30th he dined with Cromwell at the Cockpit and entered into the following conversation. He sailed on 6 November.

Whitelocke. 'My lord, I am to take my leave of your Excellency, and probably my last leave; but while God shall afford me life, I assure your Excellency, I shall be diligent and faithful in the trust reposed in me.'

Cromwell. 'My lord, if we had had the least suspicion of your fidelity, you had not been troubled with this employment; but we have had sufficient experience thereof, and of your diligence, and abilities; and I doubt not, but God will bless you, and give you a safe and honourable return to your native country; which I heartily wish, and pray for; indeed I do.'

Whitelock. 'I doubt not of your Excellency's good wishes, upon whose account chiefly I have undertaken this service; and I assure myself of the favour and assistance of your Excellency, in anything that may concern me in my absence; wherein I have two or three humble requests to you.'

Cromwell. 'You shall find me what I have said, a faithful, and affectionate friend to you, both present and absent. I pray, let me knowe, what you would particularly leave to my care, and I promise you, I shall not fail you in anything of concernment to you.'

Whitelocke. 'One of my suits is, that if, in my absence, my wife, or friends, shall have occasion to attend your Excellency on my behalf, that they may have the favour of access to you, and your Excellency's assistance.'

Cromwell. 'They shall, at any time, be welcome to me; and I shall give order for their admittance, and my best furtherance in any matter which shall concern you.'

Whitelocke. 'I humbly thank your Excellency; and do further entreat, that my bills of exchange upon the Council may be answered, and not delayed: your servant's credit will depend upon it, and a failure therein, especially in a foreign country, is a tender thing.'

Cromwell. 'I confess that is a tender point; and you may be confident, you shall not be failed nor delayed therein; our credit would be wounded thereby. I will take particular care for answering your bills speedily; nay, I will say more to you, I know your allowance is but small, I wish it had been more, yet, if I live, I will see that you shall be no looser by this employment; and though your occasions shall require the expense of more than your allowance, I will see that it shall be paid: but I would have you to be as good a husband as you can.'

Whitelocke. 'I shall not spend extravagantly, but the honour of the Commonwealth, and safety of your servant, requiring it; which I doubt my allowance will not answer.'

Cromwell. 'I will see you shall be no looser; but honourably recompensed for your service.'

Whitelocke. 'I most humbly thank your Excellency, and shall depend upon your honour; and further entreat, that a constant intelligence may be given me of your affairs here, whereby I may be enabled to give a full and clear account thereof, and have the more repute abroad by it: and your Excellency knows, that full and frequent intelligence gives life to state affairs, especially foreign.'

Cromwell. 'It is necessary your lordship should have a constant correspondence and intelligence from hence kept with you, and, for that end, your friend, Mr Thurloe, who is an able and careful man, shall not fail you.'

Whitelocke. 'I shall be very glad of his correspondence; and since your Excellency allows me this liberty, give me leave to entreat your opinion in some particulars of my instructions. If I find the queen willing to join with you, for the gaining of the Sound, and against the Dutch and Danes, and that heartily and hopefully; shall I put on that business to the utmost, and are you willing to enter into such a conjunction?'

Cromwell. 'If you find them inclinable to it, put it on as far as you can, and let us hear from you, what you judge best to be done in it. No business can be of greater consequence to us, and our trade, wherein the Dutch will endeavour to over-reach us; and it were good to prevent them, and the Dane, and first to serve our own interest.'

Whitelocke. 'I shall give your Excellency a clear account of it; and I believe it will bring the Dutch to reason as soon as anything; and that your Excellency will not much depend upon them, or the Dane, but where their own interest will be served.'

Cromwell. 'We shall freely leave that, and the whole business, to your care and prudent managing.'

Whitelocke. 'I shall do the utmost in my capacity to serve you; but must expect to have my actions traduced, and scandalized: but I hope your Excellency will give no credit to whisperings, or officious words, or letters of pickthanks behind my back.'

Cromwell. 'I shall not easily give belief to such backbiters, I hate them; and what I shall be informed of your actions abroad will hardly create in me an ill opinion of them, before I be certified from yourself.'

Whitelocke. 'It may be your Excellency will hear, that I am great with some cavaliers when I am abroad, and that I make much of them; and truly that may well be, I love a civility to all, especially to persons of condition, though enemies; and have ever used it, and perhaps may use it more than ordinary when I am abroad; and to those of the king's party, and by them I may be the better enabled to secure myself, and to understand their designs, which will be no disadvantage to your affairs: nor shall I ever betray those, or any persons by whom I am trusted.'

Cromwell. 'I think such a carriage towards them will be prudent, and fit for you to use; and it will never occasion in me, nor I hope in any other sober men, the least jealousy of your faithfulness; but it may much tend to your security, and to the good of your business.'

Whitelocke. 'I have but one thing more to trouble your Excellency with; that is, my humble thanks for all your favours, and, particularly, for the noble present I received from your hand.'

Cromwell. 'I pray, my lord, do not speak of so poor a thing; if there were opportunity for me to do honour to your lordship, I assure you that very few would go before you.'

8.

Conversation with Whitelocke, 6 July 1654

Whitelocke, back in England by 1 July 1654, was invited to see Cromwell at Whitehall. Christina before her abdication (20 May) had sent her felicitations to Cromwell and intimated a hope that her successor, Charles X, would maintain Swedish friendship for England. Whitelocke had evidently done a good job. Sweden continued as an important element in the complex foreign policy of the Protectorate.

Cromwell. 'How have you enjoyed your health in your long journey, both by sea and land; and how could you endure those hardships you were put unto in that barren and cold country?'

Whitelocke. 'Indeed, Sir, I have endured many hardships, for an old crazy carcass as mine is, but God was pleased to show much mercy to me, in my support under them, and vouchsafing me competent health and strength to endure them.'

Cromwell. 'I have heard of your quarters and lodging in straw, and of your diet in your journey: we were not so hardly nor so often put to it in our service in the army.'

Whitelocke. 'Both my company and myself did cheerfully endure all our hardships and wants, being in the service of our God and of our country.'

Cromwell. 'That was also our support in our hardships in the army; and it is the best support; indeed it is; and you found it so in the very great preservations you have had from dangers.'

Whitelocke. 'Your Highness hath had great experience of the goodness of God to you; and the same hand hath appeared wonderfully in the preservation of my company and myself from many imminent and great dangers both by sea and land.'

Cromwell. 'The greatest of all other, I hear, was in your return home upon our coast.'

Whitelocke. 'That, indeed, Sir, was very miraculous.'

Cromwell. 'I am glad to see you safe and well after it.'

Whitelocke. 'I have cause to bless God with all thankfulness for it, as long as I live.'

Cromwell. 'I pray, my lord, tell me the particulars of that great deliverance.'

After Whitelocke had given a detailed account of his remarkable escape, Cromwell went on:

Cromwell. 'Really these passages are full of wonder and mercy; and I have cause to join with you in acknowledgement of the goodness of the Lord herein.'

Whitelocke. 'Your Highness testifies a true sense thereof, and your favour to your servant.'

Cromwell. 'I hope I shall never forget the one or the other;

indeed I hope I shall not: but, I pray, tell me, is the queen a lady of such rare parts as is reported of her?'

Whitelocke. 'Truly, Sir, she is a lady excellently qualified, of rare abilities of mind, perfect in many languages, and most sorts of learning, especially history, and, beyond compare with any person whom I have known, understanding the affairs and interest of all the states and princes of Christendom.'

Cromwell. 'That is very much: but what are her principles in matters of religion?'

Whitelocke. 'They are not such as I could wish they were; they are too much inclined to the manner of that country, and to some persuasions from men not well inclined to those matters, who have had too much power with her.'

Cromwell. 'That is a great deal of pity; indeed I have heard of some passages of her, not well relishing with those that fear God; and this is too general an evil among those people, who are not so well principled in matters of religion as were to be wished.'

Whitelocke. 'That is too true; but many sober men and good Christians among them do hope, that in time there may be a reformation of those things; and I took the boldness to put the queen and the present king in mind of the duty incumbent upon them in that business; and this I did with becoming freedom, and it was well taken.'

Cromwell. 'I think you did very well to inform them of that great duty, which now lies upon the king; and did he give ear to it?'

Whitelocke. 'Yes, truly, Sir, and told me that he did acknowledge it to be his duty, which he resolved to pursue as opportunity could be had for it; but he said, it must be done by degrees with a boisterous people, so long accustomed to the contrary; and the like answer I had from the archbishop of Upsala, and from the chancellor, when I spoke to them upon the same subject, which I did plainly.'

Cromwell. 'I am glad you did so. Is the archbishop a man of good abilities?'

Whitelocke. 'He is a very reverend person, learned, and seems very pious.'

Cromwell. 'The chancellor is the great wise man.'

Whitelocke. 'He is the wisest man that ever I conversed with abroad, and his abilities are fully answerable to the report of him.'

Cromwell. 'What character do you give of the present king?'

Whitelocke. 'I had the honour divers times to be with his Majesty, who did that extraordinary honour to me as to visit me at my house: he is a person of great worth, honour, and abilities, and not inferior to any in courage and military conduct.

Cromwell. 'That was an exceeding high favour to come to you in person.'

Whitelocke. 'He never did the like to any public minister; but this, and all other honour done to me, was but to testify their respects to your Highness, the which indeed was very great, both there and where I past in Germany.'

Cromwell. 'I am obliged to them for their very great civility.'

Whitelocke. 'Both the queen, and the king, and his brother, and the archbishop, and the chancellor, and most of the grandees, gave testimony of very great respect to your Highness, and that not only by their words but by their actions likewise.'

Cromwell. 'I shall be ready to acknowledge their respects upon any occasion.'

Whitelocke. 'The like respects were testified to your Highness in Germany, especially by the town of Hamburg; where I endeavoured, in your Highness's name, to confirm the privileges of the English merchants, who, with your resident there, showed much kindness to me and my company.'

Cromwell. 'I shall heartily thank them for it. Is the court of Sweden gallant and full of resort to it?'

Whitelocke. 'They are extreme gallant for their clothes; and for company, most of the nobility, and the civil and military officers, make their constant residence where the court is, and many repair thither on all occasions.'

Cromwell. 'Is their administration of justice speedy; and have they many law suits?'

Whitelocke. 'They have justice in a speedier way then with us, but more arbitrary, and fewer causes, in regard that the boors [peasants] dare not contend with their lords; and they have but few contracts, because they have but little trade; and there is small use of conveyances or questions of titles, because the law distributes every man's estate after his death among his children, which they cannot alter, and therefore have the fewer contentions.'

Cromwell. 'That is like our gavelkind.'

Whitelocke. 'It is the same thing; and in many particulars of our laws, in cases of private right, and of the public government (especially in their parliaments) there is a strange resemblance between their law and ours.'

Cromwell. 'Perhaps ours might, some of them, be brought from thence.'

Whitelocke. 'Doubtless they were, when the Goths and Saxons, and those northern people planted themselves here.'

Cromwell. 'You met with a barren country, and very cold.'

Whitelocke. 'The remoter parts of it from the court are extreme barren; but at Stockholm and Upsala, and most of the great towns, they have store of provisions: but fat beef and mutton in the winter time is not so plentiful with them, as in the countries more southerly; and their hot weather in summer as much exceeds ours, as their cold doth in winter.'

Cromwell. 'That is somewhat troublesome to endure. But how could you pass over their very long winter nights?'

Whitelocke. 'I kept my people together and in action and recreation, by having music in my house, and encouraging that and the exercise of dancing, which held them by the ears and eyes, and gave them diversion without any offence. And I caused the gentlemen to have disputations in Latin, and declamations upon words which I gave them.'

Cromwell. 'Those were very good diversions, and made your house a little academy.'

Whitelocke. 'I thought these recreations better than gaming for money or going forth to places of debauchery.'

Cromwell. 'It was much better; and I am glad you had so good an issue of your treaty.'

Whitelocke. 'I bless God for it, and shall be ready to give your Highness a particular account of it, when you shall appoint a time for it.'

Cromwell. 'I think that Thursday next in the morning will be a good time for you to come to the Council, and to make your report of the transactions of your negotiation; and you and I must have many discourses upon these arguments.'

Whitelocke. 'I shall attend your Highness and the Council.'

9.

Debate with John Rogers, the Fifth Monarchist, February 1655/6

John Rogers was a Fifth Monarchist who had been disappointed
by the failure of the Nominated Assembly. In July 1654 he was
imprisoned at Lambeth Palace, presumably for publishing a
pamphlet attacking the Protectorate as a government oppressively
akin to that of Charles I. In February 1654/5, still not specifically
charged, he and others of his persuasion were taken to meet the
Protector and members of his 'Court' to discuss religious issues.
The subsequent extended and heated confrontation was reported
by Rogers in a characteristically prolix but circumstantial
pamphlet of twenty-seven pages. These short extracts, though
hardly satisfactory, do convey something of the tone of the debate.
Rogers was not released until January 1656/7.

Cromwell. 'I promised to send for you, for some of your friends
came and spake sharply to me, as if I had apostated from the
Cause of Christ, and persecuting godly ministers, naming Mr
Rogers and Mr Feake, and spake other things that were sharp
enough. You might have had patience in your words. Now you
have liberty to speak to those things, but do not abuse your
liberty. You told me Mr R. suffered for the Gospel. I told you he
suffered as a railer, as a seducer, and a busybody in other men's
matters, and a stirrer up of sedition, which rulers, led by just
principles, might suppress. I told you Mr Rogers suffered justly,
and not for the testimony of Jesus Christ; and, indeed, in some
degree it is blasphemy to call suffering for evil-doing suffering for
the Gospel; and if he suffers for railing, and despising those that
God hath set over us, to say that his suffering is for the Gospel, is
making Christ the patron of such things; but if it were suffering
for the Gospel something might have been said, yet not so much as
saying uncharitably he suffered for evil-doing; so that I say this is
the thing in scripture, and if we show you that you suffer for
transgression, then you abuse that scripture, which I have often
thought on, that it is to make a man an offender for a word. I wish
it were better understood in the plainness of the spirit, for (to
interpret that scripture) it was the evil of those times, which was to
lie in wait for words on purpose to catch at words without

actions, and that is a sin; but some words are actions, and words
are conjugal with actions, for actions and words are as sharp as
swords, and such things I charge you with, and you suffer not for
the testimony of Jesus Christ. I speak—God is my witness—I
know it, that no man in England does suffer for the testimony of
Jesus. Nay, do not lift up your hands and your eyes, for there is no
man in England which suffers so. There are those that are far
better than Mr Rogers, though comparisons are not good, and not
near his principles, yet if they should suffer for the testimony of
Jesus. But there is such liberty, I wish it be not abused, that no man
in England suffereth for Christ, and it is not your fancy, you must
bring strong words to acquaint me of your sharp expressions.'

Rogers. 'I desire to know in what capacity I stand before you—
as a prisoner, or as a freeman; as a Christian to a Christian, with
equal freedom that others have or as a slave?'

Cromwell. 'A prisoner is a freeman, as Christ hath made you
free, and so you are a freeman.'

Rogers. 'Since . . . [you have] the advantage of a law new made,
which they call an Ordinance of Treason . . . every word we speak
may be a snare to us.'

Cromwell. 'I know not what snare may be in this. . . . Are you
so afraid of snares? What need you fear, that will speak so
boldly? . . . You are afraid of snares and advantages taken for
your life, when there is no such thing; but I tell you, upon your
friends' Petition I sent for you, to satisfy them you suffer as an
evil-doer.'

To Rogers' protest that he was ready to answer, the Protector
replied.

Cromwell. 'Ah, we know you are ready enough . . . Take heed
you do not abuse the Scripture. If you be such a disciple, then that
promise shall be made good unto you, and then you may say you
suffer for Christ.'

Rogers. '. . . [We have had] a very dangerous passage to you
this day, an "ardua via" through swords and halberds.'

Cromwell. 'Indeed . . . and I pray who was wounded?'

Rogers. '. . . many were bruised, beaten and hurt, and among
others my wife; but who the rest be, as yet I know not.'

Cromwell. 'No, so I think! . . . But I have no time to dispute

those things . . . Then we have done; for I tell you, you came here
by a desire. I told them I would put it to the issue this meeting, and
that I would prove it you suffered for evildoing. . . .'

Cromwell. 'Ha! And thus they talk of the ministry and
Commissioners for Approbation, and say they are Antichristian. . . . You fix the name of Antichristian upon anything
. . . and so all is Antichristian, and tithes are so, too with you, but I
will prove they are not.'

Rogers. 'My Lord . . . you were once of another mind, and told
me you'd have them pulled down, and put into a treasury.'

Cromwell. 'Did I ever say so? . . . Ha! there be many gentlemen
know that I have been for them, and will maintain the justness of
them . . . See, now, how you run! It is not a national ministry that
is now established, nor can you make it appear they are
Antichristian . . . I tell you, you and you, that you cannot, for they
ordain none . . . I tell you, it is their Grace, they judge of, and not
for parts or learning Latin, Greek, or Hebrew.'

Rogers. 'And who made them judges of Grace, my Lord?' . . .

One of his followers added, 'My Lord, we are very much
dissatisfied with what you have done against these prisoners of the
Lord Jesus. . . .'

Cromwell. 'I cannot tell you, then, how to help it.'

Rogers. 'For my part, I must declare against you, and will
venture my life, if I be called to it, with these our brethren that
suffer. . . .'

Cromwell. 'Well, I'll send for some of you ere long, but I have
lost this time, and have public business upon me at this time: I had
rather have given £500!—I tell you there wants brotherly love, and
the several sorts of forms would cut the throats one of another,
should not I keep the peace.'

Rogers. 'Those you call Fifth-Monarchy-Men . . . are driven by
your sword to love one another.'

Cromwell. 'Why, I tell you there be Anabaptists . . . and they
would cut the throats of them that are not under their forms; so
would the Presbyterians cut the throats of them that are not of
their forms, and so would you Fifth-Monarchy-Men. It is fit to
keep all these forms out of the power.'

Rogers. 'Who made you, my Lord, a judge of our principles?

You speak evil of you know not what. For that Fifth-Monarchy principle, as you call it, is of such latitude as takes in all Saints, all such as are sanctified in Christ Jesus.'

[The discussion, in which others besides Rogers and Cromwell were involved on both sides, becoming overheated, was broken up. Cromwell, in response to a request for Rogers to be shortly set free, answered bluntly: 'I will take my own time; you shall not know what I will do.' Rogers was then sent back to his detention.]

IO.

Conversation with Edmund Ludlow, 14 August 1656

In July 1656 the Council, preparing for a parliament, was disturbed by rumours of plots which might involve Ireland as a base for a Spanish invasion, alongside mutinies in the forces and risings by royalists and religious dissidents. Remedial and prevent-ative precautions taken included interrogation before the Protector and Council of suspected individuals, notably such intractable republicans as Edmund Ludlow and John Bradshaw, president of the Rump court which had tried Charles I. Ludlow reported on the proceedings and their background – as he saw it.

The usurper having governed as he thought long enough by virtue of the Instrument of Government, which though drawn up by himself and his creatures, was now thought to lay too great a restraint upon his ambitious spirit; and resolving to rest satisfied with nothing less than the succession of his family to the crown, he attempted to make himself king. To this end he thought it necessary to call a parliament: and that he might engage the army to assist him in all parts to procure such men to be chosen as would be fit for his purpose, he pretended that this assembly was called only in order to raise money for the payment of the army and fleet, to confirm the authority of the Major-Generals, and that of the Instrument of Government. By this means he obtained his desires in a great measure, especially in Scotland and Ireland, where all kinds of artifice, and in many places the most irregular courses, were taken to get such men returned as were proposed by the court. But knowing the people of England not to be of so mercenary a spirit; and that as they were better instructed in the principles of civil liberty, so they were not wanting in courage to assert it, he used his utmost endeavours to disable and incapacitate such men from being chosen, whom he thought most likely to obstruct his designs. In order to this he summoned the Lord President Bradshaw, Sir Henry Vane, Col. Rich, and myself, to appear before him in Council: which we all did except Sir Henry Vane, who told the messenger he should be at his house at Charing-Cross on a certain day. Cromwell, as soon as he saw the Lord President, required him to take out a new commisson for his office of Chief Justice of Chester, which he refused, alleging that he held that place by a grant from the Parliament of England to continue *quamdiu se bene gesserit.* And whether he had carried himself with that integrity which his commission exacted from him, he was ready to submit to a trial by twelve English men, to be chosen even by Cromwell himself. Col. Rich being pressed to give security not to act against the Government, and refusing so to do, was sent prisoner to Windsor Castle. Then I drew near to the council-table, where Cromwell charged me with dispersing treasonable books in Ireland, and with endeavouring to render the officers of the army disaffected, by discoursing to them concerning new models of Government. I acknowledged that I had caused some papers to be dispersed in Ireland, but denied that they justly could be called treasonable. And though I knew not that it was a crime to debate of the several forms of government, yet that I had not done anything of that nature lately to the best of my remembrance. He then said, that he was not ignorant of the many plots that were on foot to disturb the present power, and that he thought it his duty to secure such as he suspected. To this I replied, that there were two duties required by God of the magistrate, i.e. that he be a terror to those that do evil, and a praise to such as do well; and whether my actions were good or bad, I was ready to submit to a legal trial: that I was ignorant of any other way to secure the magistrate from being afraid of the people, or the people from the dread of the magistrate, unless both will do that which is just and good. 'You do well', said he, 'to reflect on our fears; yet I would have you know, that what I do, proceeds not from any motive of fear, but from a timely prudence to forsee and prevent danger: that had I done as I should, I ought to have secured you immediately upon your coming into England, or at least when you desired to be freed from the engagement you had given after your arrival; and therefore I now require you to give assurance not to act against the government.' I desired to be excused in that particular, reminding him of the reasons I had formerly given him for my refusal, adding, that I was in his power, and that he might use me as he thought fit. 'Pray then,' said he, 'what is it that you would have? May not every man be as good as he will? What can you desire more than you have?' 'It were easy', said I, 'to tell what we would have.' 'What is that, I pray?' said he. 'That which we fought for,' said I, 'that the nation might be governed by its own consent.' 'I am', said he, 'as much for a government by consent as any man; but where shall we find that consent? Amongst the Prelatical, Presbyterian, Independent, Anabaptist, or Levelling Parties?' I answered, 'Amongst those of all sorts who had acted with fidelity and affection to the public.' Then he fell into the commendation of his own government, boasting of the protection and quiet which the people enjoyed under it, saying, that he was resolved to keep the nation from being imbrued in blood. I said that I was of opinion too much blood had been already shed, unless there were a better account of it. 'You do well', said he, 'to charge us with the guilt of blood; but we think there is a good return for what hath been shed; and we understand what clandestine correspondences are carrying on at this time between the Spaniard and those of your party, who make use of your name, and affirm that you will own them and assist them.' 'I know not', said I, 'what you mean by my party, and can truly say, that if any men have entered into an engagement with Spain, they have had no advice from me so to do, and that if they will use my name I cannot help it.' Then in a softer way he told me, that he desired not to put any more hardships on me than on himself; that he had been always ready to do me all the good offices that lay in his power, and that he aimed at nothing by this proceeding, but the public quiet and security. 'Truly, sir,' said I, 'I know not why you should be an enemy to me who have been faithful to you in all your difficulties.' 'I understand not', said he, 'what you mean by my difficulties. I am sure they were not so properly mine as those of the public; for in respect to my outward condition I have not much improved it, as these gentlemen', pointing to his Council, 'well know.' To which they seemed to assent, by rising from their chairs; and therefore I thought not fit to insist farther on that point, contenting myself to say, that it was from that duty which I owed to the public, whereof he expressed such a peculiar regard, that I durst not give the security he desired, because I conceived it to be against the liberty of the people, and contrary to the known law of England. For proof of this I produced an act of parliament for restraining the Council-table from imprisoning any of the free-born people of England; and in case they should do so, requiring the Justices of the Upper Bench, upon the application of the aggrieved party, to grant his 'Habeas Corpus', and to give him considerable damages. To this act I supposed he gave his free vote, assuring him, that for my own part I durst not do anything that should tend to the violation of it. 'But', said he, 'did not the army and Council of State commit persons to prison?' I answered, 'that the Council of State did so, but it was by virtue of an authority granted to them by the Parliament; and if the army had sometimes acted in that manner, it had been in time of war, and then only in order to bring the persons secured to a legal trial; whereas it is now pretended that we live in a time of peace, and are to be governed by the known laws of the land.' 'A Justice of Peace', said he, 'may commit, and shall not I?' 'He is', said I, 'a legal officer, and authorized by the law to do so, which you could not be, though you were King; because if you do wrong therein, no remedy can be had against you. Therefore if I have offended against the law, I desire to be referred to a Justice of the Peace, that I may be proceeded with according to law; but if I have done nothing to deserve a restraint, that then I may have my liberty.' Whereupon being commanded to withdraw into a room next to the Council-Chamber, I heard Major-General Lambert to advise that I might be peremptorily required to give the security demanded. But Cromwell said, that the air of Ireland was good, that I had a house there, and therefore he thought it best to send me thither. Immediately after Mr Scobel, one of the clerks of the Council, came to me, and acquainted me, that I might return to my lodging; where I had not been a quarter of an hour before Mr Strickland, one of the Council, came to me, and pressed me earnestly to comply: but I told him, that having contended for the liberty of others, I was not willing to give away my own, and to be made a precedent to the prejudice of my country-men, because it was the pleasure of those that had the sword to have it so. 'Why,' said he, 'was it not the sword by which you kept Warder Castle, and by which you acted during the whole course of the late war?' 'I had', said I, 'the authority of the Parliament to justify me in so doing.' He answered, 'but they governed by the sword.' To which I replied, that indeed they made use of the sword to remove the obstructions that were in the way of the civil government, and exercised that power to vindicate and establish the law of the land; and that I was heartily sorry to see one who had been so forward in the cause of the public, not to discern any difference between a sword in the hands of a parliament to restore the people to their ancient rights, and a sword in the hands of a tyrant to rob and despoil them thereof. Here our discourse was interrupted by a messenger who came from the Council with an order from them, to require me to give the security of five thousand pounds within three days after the date of the order, not to do anything prejudicial to the present government; and in case of failure, to be taken into custody. Upon the receipt of it I told the messenger, that having no power to resist, I must submit to their pleasure. A day or two after the expiration of the time limited by the order for giving the demanded security, which I had not done, Serjeant Dendy came to me with another from the Council, signed by Henry Lawrence, president, requiring and authorizing him to take me into custody. Having shewn me the order, he desired me to make choice of a chamber; but after some discourse with my near relations, who were then present, he was contented to let me remain at my lodgings. So having promised to return in a day or two, and in the mean time to advise with Lieutenant-General Fleetwood, he went away. The next day Cromwell diverting himself with hunting at Hampton-Court, asked my brother Thomas Ludlow, who was in the company, if he were not angry with him for committing me? And my brother answering, that it was not fit for him to judge concerning his actions: he thereupon assured him, that he wished me as well as any of his own children: that his desiring me to give security for my carriage to the government, was designed by him as well for my good as for his own security, and that he would have him to engage for me; to which he most readily consented. The morning following my brother came to me, and having acquainted me with what had passed between Cromwell and himself, I gave him thanks for his kind offer, but withal told him, that I would by no means desire that of him which I was not willing to do myself. Besides I told him, that should it be granted that the thing were fit for him to do, yet it might prove a snare to him, and lay an obligation upon him to gratify the usurper in another way. However after this discourse of Cromwell to my brother, and the conference of my relations with Serjeant Dendy, I ventured to accompany my father and mother Oldsworth, with my wife, into Essex, where we spent the remaining part of that summer. My stay there did in some measure answer the design of Cromwell, which was to keep me out of my own country, where he doubted I might obstruct the election of such persons as the Court had resolved by all methods to procure to be returned. But there was no need to fear my intermedling in that particular at such a time; and if I had, it should have been only to give a public testimony against any election at all, the Long Parliament being still in being, though under a present force. Besides, it was manifest that the designed assembly was to be called for no other end than to strengthen the sword, and to advance the corrupt interest of him that called them together; and if it should happen that they had either the courage or honesty to attempt anything for the service of the public, I was assured their endeavours would be rendered fruitless by a sudden dissipation.

Appendix 1: The Putney Debates, October–November 1647

Between the First and Second Civil Wars the victorious New Model Army entered into politics, initially seeking redress of professional grievances but soon drifting towards wider political and social issues as it became frustrated by the failure of parliament to respond positively. During 1647 the General Council of the Army, to which regimental rank-and-file sent elected representatives ('agitators'), met from time to time to consider the political situation and to discuss desirable reforms. In October a meeting, not formally of the Council and including some civilian members of the radical Leveller movement which was having some impact on the army, was held at Putney under the chairmanship of General Cromwell. A detailed record of the 'debates' there, which centred on the Leveller scheme for a new constitution, *The Agreement of the People*, was kept by the clerk to the Council. A transcript under the title *Puritanism and Liberty* is also published in Everyman (see Appendix 2). The following extracts express something of the style, spirit and content of Cromwell's vital contributions to the arguments. But they can only be comprehended fully in the context of the whole debates.

Cromwell. . . . 'But there may be just engagements upon us, such as perhaps it will be our duty to keep; and if so, it is fit we should consider. And all that I said was that we should consider our engagements, and there is nothing else offered, and therefore what need that anybody be angry or offended? Perhaps we have made such engagements as may in the matter of them not bind us; yet in some circumstances they may. Our engagements are public engagements. They are to the kingdom, and to everyone in the kingdom that could look upon what we did publicly declare, could read or hear it read. They are to the Parliament. And it is a very fitting thing that we do seriously consider of the things. And this is what I shall shortly offer. That because the kingdom is in the danger it is in, because the kingdom is in that condition it is in, and time may be ill spent in debates, and it is necessary for things to be put to an issue (if ever it was necessary in the world it is now),

I should desire this may be done. That this General Council may be appointed to meet against a very short time, two days — Thursday—if you would against Saturday, or at furthest against Monday; that there might be a committee out of this Council appointed to debate and consider with those two gentlemen, and with any others that are not of the Army, that they shall bring, and with the Agitators of those five regiments; that so there may be a liberal and free debate had amongst us, that we may understand really, as before God, the bottom of our desires, and that we may seek God together, and see if God will give us an uniting spirit.

And give me leave to tell it you again, I am confident there sits not a man in this place that cannot so freely act with you that, if he sees that God hath shut up his way that he cannot do any service in that way as may be good for the kingdom, he will be glad to withdraw himself, and wish you all prosperity. And if this heart be in us, as is known to God that searches our hearts and trieth the reins, God will discover whether our hearts be not clear in this business. And therefore I shall move that we may have a committee amongst ourselves to consider of the engagements, and this committee to dispute things with others, and a short day to be appointed for the General Council. And I doubt not but, if in sincerity we are willing to submit to that light that God shall cast in among us, God will unite us, and make us of one heart and one mind. Do the plausiblest things you can do, do that which hath the most appearance of reason in it, that tends to change: at this conjuncture of time you will find difficulties. But if God satisfy our spirits this will be a ground of confidence to every good man; and he that goes upon other grounds, he shall fall like a beast. I shall desire this: that you, or any other of the Agitators or gentlemen that can be here, will be here, that we may have free discourses amongst ourselves of things, and you will be able to satisfy each other. And really, rather than I would have this kingdom break in pieces before some company of men be united together to a settlement, I will withdraw myself from the Army to-morrow, and lay down my commission. I will perish before I hinder it.' . . .

Cromwell. 'I hope we know God better than to make appearances of religious meetings covers for designs or for insinuation amongst you. I desire that God, that hath given us some sincerity, will own us according to his own goodness and that sincerity that he hath given us. I dare be confident to speak it, that design that hath been amongst us hitherto is to seek the guidance of God, and to recover that presence of God that seems to withdraw from us. And to accomplish that work which may be for the good of the kingdom is our end. But it seems as much to us in this as anything, we are not all of a mind. And for our parts we do not desire or offer you to be with us in our seeking of God further than your own satisfactions lead you, but only that against to-morrow in the afternoon (which will be designed for the consideration of these businesses with you) you will do what you may to have so many as you shall think fit, to see what God will direct you to say to us, that whilst we are going one way, and you another, we be not both destroyed. This requires guidance from the Spirit. It may be too soon to say it, yet 'tis my present apprehension: I had rather we should devolve our strength to you than that the kingdom for our division should suffer loss. For that's in all our hearts, to profess above anything that's worldly, the public good of the people; and if that be in our hearts truly and nakedly, I am confident it is a principle that will stand. Perhaps God may unite us and carry us both one way. And therefore I do desire you, that against to-morrow in the afternoon, if you judge it meet, you will come to us to the Quartermaster-General's quarters—where you will find us at prayer if you will come timely to join with us; at your liberty, if afterwards to speak with us. There you will find us.' . . .

Audley. 'I shall desire to second that gentleman's motion. While we debate we do nothing. I am confident that whilst you are doing you will all agree together, for it is idleness that hath begot this rust and this gangrene amongst us.'

Cromwell. 'I think it is true. Let us be doing, but let us be united in our doing. If there remain nothing else needful but present action, let us be doing—I mean, doing in that kind, doing in that sort. I think we need not be in council here if such kind of action, action of that nature, will serve. But if we do not rightly and clearly understand one another before we come to act, if we do not lay a foundation of action before we do act, I doubt whether we shall act unanimously or no. And seriously, as before the Lord, I knew no such end of our speech the last night, and our appointing another meeting, but in order to a more perfect understanding of one another, what we should do, and that we might be agreed upon some principles of action. And truly if I remember rightly, upon the delivery of the paper that was yesterday, this was offered, that the things that are now upon us are things of difficulty, the things are things that do deserve therefore consideration, because there might be great weight in the consequences; and it was then offered, and I hope is still so in all our hearts, that we are not troubled with the consideration of the difficulty, nor with the consideration of anything but this: that if we do difficult things, we may see that the things we do, have the will of God in them, that they are not only plausible and good things, but seasonable and honest things, fit for us to do. And therefore it was desired that we might consider, before we could come to these papers, in what condition we stood in respect of former engagements, however some may be satisfied that there lie none upon us, or none but such as it's duty to break, it's sin to keep. Therefore that was yesterday premised, that there may be a consideration had of them—and I may speak it as in the presence of God, that I know nothing of any engagements, but I would see liberty in any man as I would be free from bondage to anything that should hinder me from doing my duty— and therefore that was first in consideration. If our obligation be nothing, or if it be weak, I hope we shall receive satisfaction why it should be laid aside, and be convinced that the things that we speak of are not obliged. And therefore, if it please you, I think it will be good for us to frame our discourse to what we were, where we are, what we are bound to, what we are free to; and then I make no question but that this may conclude what is between us and these gentlemen, in one afternoon. I do not speak this to make obligations more than what they were before, but as before the Lord. You see what they are (*producing the printed volume of Army Declarations*); and when we look upon them we shall see whether we have been in a wrong way, and I hope it will call upon us for the more double diligence.'

Appendix 2: Sources

A. Speeches

1. *At the General Council, 23 March 1648/9*, Stainer No. 10. From Clarke MSS, Worcester College, Oxford. 12 folios 147–150; *Clarke Papers*, ii, pp. 200 ff.

2. *To the Nominated Assembly, 4 July 1653*, Stainer No. 17. A difficult text to establish. Stainer, followed generally here, brings together two overlapping versions modifying and supplementing each other. His first part derives from *The Lord General Cromwels Speech delivered in the Council-Chamber, Upon the 4 of July 1653*, claiming to be 'a true copie. Published for information and to prevent mistakes. Printed in the year 1654.' Its page of errata has been incorporated in this text. The second part draws on a version in *Original Letters and Papers of State of . . Mr John Milton*, ed. J. Nickolls, 1743. An appendix to A. H. Woolrych, *Commonwealth to Protectorate*, Oxford, 1982, considers critical material for an acceptable version and cites an abridgment in Tanner MS, No. 52, folios 20–23 in the Bodleian Library. This includes phrases not in Nickolls or the pamphlet, among them an emphatic assertion that at the conference the night before the dissolution 'we found from their (the Rumpers') own mouths that they did intend a perpetuation of themselves. We did not guess at this. We know it.' This is relevant to B. Worden's assessment of the missing bill for a new representative which precipitated the dissolution (*The Rump Parliament*, Cambridge, 1974). Cromwell may have said that 4 July 1653 was '*the* day of the Lord' or '*a* day' – a matter of some significance.

3. *To the First Protectorate Parliament, 4 September 1654*, Stainer No. 24. From *His Highnesse the Lord Protectors Speeches in the Painted Chamber, the one on Monday the 4th of September; the other on Tuesday the 12th of September 1654*. Taken by one who stood very near him and published to prevent mistakes . . . 1654. See also *The Speech of His Highness . . . to the Parliament . . . Examined by the Original Copy. Published by Order and Authority . . . 1654*, which

reports Cromwell speaking for about an hour and a half.

4. *To the First Protectorate Parliament, 12 September 1654,* Stainer No. 25. From *His Highness ... Speech to the Parliament in the Painted Chamber,* on Tuesday. Taken by one who stood very near him, and published to prevent mistakes, 1654.

5. *To the First Protectorate Parliament, 22 January 1654/5,* Stainer No. 27. From *His Highness Speech to the Parliament in the Painted Chamber, at their Dissolution, upon Monday the 22nd of January 1654.* Published to prevent mistakes, and false copies ... Printed by Henry Hills, printer to ... the Lord Protector ... 1654(/5). A note at the end reports a Council order of 5 February that 'no person or persons whatsoever presume at their perils, on any pretence whatsoever, to print, or reprint, either in part or whole' this speech 'other than Henry Hills . . .'. *Clarke Papers,* iii, p. 21, reports Cromwell himself perusing and correcting a copy of the speech transcribed from shorthand.

6. *To the Lord Mayor etc of the City of London, 5 March 1655/ 6,* Stainer No. 32. From Clarke MS 28, folio 5; *Clarke Papers,* iii, pp. 65–6. Also reported in *Mercurius Politicus,* 25 February–6 March, and Whitelocke *Memorials,* 1682, p. 622.

7. *To the Second Protectorate Parliament, 17 September 1656,* Stainer No. 34. From B. L. Add. MSS Ayscough 6125, folios 34–60b. Abstract in *Clarke Papers,* iii, pp. 72–4. This text is certainly incomplete. The speech was reported to have run for three hours.

8. *To the Commons on accepting public and private bills, 27 November 1656,* Stainer No. 35. From Clarke MS 28, folio 117b. *Clarke Papers,* iii. pp. 83–4. See *C.J.,* vii, p. 460 for an account of the proceedings and a list of the bills.

9. *Reply to the Commons' congratulations on the failure of Sindercombe's assassination plot, 23 January 1656/7,* Skinner No. 36. From B. L. Lansdowne MS 155, folio 40. See also *C.J.,* vii, p. 481 and *Clarke Papers,* iii, p. 87.

10. *To a meeting of army officers, 28 February 1656/7,* Stainer No. 37. From Ayscough 6125, folios 61b–63.

11. *To the Commons on presentation of the new constitution with the title of King, 31 March 1657,* Stainer No. 38. From Ayscough 6125, folios 74–5. Other versions in Lansdowne 754, folio 153 and Clarke MS 29, folio 296.

12. *To a Commons Committee urging acceptance of the title, 3 April 1657*, Stainer No. 39. From Carte MS lxxx, folios 755–6, Bodleian Library. Other versions in Ayscough 6125 and Clarke MS 29, folio 1033b.

13. *Similar meeting, 8 April 1657*, Stainer No. 40. From Clarke MS 29, folio 39. Other versions in Ayscough 6125, folios 78b–80b, and B. L. Sloane MS 4157, folios 180–1.

14. *Similar meeting, 11 April 1657*, Stainer No. 41. From *Monarchy Asserted to be the best, most Ancient and Legall form of Government, in a conference had at White Hall with Oliver Lord Protector and a Committee of Parliament* ... 1660.

15. *Similar meeting, 13 April 1657*, Stainer No. 42. From Ashmole MS 749, Bodleian Library. Another version in *Monarchy Asserted*.

16. *Similar meeting, 20 April 1657*, Stainer No. 43. From *Monarchy Asserted*. Another version in Ayscough 6125, folios 11–15.

17. *Similar meeting, 21 April 1657*, Stainer No. 44. From Ayscough 6125, folios 15–31b. Another version in *Monarchy Asserted*.

18. *To the Commons on the Humble Petition and Advice, 8 May 1657*, Stainer No. 45. From *C.J.*, vii, p. 553. Other versions in Clarke MS 29, folio 58b; Ayscough 6125, folios 32–3; B. L. Harleian MS 6846, folio 237; *Monarchy Asserted*; *Thurloe State Papers*, vi, p. 267.

19. *To the Commons accepting the revised Petition and Advice, 25 May 1657*, Stainer No. 46. From *C.J.*, p. 559. Other versions in Clarke MS 29, folio 75b; Ayscough 6125, folio 51; *T.S.P.*, vi, pp. 309–10.

20. *To the Commons accepting bills, public and private, 9 June 1657*, Stainer No. 47. From *C.J.*, vii, p. 352. Also in *The Public Intelligencer*, No. 86.

21. *To 'the Other House' and the Commons at opening of the second session of Parliament, 20 January 1657/8*, Stainer No. 48. From *C.J.*, vii, p. 579 . Other versions in *The Public Intelligencer* No. 118; Harleian 6801, folios 282–7.

22. *To both Houses in 'the Banqueting House' at Whitehall, 25 January 1657/8*, Stainer No. 49. From Lansdowne 754, folio 330–1. Other versions in Ayscough 6125, folios 82b–89 and Sloane 2905.

23. *To a Commons Committee, 28 January 1657/8*, Stainer No. 50. From *C.J.*, vii, p. 589.
24. *To both Houses on dissolving Parliament, 4 February 1657/ 8*, Stainer No. 51. From Lansdowne 745, folio 342. Another version in Clarke MS 30, folio 17.
25. *To Army officers about the dissolution, 6 February 1657/8*, Stainer No. 52. From *Clarke Papers*, iii, pp. 139–40.
26. *To the Lord Mayor etc of the City of London, 12 March 1657/8*, Stainer No. 53. *Fr*ɔ*m A Discovery Made by His Highness the Lord Protector to the Lord Mayor . . . 1658*. Also in *Clarke Papers*, iii, p. 143, *T.S.P.*, vii, p. 3, etc.

B. Conversations

1. *With Fairfax and others about the invasion of Scotland, 24 June 1650*. From Bulstrode Whitelocke, *Memorials of the English Affairs, 1682*, pp. 460–2.
2. *With Ludlow about Irish problems, c. June 1650*. From *Ludlow's Memoirs* (ed C. H. Firth), Oxford, 1894, i, pp. 244–8.
3. *At the Speaker's house about a settlement, October 1651*. From Whitelocke, *Memorials*, pp. 516–17.
4. *With Whitelocke about monarchy, November 1652*. From Whitelocke, *Memorials*, pp. 548–51.
5. *With Whitelocke about the embassy to Sweden, 5 September 1653*. From Whitelocke, *Journal of the Swedish Embassy, 1772*, i, pp. 12–15.
6. *Similar meeting, 13 September 1653*. From Whitelocke, *Swedish Embassy, 1772*, i, pp. 31–6.
7. *With Whitelocke, Farewell meeting, 30 October 1653*. From Whitelocke, *Swedish Embassy, 1772*, i, pp. 95–6.
8. *With Whitelocke on his return from Sweden, 6 July 1654*. From Whitelocke, *Swedish Embassy*, ii, pp. 385–92.
9. *With John Rogers, the Fifth Monarchist, February 1654/5*. From *The Faithfull Narrative of the Testimony and Demands made to Oliver Cromwell and his powers on behalf of the Lords Prisoners . . .* Published by *Faithful Hands, 1654* as reprinted in F. Rogers, *The Life and Opinions of a Fifth Monarchy Man, 1867*.

10. *With Ludlow before the Council, 14 August 1656.* From *Ludlow's Memoirs*, ii, pp. 9–15.

C. *Appendix 1*

Cromwell at 'the Putney Debates', October–November 1657. From A. S. P. Woodhouse (ed.), *Puritanism and Liberty*, 3rd ed., Everyman History Classics, 1984 (Preface by I. Roots), pp. 16–17, 23, 44–5.

Appendix 3: Suggestions for Further Reading

Cromwell's *Letters and Speeches* were first collected and edited (idiosyncratically) by Thomas Carlyle in 1845. Of numerous later editions the best is by C. S. Lomas, 3 vols, 1904. Almost every scrap of Cromwell's *Writings and Speeches* is presented, with a ponderous commentary, in W. C. Abbot, ed., 4 vols, Cambridge, Mass, reprint Oxford, 1988. (See J. Morrill, 'Textualizing and Contextualizing Cromwell', *Historical Journal*, 33, 1990.) C. L. Stainer, ed., *Speeches of Oliver Cromwell* is valuable for the notes as well as the texts.

The fullest context for this volume is provided in S. R. Gardiner, *The History of the Great Civil War*, 4 vols, 1893, and *The History of the Commonwealth and Protectorate*, 4 vols, 1903, continued by C. H. Firth, *The Last Years of the Protectorate*, 2 vols, 1910. G. Davies, *The Restoration of Charles II*, Oxford, 1955, completes the narrative. More detailed studies include A. H. Woolrych, *Soldiers and Statesmen: the General Council of the Army and its Debates*, 1647–48, Oxford, 1987; D. Underdown, *Pride's Purge*, Oxford, 1971; B. Worden, *The Rump Parliament*, Cambridge, 1974, and A. H. Woolrych, *Commonwealth to Protectorate*, Oxford, 1982. A more general background is offered by, *inter alia*, G. E. Aylmer, *Rebellion or Revolution? England, 1640–1660*, Oxford, 1986; B. Coward, *The Stuart Age*, 2nd ed., 1999; D. Hirst, *Authority and Conflict: England, 1603–1658*, 1986; I. Roots, *The Great Rebellion, 1642–1660*, 5th ed., 1995, and R. Hutton, *The British Republic, 1649–1660*, 1990. Among biographies of Cromwell C. H. Firth, *Oliver Cromwell and the Rule of the Puritans*, 1901, etc. is a classic. Other lives include R. Howell, 1981, P. Gregg, 1988; B. Coward, 1991; P. Gaunt, 1996 and J. C. Davis, 2001. Collections of articles on particular aspects of Cromwell include C. Hill, *God's Englishman*, 1970; I. Roots, ed., *Cromwell: A Profile*, 1973, J. Morrill, ed., *Cromwell and the English Revolution*, 1990; and R. C. Richardson, ed. *Images of Oliver Cromwell*, 1993.

Further relevant articles are to be found in G. E. Aylmer, ed., *The Interregnum: The Search for a Settlement*, 1972; K. Thomas and D. H. Pennington, eds, *Puritans and Revolutionaries* (for Christopher Hill), Oxford, 1978, C. Jones, M. Newitt and S. K. Roberts, eds, *Politics and People in Revolutionary England* (for Ivan Roots), Oxford, 1986 and R. Ollard and P. Tudor Craig, eds, *For Veronica Wedgwood These: Studies in Seventeenth-Century History*, 1986. *Cromwelliana*, the journal of the Cromwell Association, gives wide coverage to the Protector and his times.

For major documents see S. R. Gardiner, ed., *Constitutional Documents of the Puritan Revolution*, Oxford, 1904, and J. P. Kenyon, ed., *The Stuart Constitution*, Cambridge, 2nd ed, 1986. Debates in the Protectorate parliaments are well reported in J. R. Rutt, ed, *The Diary of Thomas Burton, M. P.*, 4 vols, 1828; reprinted, with additional material edited by I. Roots, New York, 1974. Many of Cromwell's contemporaries appear in the *Dictionary of National Biography*–and will in the *New D. N. B.* (from 2005)–and in R. L. Greaves and R. Zaller, eds, *Biographical Dictionary of British Radicals in the Seventeenth Century*, Brighton, 1982–84. R. C. Richardson, ed. *The Debate on the English Revolution*, 2nd ed., 1987, usefully surveys three and a half centuries of historiography. See also B. Worden, *Roundhead Reputations. The English Civil Wars and the Passions of Posterity*, 2001.

Appendix 4: Chronology

1599	25 April	Birth of Oliver Cromwell
1616		Cromwell at Sidney Sussex College, Cambridge
1625		Accession of Charles I
1628–9		Cromwell MP for Huntingdon in Charles I's Third Parliament
1637		The Scottish National Covenant
1640	May	Cromwell MP for Cambridge City in Short Parliament
	November	Cromwell *do.* in Long Parliament
1641		Cromwell speaks on The Root and Branch Bill
	November	The Irish (Ulster) Rebellion
	December	The Grand Remonstrance
1641/2	January	Charles I's attempted arrest of the five MPs
	March	The Militia Ordinance
1642	June	The 19 Propositions
	22 August	Outbreak of Civil War
		Battle of Edgehill
		Cromwell's rise as military commander begins
1643		The Solemn League and Covenant
	December	Death of John Pym
1644		Milton's *Areopagitica*
		Cromwell Lt. Gen. of Eastern Association
	July	Battle of Marston Moor
1645		Raising of New Model Army

		The Self Denying Ordinance
	June	Battle of Naseby
1646		Charles I surrenders to Scots
		End of First Civil War
1647		Army seizes Charles I
	August	The Heads of the Proposals
		The Agreement of the People
	October–November	The Putney Debates
		Charles I's 'Engagement' with the Scots
1648		The Second Civil War
	December	Pride's Purge
1648/9	January	The Trial and Execution of Charles I
		Abolition of monarchy and the Commonwealth established
1649		Abolition of House of Lords
		Suppression of Army Levellers
		Eikon Basilike
		Cromwell in Ireland
1650		Marvell's *Horatian Ode on Cromwell's Return from Ireland*
	June	Fairfax resigns as C. in C.
		Cromwell invades Scotland
	3 September	Battle of Dunbar
1651		Death of Henry Ireton
		Hobbes's *Leviathan*
		The Navigation Act
	3 September	The Battle of Worcester
1652–4		The First Dutch War
1653	April	Rump's Bill for a new representative
	20 April	Cromwell ejects the Rump
	4 July	The Nominated Assembly (Barebone's Parliament)
1653	October–June 1654	The Swedish Embassy

	December	Resignation of Barebone's
	12 December	The Instrument of Government
		Inauguration of the Protectorate
1654	January–August	Cromwell's Ordinances (including Union with Scotland, reform of Chancery, the Triers and Ejectors, etc)
	3 September	The First Protectorate Parliament
	12 September	Cromwell's Fundamentals and Circumstantials
	September–January 1654/5	Formulation of proposed parliamentary constitution
1654/5	22 January	Dissolution of Parliament
1655	March	Penruddock's Rising
		The New Militia and the Major-Generals
		The Decimation Tax
	November	War with Spain
		Capture of Jamaica
1656		Harrington's *Oceana*
	17 September	The Second Protectorate Parliament
		Exclusion of Commonwealthsmen, etc
	October–December	The Case of James Nayler
	December–January 1656/7	The Decimation Bill
1656/7	January	Sindercombe's Plot
	23 February	Sir Christopher Packe's 'Paper'
	March	Alliance with France
1657	March–May	The Offer of the Crown and Humble Petition and Advice
	April	Confirmation of Cromwell's Ordinances

	May	Rejection of 'the title'
		Killing No Murder
		Blake's victories at sea over Spain
	June	Acceptance of the revised Humble Petition and Advice
		The Additional Petition
	25 June	End of first session of Parliament
	26 June	Second installation of the Protector
		Resignation of Lambert
		Nomination to 'the Other House'
1657/8	January	Second session of Parliament (with 'the Other House')
	4 February	Dissolution of Parliament
1658	June	Battle of the Dunes and acquisition of Dunkirk
	August	Cromwell's illness
	3 September	Death of Oliver Cromwell
		Succession of Richard Cromwell as Protector
	November	Oliver's funeral
1658/9	January–April	Third Protectorate Parliament
1659	April	The fall of the Protectorate
		The Rump recalled, dismissed and recalled again
1659/60	January	Monck marches on London
	February	The Long Parliament dissolves itself
1660	March	The Convention Parliament (with the House of Lords)
		The Declaration of Breda
	May	Vote for government 'by King, Lords and Commons' leading to the Restoration of Charles II

1660/61   30 January   Cromwell's corpse dis-
                              interred, hanged at
                              Tyburn and cast into an
                              unmarked pit.